creating effective programs
for gifted students
with learning disabilities

creating effective programs
for gifted students
with learning disabilities

Ann Rowe, Ph.D., Julie F. Pace, Ph.D.,
and Karin Tulchinsky Cohen

PRUFROCK PRESS INC.
WACO, TEXAS

Prufrock Press Inc.
P.O. Box 8813
Waco, TX 76714-8813
Phone: (800) 998-2208
Fax: (800) 240-0333
http://www.prufrock.com

Table of Contents

Introduction

We, the authors, came together as a result of a conference held in March 2010 in Shady Grove, MD: "Diamonds in the Rough: Smart Kids Who Learn Differently." Parents, educators, and professionals flocked to presentations on a range of topics designed to address how to educate the wonderful and bewildering students who continue to "stump the experts." These quirky and often brilliantly insightful students are fascinating, yet also infuriating, due to their unpredictable and wildly variable performance. The intense interest in the conference indicated that parents and educators alike recognized the promise of these students, but also saw the need for better or different tools to help them actualize their potential.

Each of us brings a different perspective to the issues addressed in this book. Julie worked for many years as a psychologist evaluating underachieving gifted students through the Diagnostic and Counseling Center at the Johns Hopkins Center for Talented Youth. Ann, also a clinical psychologist, has extensive experience in evaluating the broad spectrum of children with learning disabilities, as well as consulting at a full-time special education school. Karin has wide-ranging experience as an educator and educational advocate in the area of gifted students with learning disabilities. Although we have arrived at this point from different paths, we share a commitment to this population of intriguing and admirable individuals.

It is perhaps important to point out that we present a clinical or child-centered approach to the issue of giftedness in the presence of learning challenges. Our more individualized approach suggests programmatic changes from the bottom up rather than speaking to the broad-scale needs of policy development for large public school systems. Although we feel that our experience and understanding of specific individuals with learning challenges can inform public school system policies, we recognize that decisions on a large scale cannot always have the level of specificity that we might use in programming for individual students. However, we hope that the increased interest in differentiated instruction will increase the relevance of our discussion in both public and private school settings.

In Chapter 1, we place the concept of gifted students with learning disabilities in the context of current controversies in both the definitions of learning disabilities and of giftedness. In Chapter 2, we review theories of giftedness that provide insight into the gifted aspects of our students, with particular emphasis on the Munich Model of Giftedness (Heller, 2004), which identifies important factors that affect a student's ability to demonstrate his or her strengths. We elaborate on these issues to add an additional factor, information processing, which is also an important determinant for talent production in gifted students with learning disabilities. Through case studies, we demonstrate the developmental course of a group of gifted students whose academic fluency challenges result in a gradual divergence between efficiency and higher order thinking skills. The information processing challenges of these students gradually become evident in test scores through the impact of poor working memory and weak executive skills. The experiences of these young people illustrate the importance of early identification and intervention, as well as appropriate accommodations to help with a successful transition to adulthood.

In Chapter 3, we discuss important reasons to provide programming for gifted students with learning disabilities. Twice-exceptional students are at significant risk for underachievement. Many gifted students do not demonstrate their early intellectual promise, and students with learning disabilities typically underperform in terms of their participation in advanced coursework and completion of college coursework. A large group of college students with disabilities are not identified until college, when their self-styled compensatory strategies can no longer meet academic demands. Many of these students could have been identified earlier and could have received accommodations and strategy instruction in metacognition to improve their academic success.

The provision of a program for students who are gifted and talented with learning disabilities (GTLD) can provide important benefits to the school as a whole. Broadening the skill base of classroom teachers increases the level of rigor in the classroom, and we will discuss research that shows that professional development training in special populations increases teacher effectiveness overall. Training in identifying learning problems in the gifted population is likely to build observation skills and sensitivity of teachers to other underserved populations. In addition, twice-exceptional identification and programming can provide needed social and emotional support to address the negative impact of underachievement.

In Chapter 4, we go on to discuss the characteristics that twice-exceptional students share with mainstream gifted students as well as unique characteristics that need to be addressed in programming. In Chapter 5, we discuss the more complex issues that emerge when gifted students with learning disabilities also have Attention Deficit/Hyperactivity Disorder (ADHD) or autism spectrum disorders (ASD). The overlap between learning disabilities and ADHD and/or ASD in gifted students creates a highly complex set of issues that needs to be addressed to meet the needs of these students.

In Chapter 6, we discuss issues in the assessment and identification of gifted students with learning disabilities. These students can be difficult to identify due to the interactions of their giftedness and their learning challenges. We will illustrate diagnostic challenges with case studies of three types of students: students whose gifts mask their disabilities, students whose disabilities mask their gifts, and the most challenging group—students whose gifts and disabilities mask each other. We draw a distinction between the process of identification—selecting students for programming and services—and the assessment process, which provides a rich analysis of a student's learning profile that meets many purposes beyond providing data for identification purposes. A good diagnostic evaluation guides teacher intervention and also demystifies the relationship between gifts and weaknesses for twice-exceptional students and their parents.

GTLD students can be identified in the classroom by attention to a number of red flags including inconsistent performance, slow work pace, and social and emotional difficulties. In Chapter 7, we discuss these classroom indicators. In Chapter 8, we go on to describe the formal assessment process and the special features of test performance in twice-exceptional students that require clinical judgment and careful analysis to fully grasp the range of a student's learning strengths and weaknesses. We advocate a neuropsychological approach that looks at learning from an information processing perspective. This approach does not require special training in neuropsychology but could be accomplished by a school psychologist with the addition of a few readily available tests to the standard psychoeducational battery. Teachers who receive professional development in information processing challenges in learning can also make more informed observations and instructional interventions. We identify best practices in assessment including careful analysis of variability in test performance, the collection of contextual information from teachers and parents in real-world challenges, and careful attention to qualitative data gleaned from observations during the testing process.

In Chapter 11, we begin to develop recommendations for programming with the recognition that school budgets are tight and there is already a struggle to make gifted education a funding priority. Effective instruction for twice-exceptional students requires a fundamental shift in teacher orientation. Teachers typically do not have the necessary skill set to address the complexity of GTLD issues. The training of most teachers focuses on one aspect of the picture: general education strategies, special education strategies, or gifted education. With professional development and mentoring, teachers can broaden their skills to flexibly address the changing needs of students who need more individualized attention. We discuss the paradoxical nature of twice-exceptional students in terms of their need for structure and flexibility, their need for clear expectations but empathy for their challenges, their desire for relationships but the need to develop social skills, and the need to recognize both their strengths and their weaknesses.

In Chapters 12–17, we illustrate best practices for programming for twice-exceptional students through a series of case studies from a variety of school settings. We identify the importance of teaching to student strengths and interests, as well as providing an accepting and supportive climate in the classroom. Helping parents understand the disparity of student strengths and weaknesses is particularly important in developing a strong support system for students. We also address the important role of accommodations and adaptations in removing barriers for students to participate successfully in gifted programming. In terms of particular curriculum models, we discuss the importance of programs that explicitly teach higher order thinking and metacognitive strategies. Many of these programs are elegant in their simplicity and can be introduced school-wide to good effect. We also emphasize the importance of embedding supports and accommodations into the school program as seen in the Universal Design for Learning movement.

The issues regarding the value of GTLD programming must be seen in the context of a current transformation in educational policy. Standards for diagnosis of learning disabilities are in flux with the rise of the Response to Intervention (RtI) movement and impending changes in the American Psychiatric Association's *Diagnostic and Statistical Manual* (DSM), the manual used by clinicians as a standard for diagnosis. As these changes occur, students with disabilities, particularly those students who are GTLD, are vulnerable to losing the support they need. With the advent of RtI, a document gap has emerged where students who have received interventions via RtI do not have the testing documentation required by most colleges. In Chapter 18, we discuss the issues regarding documentation for college and also point to the importance for high school programs to provide a structured transition to college.

Gifted students with learning disabilities challenge many assumptions in both special education and gifted education. We hope you will come to appreciate the courage and perseverance of these students, as well as the complex issues in assessment and programming they present. We believe this pursuit is worthwhile as a way to organize thinking about all students who don't readily fit the mold.

chapter 1

GTLD Versus Twice-Exceptional— What's in a Name?

Fashions change in the world of gifted education as they do in the world at large, and labels often convey particular conceptual orientations. In the latter portion of the 20th century, the terms *gifted* and *learning disabled* developed through separate channels due to the public laws governing the provision of educational services for special populations. Definitions of specific learning disabilities emerged in 1975 with the Education for All Handicapped Children Act (Public Law 94-142) and were further codified in the 1990 Individuals With Disabilities Education Act. Although the definition of giftedness has a long theoretical and research basis, legal definitions of giftedness emerged through the 1988 Jacob K. Javits Gifted and Talented Education Act. The concept that a student could be both "learning disabled" and "gifted" arrived much later on the scene. For many students, having a learning disability meant that they were not considered eligible for gifted programming. The inclusion movement has led to the recognition that students may have multiple academic needs that should be addressed, and it is no longer acceptable to exclude students from academically rigorous programs because they might need special accommodations or adaptations to participate (Neihart, 2008).

In recent years, the term *twice-exceptional* has gained parlance as a descriptor that recognizes that many factors can interfere with the expression of talent. Seeking to attract a larger advocacy community, organizations for gifted students with learning disabilities have broadened the scope of their mission to include students with attention disorders, hearing and speech impairments, and emotional disturbance, in addition to students with specific learning disabilities (Kavale & Forness, 1998). Each of these co-occurring conditions introduces a complex set of educational and assessment considerations in planning programs for gifted students. This book will focus on the narrower range of specific learning disabilities and attention disorders, but we will also touch on the impact of emotional concerns in the course of our discussion of programming challenges, with particular attention devoted to students on the autism spectrum. These students represent a significant portion of students with both gifts and learning challenges who require specific classroom adaptations to address their social and emotional needs.

One motivation for the current use of the term twice-exceptional is the desire to avoid identifying students specifically on the basis of their weaknesses. The labeling of learning deficits is particularly painful for parents and teachers of students who are both intellectually gifted and who have learning challenges. These students constantly hold out the promise of extraordinary capacity but often stumble in the execution of tasks designed to demonstrate their talent, a matter of constant frustration for both students and their adult support teams. However, in our experience, it is important not to gloss over the diagnosis of a specific learning disability. The term learning disability provides a legal mandate for students to receive needed services and accommodations. Glossing over a child's deficits has the unfortunate impact of weakening a mandate to address academic difficulties with publicly funded services and accommodations. For many gifted students with disabilities, these services and accommodations are crucial to their ability to succeed in advanced academic settings.

The Concept of GTLD Stretches the Definition of Learning Disability

As Kavale and Forness (1998) indicated, the definition of learning disability (LD) has both scientific and political aspects. The concept of LD was originally defined in the 1970s as relating to specific learning deficits rather than generalized learning failure. Inherent in the original definition was the concept of "unexplained learning failure" or underachievement; the notion was that there was an unexpected level of academic performance that did not mesh with the student's other academic or cognitive skills. Also integral to the original definition of LD was the notion that learning deficits were caused by brain-based processes that created these specific problems. Kavale and Forness noted that as the criteria for intellectual disabilities (formerly called mental retardation) and emotional disturbance were tightened, students who obviously needed services were excluded from special education. Subsequently, the functional definition of LD expanded and became less rigorous. In a sense, the category of LD became a "catch-all."

Early definitions of specific learning disabilities were based on the use of a discrepancy model. In this approach, a significant disparity between a person's performance on a measure of intellectual ability (e.g., an IQ test) and measures of academic achievement in a particular domain was deemed to indicate the presence of a specific learning disability. This approach was codified in the Individuals With Disabilities Education Act (IDEA), which provides a categorical definition for learning disabilities. That is, a child had to meet diagnostic criteria for a learning disability within a particular academic domain (e.g., reading, written expression).

Controversies Over Discrepancy Models

Discrepancy models came under criticism following a large-scale, multisite research study conducted by the National Institute of Child Health and Human Development (NICHD; Lyon & Moats, 1997), which found that poor readers who also had an ability/achievement discrepancy were not significantly different in their reading problems or progress from poor readers who had both poor reading skills and low cognitive functioning. This research challenged the practice of excluding cognitively low-functioning students from reading remediation and research on dyslexia based on the belief that their poor reading resulted from low intelligence. The NICHD study concluded that students at all ability levels who are reading below grade level can profit from structured reading remediation using phonologically based methods.

Subsequent brain imaging research has found that students with high and low IQs have similar patterns of brain dysfunction in relation to phonological processing (Tanaka et al., 2011). Interestingly, the *Los Angeles Times* reported that this study indicated that IQ testing should not be used to diagnose reading disabilities (Roan, 2011). This position has been taken to a greater extreme by proponents of the low-achievement model (Fletcher, Francis, Morris, & Lyon, 2005), who claim that diagnostic testing is not helpful and that looking at test profiles is suspect. The low-achievement model focuses solely on academic performance and Response to Intervention (RtI).

As a result of this reading research, the RtI model was developed to provide early intervention when students fall behind in basic academics. In this approach, students with low achievement scores are assumed to require remedial instruction, which is provided without formal diagnostic assessment. Students who do not respond to this more intensive intervention are then referred for further assessment and may progress through increasing intensity of special education services. The debate over the relative merits of RtI versus the cognitive hypothesis-testing model has developed in an unfortunate direction with each side caricaturing the claims of the other point of view. The RtI movement claims that advocates of the benefits of testing want to return to the old model of waiting to fail until the student is evaluated and that there is limited evidence to support the benefits of doing diagnostic testing. Testing advocates dismiss the real improvements in intervention made by the RtI approach (Learning Disabilities Association of America, 2010). Both points of view tend to dismiss the insights and contributions of the other side and to exaggerate the empirical support for their general claims. Fortunately, IDEA splits the difference and allows for multiple ways to define learning disabilities.

The range of learning disabilities profiles is sufficiently complex that a single model is unlikely to address the issues for all of the relevant subgroups of students. For example, many students do respond to intensive phonological intervention in early elementary school. However, a subset of poor readers doesn't improve in overall reading skills despite intensive phonologically based instruction. Challenges in addressing the needs of this group tend to get swept under the political carpet when people defend RtI, because RtI does not yet provide a way to effectively address these students' needs. For these students, diagnostic assessment is important to identify the information processing challenges that are interfering with their acquisition of basic academic skills (McKenzie, 2009). It is our contention that twice-exceptional students comprise another group that does not readily fit the mold.

Learning Disabilities Are Associated With Neuropsychological Deficits

The more extreme proponents of RtI (e.g., Fletcher et al., 2005) contend that neuropsychological testing has not been found to be useful in diagnosing learning disabilities. However, a meta-analysis of 32 peer-reviewed articles conducted by Johnson, Humphrey, Mellard, Woods, and Swanson (2010) found strong effects for neuropsychological deficits in students with specific learning disabilities as compared to their typically performing peers. In the area of reading disabilities, the strongest deficits were found in phonological processing, verbal working memory, and processing speed. Language ability was also a significant deficit. For mathematics disabilities, deficits in executive functions were large. Despite these results, the claim is that there is not sufficient specificity to claim a causal relationship. That is, the connection between these cognitive processes and specific academic skills is not clear-cut and the fact that cognitive deficits can be related to more than one academic process suggests a lack of causality.

The successful identification of specific neuropsychological processes underlying basic reading skills has perhaps led to unrealistic expectations regarding the further specificity possible in relating neuropsychological processes to discrete academic skills. Phonological processing and rapid retrieval of sound/symbol associations, the processes underlying basic decoding skills, are fairly discrete functions. However, students who are still struggling with reading comprehension after having "cracked the code" are likely struggling with more complex and general processing challenges (i.e., language, memory, and executive functions) that affect multiple academic domains. We may find specific information processing deficits related to math and writing acquisition as research progresses in these areas, but again, the more complex problems in these academic domains likely have an overlay of broader cognitive dysfunction.

Research has found that the students most resistant to RtI intervention are students who have average ability but score below average in reading achievement (Swanson, 2008). Johnson et al. (2010) found that these students have the greatest neuropsychological deficits as well. Although twice-exceptional students have overall higher cognitive ability and academic skills, they also experience complex processing challenges as students who fail to respond to RtI intervention.

To date, little has been written about the use of RtI with twice-exceptional students (Crepeau-Hobson & Bianco, 2011). The movement toward the RtI model has presented challenges for gifted students with learning disabilities. Psychologists have long relied on the ability-achievement discrepancy model to diagnose learning disabilities in gifted students. Twice-exceptional learners use their strong intellect, together with hard work and determination, to compensate for their learning challenges. The result of these efforts may mean that their achievement is in the average range relative to peers—yet a significant weakness compared to their intellectual capability. Using an RtI approach increases the likelihood that the needs of these students—both their gifts and their disabilities—will remain masked (Assouline, Foley Nicpon, & Whiteman, 2010; McKenzie, 2010). Because the abilities of twice-exceptional students often mask the impact of their learning challenges, they are unlikely to be identified as needing intervention. In addition, because of the decreased emphasis on assessment with the RtI approach, the gifts of these students may go unidentified as well. Until we have more complete information about the relationship between cognition and learning, the intuition that a person should roughly achieve at the level of his or her intellectual ability is a practical and reasonable approach to identify significant learning problems.

Although similar brain processes appear to underlie dyslexia across the range of intellectual ability, students with stronger overall cognitive ability are likely to manage their learning challenges differently than students of low cognitive ability. Reading is a complex process that involves a range of skills beyond phonological processing. Brighter students make use of a broader arsenal of cognitive skills to compensate for phonological deficits. High-ability students who meet the low achievement criteria are likely to be the most extreme members of this group and may face important additional challenges that interfere with their ability to use their cognitive skills to compensate for basic phonological weaknesses.

The understanding of these complex learners would be facilitated by the use of the sophisticated tools available to measure neuropsychological functions. Gifted students with learning disabilities identified via a discrepancy model typically have a clear pattern of processing deficits. Indeed, a best practices approach in diagnosing specific learning disabilities requires more than a simple discrepancy between intellect and achievement, but also dictates that a relevant processing deficit be identified to explain the observed discrepancy (Brody & Mills, 1997).

Unfortunately, the current focus on low academic outcomes in the Individuals With Disabilities Education Improvement Act (IDEA; 2004) and the Americans with Disabilities Act (ADA; 1990) has led to a decline in the use of psychological testing in the public school system. This situation is particularly tragic given the significant advances in research on the underlying processing issues that affect learning, particularly in the areas of executive functioning and working memory. Just when we have the tools to really explain *why* someone is unable to learn adequately, society is turning away from these more sophisticated measures.

Although the decline in the use of psychological testing results from the reading debate stimulated by the NICHD research program and the RtI movement, it is also a matter of convenience due to the costs of conducting diagnostic evaluations. Diagnostic testing is time-consuming and requires an increasingly specialized set of skills to provide state-of-the-art evaluations. To some extent, relying solely on outcomes to guide instruction dooms educators to a trial-and-error approach in addressing learning difficulties beyond basic skills. Classroom teachers are not equipped with the tools to assess most important neuropsychological processes involved in learning.

An appropriately designed comprehensive evaluation will produce a consistent and coherent explanation for an individual's learning challenges and also identify strengths best used to compensate for areas of neuropsychological weakness. Learning disabled students of all ability levels struggle with academics due to significant information processing weaknesses that show up both on neuropsychological tests and also can be observed in the way that individuals approach standardized tests. Often, compensatory strategies can be observed or inferred from a person's performance. Reevaluations of students over the course of their academic careers often demonstrate that neuropsychological patterns tend to be stable over time.

Gifted Students With Learning Disabilities Are Often Overlooked

Gifted students with learning disabilities are often overlooked both for having learning problems and also for having intellectual gifts because they can muddle through with roughly average school performance. The tragedy of overlooking these learning issues is that eventually these students reach a point where their homegrown compensatory strategies are unable to successfully manage complex academic tasks. At that point, the students begin to struggle to maintain even average performance—not to mention the level of performance that might be expected given their intellectual horsepower. Hitting this wall can occur at third grade, sixth grade, 10th grade, college, or even graduate school. Perhaps it is not surprising that a recent study found that 31% of participants with a specific learning disability (i.e., a disability in reading, mathematics, or written expression) indicated that their disability was first identified at the postsecondary level (Stodden & Conway, 2002). It is likely that a large portion of these students were GTLD.

Twice-exceptional students are caught in the vortex of the debate over the definition of learning disability, as they are most often identified via a discrepancy model and do not necessarily perform below age or grade expectations due to their ability to partially compensate for their processing challenges. The performance of these students challenges the traditional definition of disability as a numerical equation and also raises issues of equity in identifying an appropriate frame of reference: Should individuals in advanced academic situations who are competing with intellectually gifted peers be held to a standard that compares them to the average American? Many of these students struggle in academically challenging situations but perform in the average range in standardized testing terms. This issue becomes particularly salient as students move into college and work situations. It is important to keep in mind that these students are floundering largely due to deficits in basic academic fluency—not in intellectual capacity. They struggle with the input and output of information but can function at an advanced level to "connect the dots"—once they have the dots.

Focusing solely on test scores also ignores the painful reality for twice-exceptional individuals, many of whom invest extensive time and effort in convoluted and laborious procedures to work around their processing difficulties. These students often work diligently into the night with mediocre results. Before we gloss over their struggles by considering their outcomes "good enough," consider that we may actually be punishing these students for their often admirable motivation and perseverance—if they did not work so hard, their performance would deteriorate to a level that would qualify for LD services. These individuals are the ones most penalized by the gatekeeping function that standardized testing performs at the college, postgraduate, and professional levels. Entrance to college, graduate, or professional school and licensure examinations all hinge on performance on timed tests where students are expected to work intensively for a relatively brief period of time. Students who need additional time to process and retrieve information have to meet increasingly stringent standards to demonstrate a disability. It is particularly frustrating to recognize that the same time constraints and performance demands do not actually exist in most professional work environments. As you will see in later portions of this book, what these students need are fairly simple changes—accommodations in terms of extended time and output modality, as well as instruction in metacognitive strategies—to increase the efficiency of their compensatory strategies.

Who Are GTLD Students?

Case Study 1: Carolyn

Carolyn is a typical gifted student with learning disabilities. She initially attended public school and had early difficulty learning numbers, colors, and the alphabet. Her handwriting skills were slow to develop, and she reversed letters and was a poor speller. Despite these difficulties, Carolyn made good grades, and her teachers rated her academic performance as strong for her age. It was not until she was 11 years old that Carolyn began to have significant struggles that led her parents to seek a private diagnostic evaluation. Her parents were particularly concerned that a bright girl like Carolyn did not enjoy going to school, and they were worried about her frequent somatic complaints.

Carolyn received a comprehensive evaluation at age 11 that looked at her overall cognitive ability, as well as her basic academic skills. In addition, neuropsychological tests were included in Carolyn's evaluation. These tests provide insight to Carolyn's information processing strengths and weaknesses, which can help explain disparities in ability and academic performance. We will go into Carolyn's diagnostic profile in some detail because it illustrates some important points regarding testing and performance in gifted students with learning disabilities.

Table 1.1

Carolyn's Scores on the Wechsler Intelligence Scale for Children-Third Edition (WISC-III)

Scale	Composite Score	Percentile Rank	Qualitative Description
Verbal Comprehension	130	98	Very Superior
Perceptual Organization	114	82	High Average
Freedom from Distractibility	106	66	Average
Processing Speed	111	77	High Average
Verbal IQ	128	97	Superior
Performance IQ	112	79	High Average
Full Scale IQ	123	94	Superior

Note. IQ and index scores range from 50 to 150. The average range is 90–109.

Table 1.1 provides the intelligence testing profile for Carolyn at age 11. Later, we will review her subsequent performance on intelligence tests over the years, which show a decline in cognitive skills that can be characteristic of gifted students with learning disabilities. At age 11, Carolyn's testing on the Wechsler Intelligence Scale for Children-III (WISC-III) indicated superior overall ability with a Full Scale IQ score of 123, a level of performance at the 94th percentile compared to Carolyn's age peers. IQ tests are composed of subtests that can be statistically grouped to examine clusters of ability. On the WISC-III, Carolyn obtained a Verbal IQ score of 128, which fell at the 97th percentile. This score is comprised of scores on subtests measuring various aspects of verbal reasoning and knowledge. Clearly, Carolyn demonstrated giftedness in the area of verbal ability. Somewhat in contrast, her performance on measures of nonverbal reasoning fell in the high average range with a Performance IQ score of 112 (79th percentile).

A more in-depth understanding of Carolyn's skills can be seen through the level of indices (see Table 1.2). The Verbal Comprehension Index and Perceptual Organization Index measure aspects of higher order thinking. Looking at her individual subtest scores, Carolyn had some exceptionally strong scores on the Information, Vocabulary, Comprehension, and Picture Arrangement subtests. These scores indicate an advanced knowledge base in terms of Carolyn's general fund of knowledge and vocabulary as well as highly developed awareness of social conventions.

Looking back at Table 1.1, note that Carolyn's two other indexes, the Freedom from Distractibility Index of 106 (66th percentile) and the Processing Speed Index of 111 (77th percentile) are quite a bit lower and range from aver-

Table 1.2
Carolyn's Scores on the WISC-III Subtests

Subtests	SS*	Percentile
Verbal Comprehension		
Information	17	99
Similarities	13	84
Vocabulary	15	95
Comprehension	16	98
Perceptual Organization		
Picture Completion	12	75
Picture Arrangement	18	99
Block Design	9	37
Object Assembly	10	50
Freedom from Distractibility		
Arithmetic	13	84
Digit Span**	9	37
Processing Speed		
Coding	10	50
Symbol Search**	14	91

Note. Scaled scores range from 1 to 19 with 10 as average. Percentiles range from zero to 100 with 50 as average.
*Subtest Scaled Score Mean = 10; SD = 3. **Optional subtest

age to the low end of the high average range. These scales represent measures of cognitive efficiency. The disparity between Carolyn's higher order skills and her cognitive efficiency indicates that she has exceptional reasoning skills, but performs more similarly to an average person in the input and output of information. Both Carolyn and her teachers may feel frustrated that her pace of production is not as rapid as her overall intelligence might indicate.

Gifted individuals in general have greater disparities in subtest scores than their mainstream peers, with some exceptional skills and other scores that are more within the average range. The discrepancy between higher order reasoning and cognitive efficiency is a common finding among gifted individuals. In Carolyn's case, this disparity reflected underlying processing challenges that affect her overall cognitive efficiency.

Intelligence testing is used in diagnostic evaluations to provide an overall estimation of intellectual potential. A child would be expected to roughly score in academics at the level of his or her overall intelligence. A person with

Carolyn's superior score/intelligence would be expected to score at least in the high average range in her academics. However, when we examine Carolyn's achievement test scores, she scored in the average range for reading comprehension and basic reading skills, as well as for written expression and math calculation. In the current educational climate, Carolyn would not qualify for special education because her achievement, while discrepant from her ability, is in the average range.

However, Carolyn's neuropsychological testing indicated that there were underlying processing deficits that account for her struggles with academics and for which she was compensating with her strong intellectual horsepower and personal work ethic. Neuropsychological tests assess the input and output of information, in terms of auditory and visual processing, language processing, memory, and organization and planning skills. Pinpointing strengths and weaknesses in information processing tells us why a person might be struggling with particular academic tasks. Much research on reading disabilities has found two cognitive processes that underlie reading disabilities: phonological processing, or the ability to discriminate and manipulate sound/symbol associations, and lexical retrieval, or the ability to "see and say." How quickly a student can accomplish these basic tasks determines her overall reading fluency, which, in turn, affects reading comprehension. Carolyn had weaknesses in both of these dimensions.

Because she was tested privately, Carolyn received a diagnosis of a learning disability due to reading and writing skills that were below expectations based on her overall intelligence. Note that this diagnosis relies on a discrepancy model definition of learning disabilities: Carolyn did not score below average on measures of academic achievement. Clinicians in the private sector tend to rely on the text revision of the fourth edition of the *Diagnostic and Statistical Manual* (DSM-IV) of the American Psychiatric Association (APA; 2000), which gives greater latitude for professional judgment than is allowed in a public school setting. As a result, it is possible for a psychologist to diagnose a specific learning disability based on DSM criteria while the public school does not view the student as qualified for special education or accommodations.

Subsequent to her diagnosis, Carolyn received tutoring in reading and went on to attend a selective college preparatory school. Although she made excellent grades, Carolyn struggled to complete her work within the time limits given. In ninth grade, she returned for a diagnostic evaluation due to her parents' concerns that she was spending excessive amounts of time on her schoolwork. Although Carolyn was deemed eligible for extended time accommodations for classroom tests, she was reluctant to make use of this accommodation. Her parents were concerned about her high stress level, increasingly rigid work habits, and lack of time for nonacademic pursuits. Her teachers commented that

Carolyn was an outstanding and hardworking student, but they felt that she overprepared for assignments and tests. Carolyn went on to successfully complete her high school career with an A average, including taking a number of Advanced Placement courses.

Carolyn was accepted to a highly competitive and selective public university and returned for diagnostic testing to document her need for accommodations, as required by the Americans with Disabilities Act. Carolyn indicated that her main concerns were her difficulties with note taking and with identifying important information. Carolyn reported that she had to memorize everything because she could not pick out what was important, and she spent many hours writing practice essays for tests.

As can be seen in Table 1.3, by the time of this final assessment at age 18, Carolyn's overall IQ score as measured by the Wechsler Adult Intelligence Scale (3rd ed., WAIS-III) had fallen from the superior range to the average range (FSIQ = 104, 61st percentile). In part, this drop in scores reflects a change in the relative weights of subtests in constructing the Full Scale IQ score. On earlier versions of the Wechsler scales, the higher order reasoning scores were more highly weighted than the measures of cognitive efficiency. However, the current versions of the Wechsler tests equally weight both dimensions due to the belief that efficiency is an important part of intelligence in the real world. Similar to her performance at age 11, Carolyn's verbal comprehension was superior and her perceptual reasoning was high average. However, the earlier divergence between higher order thinking and cognitive efficiency has increased, with Carolyn then performing in the low average range for working memory and low in the average range for processing speed. Measures of cognitive efficiency typically require individuals to complete simple tasks under timed conditions. The drop in Carolyn's IQ scores over time, illustrated in Table 1.3, is not uncommon in the learning disabled population and represents the impact of increased demands on working memory and executive functioning skills placed on individuals at different ages. Figure 1.1 shows the drop visually.

A stark picture emerges in Carolyn's neuropsychological test profile. As Table 1.4 and Figure 1.2 illustrate, Carolyn had areas of both extreme competence and extreme deficit. Consistent with her earlier testing, Carolyn continued to show underlying deficits in phonological processing and lexical retrieval. Carolyn's profile indicated the classic pattern of dyslexia. She had difficulty breaking individual words down into component sounds and also in accessing letter and number names quickly. When individuals struggle with these skills, particularly as young adults, it indicates that these processes are not sufficiently automatic and that more effort is being exerted to execute basic reading functions than is expected. For most young adult readers, basic decoding and sight reading skills require minimal effort or brain resources. For the dyslexic young

Table 1.3
Carolyn's IQ Scores Over Time

Scale	Age 11	Age 15	Age 18
Full Scale IQ	123	110	104
Verbal Comprehension Index	130	128	124
Perceptual Organization Index	114	108	111
Working Memory Index/ Freedom from Distractibility Index	106	88	82
Processing Speed Index	111	100	91

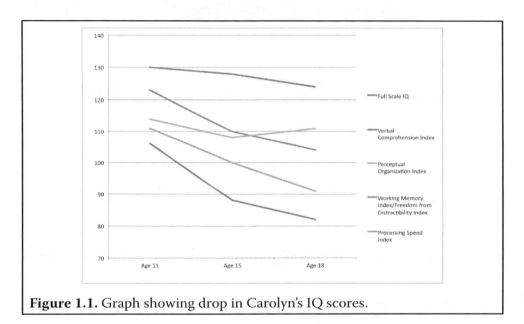

Figure 1.1. Graph showing drop in Carolyn's IQ scores.

adult, some conscious effort is still involved in just determining what the words on the page are, leaving fewer mental resources available for other functions such as comprehension and inferential thinking.

In addition to prerequisite reading skills, Carolyn struggled in the area of working memory, as indicated by her difficulty recalling sequences and retrieving specific information on demand. Working memory serves as the dispatcher that matches incoming information demands with the relevant aspects of the memory system, similar to the 911 dispatcher who must decide which ambulance and hospital system to utilize based on the location and specifics of the emergency situation. The working memory system must evaluate the demands of a particular cognitive task in the moment and then access the necessary brain

Table 1.4
Carolyn's Neuropsychological Profile at Age 18

Subtest	Percentile
Language Processing	
Phonological Processing	16
Rapid Naming	2
Letter Fluency	37
Category Fluency	1
Sight Word Efficiency	4
Decoding Efficiency	10
Memory and Learning	
Narrative Memory	75
List Learning	25
Sequences	9
Executive Functioning	
Category Switching	37
Number Sequencing	63
Number-Letter Switching	37
Sorting	84
Sort Recognition	84
Word Context	16
Proverb	91
Visual Motor	
Motor Speed	37
Rey Copy	14
Rey Delay	79

functions to meet the demand. Students with weak working memory constantly struggle to hang on to enough information to accurately assess the task demand and then to make the necessary connections. This means they struggle to manage information in the moment and they need to fill in missing pieces after the fact using reasoning or past experiences. Students like Carolyn need additional time to get organized and get the required brain processes rolling.

Neuropsychological testing also identifies strengths. Carolyn had a strong narrative memory, which is a common finding in gifted students with learning disabilities. When information is presented in a story format or is highly organized with a narrative framework, Carolyn had advanced skills that help

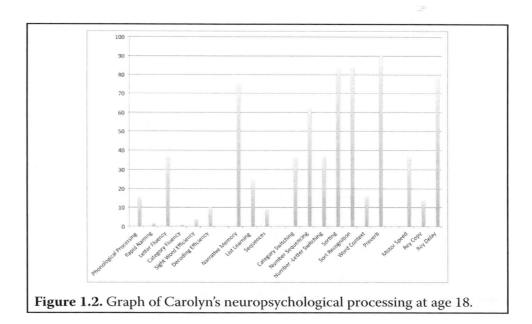

Figure 1.2. Graph of Carolyn's neuropsychological processing at age 18.

her compensate for other memory weaknesses. As Carolyn herself indicated, she often relied on memorization as a learning strategy. When she loses track of what she is doing, Carolyn was able to fill in the gaps in information by using her sense of the "story" and her comprehensive knowledge base. Carolyn also demonstrated strong problem-solving skills that likely helped her to use logic to fill in missing information.

Carolyn's academic profile at age 18 demonstrated the dramatic contrast between her advanced conceptual skills and the weak underpinnings of basic processes. Carolyn had strong reading comprehension, particularly when given extended time accommodations, but her basic reading skills and reading fluency were deficient. Similarly, in mathematics, Carolyn had very poor recall of basic math facts and struggled to complete computations in a timely manner, but is able to excel in calculations in an untimed format. Carolyn had poor spelling and struggled to write simple sentences quickly on a measure of writing fluency, yet can write complex writing assignments with sophistication. As noted in Figures 1.3 and 1.4, over time, the discrepancy between Carolyn's advanced conceptual skills and basic fluency increasingly diverged and her academic fluency fell to the below average range as her conceptual skills accelerated.

Carolyn went on to become a successful college student with a high college GPA and demonstrated her gifts in her placement in a selective science program. After college, she entered a doctoral program in biology at a major research university. Carolyn indicated that the single most important recommendation arising out of her evaluation was the provision of extended time for tests. She also profited from planning her course of study to spread out courses.

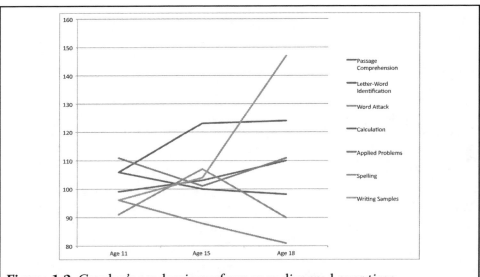

Figure 1.3. Carolyn's academic performance diverged over time.

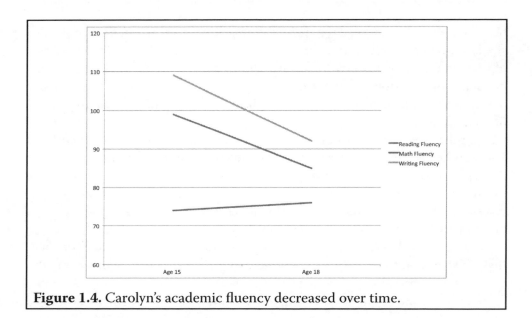

Figure 1.4. Carolyn's academic fluency decreased over time.

Although Carolyn's story has a happy ending, many other twice-exceptional students face a long road of misunderstandings and frustration. As you will note, Carolyn's teachers never actually identified that she had learning challenges but were more attuned to her level of work and stress. She was lucky to have attentive parents who sought answers to the mismatch of her ability and her performance and to have the family resources available to address her real but subtle learning challenges. Often, parents are the most aware of the toll that learning disabilities take on gifted students.

Case Study 2: Edgar

In many ways, Carolyn illustrates the best-case scenario for twice-exceptional students. Despite her learning challenges, Carolyn was able to remain hopeful and resilient in dealing with these problems. Not all GTLD students face such a relatively easy road.

Edgar originally came for testing as a junior in high school. He was failing his classes and getting into various social problems including drug and alcohol use, reckless driving, and truancy. He was a middle child in a large middle class family with concerned parents who had actually begun having diagnostic evaluations for Edgar when he was 7 years old. His family also sought support from his school but was somewhat less successful than Carolyn's family, as Edgar attended a public school where he was not deemed to qualify for special education. Edgar received several evaluations over the years and was given clinical diagnoses including ADHD and Disorder of Written Expression. By age 17, family tensions were high due to his parents' frustration with Edgar's apparent lack of motivation and effort. Edgar reacted to parental frustration and disappointment by avoidance or angry rebellion. Both Edgar and his parents regretted that he was not eligible to receive an advanced state diploma and that he was struggling to make postsecondary plans while his friends were pursuing admission to selective colleges.

Looking into his history, it was apparent that Edgar's parents had been concerned about his academic and classroom performance for many years, paying repeatedly for diagnostic evaluations and requesting evaluation by his public school system. Perhaps surprising given his subsequent reading performance, Edgar was an early and precocious reader; however, he gradually gave up recreational reading. Early test reports indicate some mild concerns with attention and motivation dating back to elementary school. Edgar's parents indicated that his grades began to decline in seventh grade, but that he had never given his best effort in school. They believed that he was "able to get by" because of his strong intelligence. Current teacher ratings indicated that Edgar was viewed as "a very capable student when he wants to be successful." Edgar was described as making limited effort, missing assignments, sleeping in class, and not taking advantage of extra help offered by his teachers. Some issues with managing materials, prioritizing tasks, paying attention, staying on task, and taking responsibility for his actions were also identified. Despite his poor attitude at school, Edgar was active on a travel sports team and successfully held a summer job.

At age 17, Edgar clearly demonstrated the profile of an individual with dyslexia. On the WAIS-III, Edgar's overall skills fell in the high average range (Full Scale IQ = 112; 79th percentile) with superior verbal comprehension (VCI = 120; 91st percentile) and average perceptual organization (POI = 105; 63rd percentile), working memory (WMI = 108; 70th percentile), and processing speed (PSI = 96, 40th percentile).

When Edgar's academics were considered, he scored solidly within the average range for math and writing skills, but there was variability in his reading skills. Assessment of his basic reading skills showed skills in the average range, although he did demonstrate some inefficiency in the automaticity of his reading. Edgar's reading fluency and comprehension were below age expectations on two more extensive reading tests, including a test (the Nelson-Denny Reading Test) that includes passages similar to those found on the SAT. These results indicated the presence of a specific learning disability in reading.

Edgar's neuropsychological testing profile is less dramatic than Carolyn's. He also had difficulty retrieving information from memory, as well as some challenges with visual-motor integration. For the most part, though, he scored within expected ranges for most language, memory, and executive functions. Given his history of early attention problems and current parent ratings, he was also diagnosed with ADHD.

So far, Edgar's testing seems rather straightforward, until his developmental profile is considered. In the area of intelligence, over the four evaluations, Edgar's scores measured in the superior to very superior range until a significant drop after age 13 (See Table 1.5 and Figure 1.5). A more dramatic decline was evident in Edgar's performance on measures of academic achievement, which began to decline after age 11 (See Table 1.6 and Figure 1.6). Similar to Carolyn, Edgar also demonstrated a drop in basic academic fluency over time.

To further complicate the picture, Edgar was experiencing significant social and emotional concerns that could have a negative impact on his academic and cognitive performance. So how did a gifted 7-year-old with highly advanced academic skills devolve into a bright teenager with a reading disorder and emotional difficulties? Given the complexity of the situation, it is likely that the answer is subtle. It is perhaps important to note that Edgar was evaluated at each point when academic demands increased: entering third grade, entering middle school, entering high school, and during 10th grade. Although Edgar did receive diagnoses along the way, these findings did not lead to interventions or accommodations. He was also not identified as gifted after early elementary school. The results suggest that, despite Edgar's early reading success, he did have an underlying reading disorder that eventually became apparent as academic demands increased.

Table 1.5
Edgar's IQ Scores Over Time

	Age 7	Age 9	Age 13	Age 17
	WISC-III	**WISC-III**	**WISC-IV**	**WAIS-III**
Verbal IQ	134	134	*	117
Performance IQ	112	112	*	105
Full Scale IQ	126	126	132	112
Verbal Comprehension Index	134	131	140	120
Perceptual Organization Index	113	116	123	105
Working Memory Index	*	134	138	108
Processing Speed Index	*	109	97	96

Note. * represents missing data from Edgar's file.

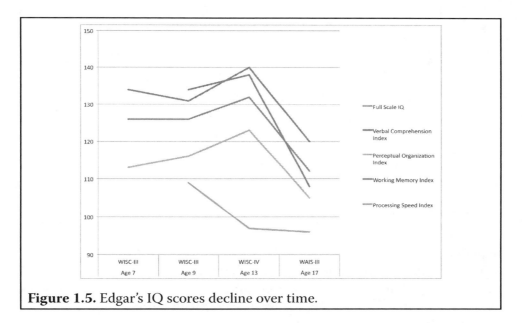

Figure 1.5. Edgar's IQ scores decline over time.

Edgar's profile is illustrative of the complex assessment issues that we will address later in this book. The issue of how to understand declines in cognitive and academic skills over time is complex. At one time it was thought that cognitive skills were generally stable over the course of an individual's life. However, recent research by Ramsden et al. (2011) has found that both verbal and nonverbal skills can change—either grow or decline—in adolescence. The decline

Table 1.6
Edgar's Academic Skills Over Time

	Age 7	Age 9	Age 13	Age 17
Letter-Word Identification	131	111	*	96
Passage Comprehension	125	115	110	115
Calculation	146	118	111	107
Applied Problems	143	127	107	105
Writing Samples	118	97	116	105

Note. * represents missing data from Edgar's file.

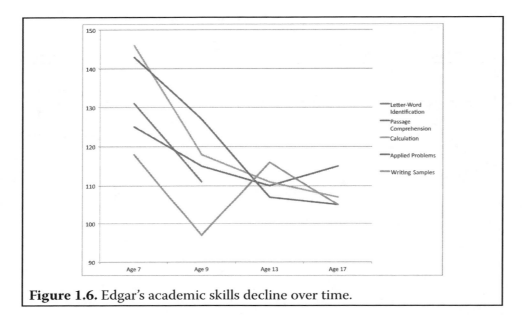

Figure 1.6. Edgar's academic skills decline over time.

in performance on IQ tests likely reflects some features of the test, namely that subtests are made more difficult by increasing the executive function demands of tasks. For example, more advanced items may require the juggling of a larger amount of information rather than dealing with more advanced content. Cognitive declines can also reflect processing speed issues. A further complication is that significant social and emotional difficulties, particularly anxiety and depression, can affect student performance on IQ tests. These difficulties are often a factor for students with significant learning challenges.

Declines can also occur in the academic skills of mainstream students. Xiang, Dahlin, Cronin, Theaker, and Durant (2011) examined longitudinal data from the Measures of Academic Progress (MAP) assessments by the Northwest

Evaluation Association. Using an extensive database, the researchers looked at elementary and middle school cohorts who had scored above the 90th percentile in math and reading. Over the course of 5 years, "Consistent High Flyers" (scorers above the 90th percentile at both points) represented between 55% and 70% of the groups. "Descenders" (students who scored above the 90th percentile pretest and scored below that level posttest) represented a significant portion of the group, from 30% to almost 50% of the group. However, the amount of decline in relative academic performance was very modest, with a high majority of students scoring in the top 30% of scorers. The level of decline seen in Carolyn's and Edgar's profiles is significantly greater than would be suggested by these data.

Edgar and his family were aware of the relative decline of his skills compared to his early potential and compared to his cohort of high-achieving classmates. At the time of the evaluation, Edgar had only tenuous hope that things could improve and was becoming significantly depressed, which further compromised his cognitive capacity and efficiency. His postsecondary plans at the time were to take courses at a community college or to enter the military. We have lost touch with Edgar, but hope that he has been able to explore alternate routes to success.

Conclusion

As the case studies of Carolyn and Edgar illustrate, twice-exceptional students test the limits of traditional understandings of both giftedness and the nature of learning disabilities. These students often face learning challenges that are difficult to capture in numbers; it can also be difficult to measure their strengths. Although twice-exceptional students create a challenge for assessment and identification (which we will begin to address in Chapter 8), intervention is important to prevent underachievement. In addition, GTLD programming can be beneficial to the school environment in the gains in sensitivity to the needs of diverse learners.

chapter 2

Models of Giftedness and Twice-Exceptionality

Statistical Definitions of Giftedness Underidentify Gifted Students With Disabilities

The original definitions of giftedness relied on a statistical definition based on the bell curve. Somewhat arbitrarily, giftedness was defined as having an IQ score more than two standard deviations above the mean, or above the 98th percentile. Although it is true that this criterion identifies a small group of individuals with rare IQ scores, this distinction is not based on a particular theoretical model or even research studies that demonstrate that individuals in this range are significantly different in an observable way from, say, individuals scoring above the 95th percentile. This issue became more pressing as the use of this somewhat arbitrary standard resulted in the underrepresentation of various groups within the pool of gifted students. Over time, it has become clear that other factors, such as exposure to multiple languages or socioeconomic conditions, do in fact have an impact on test performance. To accommodate this issue, most public school systems have used more generous numeric criteria and have incorporated other types of assessments to identify gifted potential.

Numeric criteria, however generous, continue to be problematic for individuals with learning disabilities. As we saw with Carolyn, individuals with learning disabilities typically have significant variability among subtest scores on intelligence tests that make the various summary scores, such as a Full Scale IQ score, unrepresentative of the full story of their strengths and weaknesses. Particularly for these individuals, people cannot be reduced to a single number.

Recognizing the difficulties with a statistical definition of intelligence, more recent models of giftedness have focused on the idea that innate talent is only one part of the puzzle. Complications arise in defining giftedness when some children who show early promise do not go on to appear gifted as adults and conversely, individuals who were not seen as gifted initially go on to develop extraordinary talent.

Multitrait Models of Giftedness Identify Factors That Determine Gifted Production

Renzulli's Three-Ring Conception of Giftedness

Multitrait models of giftedness rely upon the idea that talent is a potential within a person that is somewhat separate from but interacts with other factors of personality and cognitive functioning. For example, Joseph Renzulli and his colleagues at the University of Connecticut have identified additional attributes beyond advanced cognitive ability that are necessary components to gifted intellectual performance. In the Renzulli Three-Ring Conception of Giftedness model (Renzulli, 2005), motivation and creativity are viewed as moderating factors that determine whether an individual displays gifted behavior or produces gifted work. In Renzulli's view, having intellectual horsepower is a necessary but not sufficient condition for being gifted. Although the insight that it takes more than "being smart" to be gifted is helpful in understanding discrepancies between ability and achievement, Renzulli's model is fairly general in defining the other factors that go into the mix.

Despite its vague theoretical underpinnings in the Renzulli Three-Ring Conception of Giftedness, the Schoolwide Enrichment Model (Renzulli & Reis, 1997) represents a fairly unique contribution to the field in its level of empirical support. The Schoolwide Enrichment Model (SEM) applies the principles of gifted education to promote both the intellectual development of gifted students, as well as higher order thinking in a broad range of students whether gifted or not. Avoiding some of the inequities inherent in strict cutoff criteria for participation in gifted programming, the SEM exposes a broader range of students to enrichment activities to allow students with talent to bubble to the surface. Students are exposed to a gradually more specialized gifted curriculum beginning with whole-school exposure to new topics and enrichment clusters that teach students new skills from an expert, culminating in individual projects that students conduct to address a particular area of personal interest. In this approach, students pursue their own interests in a structured format that teaches them metacognitive skills.

Developmental Models of Giftedness

In contrast to the multitrait models, Russian theorists have pursued a developmental explanation for talent development (Jeltova & Grigorenko, 2005). Similar to the general development of human capacities for language and motor skills that develop at critical periods, these theorists propose that there are sensitive periods for giftedness. Under this view, various developmental capacities and experiential factors converge to create periods of heightened and accelerated talent development. The study of child prodigies as a special case illustrates the importance of realizing that giftedness is neither static nor a smooth progression (Shavinina, 2010). Child prodigies experience periods of very rapid acquisition of skills followed by periods of fundamental reorganization or consolidation of skills.

Walters and Gardner (1986) have pointed to the importance of "crystallizing experiences" in which individuals with potential encounter an experience that fundamentally alters their perception of a particular domain. Typically these crystallizing experiences involve another person, likely an expert in the field. The Russian view of the importance of the convergence of internal and external factors speaks to the role that the "goodness of fit" of the environment plays in whether a student actualizes gifted potential. When there is a lack of convergence between internal and external factors, potential may not be actualized.

Cross and Coleman (2005) also took a developmental approach in their conception of giftedness, but view the development of talent as a continuous process. In their view, giftedness equates to advanced development in a particular domain. In the early elementary years, gifted students have more generalized advanced ability that may be identified by the students' high performance on norm-referenced cognitive testing, high academic performance, or a more rapid learning rate than the typical student. Cross and Coleman viewed giftedness at this stage of development as normally distributed in the population (although they present no data to support this claim). Over time, students who continue to warrant the label of "gifted" move to advanced performance in an area of talent. At this later stage, which occurs by secondary school, giftedness should be judged by performance criteria; in other words, potential should have morphed into advanced talent. In the view of Cross and Coleman, although talent potential is normally distributed, advanced talent development is not. Having the opportunity to develop talent and the commitment to persevere in developing skills determine whether a person reaches an advanced level of talent. Cross and Coleman questioned the concept of gifted underachiever and feel that by secondary school, students who don't reach their potential in talent development should no longer be seen as gifted.

Although there is merit in considering how long students should be given additional opportunities when they don't seem to take advantage of them, the situation for twice-exceptional students is more complicated because they are wrestling with deficits in basic skills that place them on a competing downward trajectory. As in the case of Carolyn, over time her basic skills did not keep pace with those of her peers, and she increasingly was pedaling uphill when others were coasting down. Given the emotional baggage that often accompanies this level of disparity in skills, it is perhaps not surprising that these often very dedicated and motivated individuals don't always have the capacity to develop their talent independently. GTLD instructional strategies provide the supports that will allow these students to have greater emotional and mental energy to develop areas of potential talent.

Overt Versus Covert Giftedness

Russian psychologists further recognized the complexity of talent development through the concept of "overt" versus "covert" giftedness (Jeltova & Grigorenko, 2005). Covertly gifted individuals present with atypical patterns that may mask giftedness. Albert Einstein is the poster child for this concept. Einstein was not viewed as gifted as a youngster, likely due to behavioral and social oddities that today might be recognized as features placing him on the autism spectrum. Russian researchers such as Leitis (as cited in Jeltova & Grigorenko, 2005), through observations and case studies, have identified the important role of creativity, particularly for these more atypical students who may be more likely to engage in exploration and experimentation in the world through creative outlets. For these students, efforts to change their unusual behaviors may create more stress that further blocks the development of their gifts, or they may not respond well to acceleration as an approach to gifted education. These students may need more time to use creative outlets to improve self-regulation and mental energy. Twice-exceptional students are more likely to exhibit atypical behaviors that mask their gifts.

Giftedness as Successful Intelligence

The notion that there should be a progression to the development of talent makes intuitive sense. Sternberg (2005) has developed the concept of giftedness as a development of expertise or as *successful intelligence*. In this view, success includes the ability to achieve personal goals in relation to gifts, to calibrate strengths and weaknesses to maximize success, and to address resources (or the absence thereof) in the environment. Sternberg identified metacognitive components of intelligence (i.e., common processes that underlie intelligent behavior in academic, social, and practical situations). These skills consist of executive functions: planning what to do, monitoring progress toward a goal, and evaluating the outcome. Further executive functions come into play in the selective acquisition of knowledge: deciding what is relevant to the situation, relating prior experience relevant to the current situation, and combining relevant information with prior knowledge in innovative ways. This issue is relevant to the GTLD discussion because executive functions are typically weak in students with learning disabilities. However, Sternberg pointed to three domains of intelligence: analytical, creative, and practical. Although GTLD students may struggle with executive functions in one domain, they may have strengths in other domains, such as in creative outlets or practical situations. Twice-exceptional students often do well in multisensory or hands-on situations that get them away from symbols and text. Even in the area of analytical executive skills, students can be taught these skills, and GTLD programming is an ideal way to develop them.

To further illustrate the importance of these broader conceptions of gifts, Sternberg worked for several years with the College Board to develop the Rainbow Project (Sternberg & Rainbow Project Collaborators, 2006), which attempted to improve the ability of the SAT to predict first-year college grades. Sternberg developed measures of both creativity and practical problem-solving skills to supplement the basic SAT and SAT II scores as predictors of freshman grades. Interestingly, the addition of these two additional facets of giftedness increased the predictive validity of the SAT and also did not show the inequities based on socioeconomic status and race that plague the SAT. In further research, Sternberg utilized this approach in selecting students for a precollege summer program and assigned students to a psychology course either taught in a way that matched their strengths (analytical, practical, or creative) or one that was discordant with their strengths. When instruction was matched to the students' strengths, they learned more.

Production Models of Giftedness

The Schoolwide Enrichment Model also provides guidance in terms of evaluating criteria for gifted production. Often, special talents are difficult to measure in terms of objective standards. The Student Performance Assessment Form (Renzulli & Reis, 1997) provided clear criteria for recognizing giftedness in student projects. Students should demonstrate a clear and fairly specific definition of their purpose or question to be answered, use more varied and advanced resources or materials than would be expected at their age, make a good match between the question of interest and the type of resources used, and demonstrate a logical process. In addition, students should have an "action" orientation that leads to some type of change, either in the problem or in the audience's perception of the problem, rather than simply report on the facts. Students should demonstrate originality, attention to detail, and commitment of time to the project, and they should make an original contribution for someone of their age.

Product-oriented definitions provide criteria by which to evaluate the giftedness of an individual's productive output. Having a clear idea of what constitutes gifted output makes it possible to demonstrate that individuals who don't meet traditional psychometric definitions of giftedness do in fact have the capacity to engage in gifted intellectual activity. Often for students with learning disabilities, the base conditions for intellectual activity may need to be modified in terms of time constraints and the use of assistive technology to allow them to overcome the limitations of deficient basic academic skills.

Product-oriented definitions of gifted work can also provide guidance in terms of evaluating progress toward advanced quality work. At the Kingsbury Day School in Washington, DC, a pioneering project is being conducted to engage students with complex learning disabilities in gifted programming. Many of these students have significant speech/language or motor challenges, as well as attentional and/or social-emotional challenges. Although the students receive accommodations such as text-to-voice software and scribing, they continue to face significant struggles due to their past history of learning challenges. Students in the Kingsbury GTLD program use the Renzulli Learning System (http://www.renzullilearning.com), a Web-based personalized search engine and learning platform, to structure student exploration of advanced topics and to produce long-term projects. Initially, students struggled to grasp the scope of gifted projects, and the Renzulli project evaluation criteria provided a means of evaluating the students' progress in demonstrating higher order thinking. Over time, these students are making progress in demonstrating their gifts with appropriate scaffolding and accommodations.

Munich Model of Giftedness

Understanding giftedness as a potential that may or may not be manifest under certain conditions helps us to better understand why bright individuals with learning disabilities may not be able to demonstrate their giftedness under typical circumstances. These moderating factors can point to interventions that may increase the ability of these bright individuals to function at a gifted level.

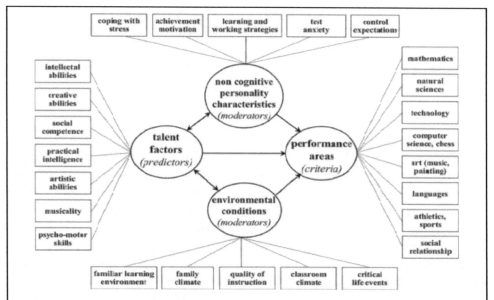

Figure 2.1. The Munich Model of Giftedness. From "The Munich Model of Giftedness Designed to Identify and Promote Gifted Students" by K. A. Heller, C. Perleth, and T. K. Lim, in *Conceptions of Giftedness* (2nd ed., p. 149), by R. Sternberg and J. Davidson (Eds.), 2005, Cambridge UK: Cambridge University Press. Copyright 2005 by Cambridge University Press. Reprinted with the permission of Cambridge University Press. All requests from third parties to reproduce this material must be forwarded to Cambridge University Press.

The Munich Model of Giftedness (Heller, 2004), a potentiality model, is particularly useful for understanding factors that may block or contribute to the actualization of talent or giftedness (see Figure 2.1). Heller's model is helpful in understanding the challenges for learning disabled students, as well as factors that may limit their ability to show their talents.

Moderator: Noncognitive personality factors. The Munich Model identifies noncognitive personality factors as important moderating variables. These variables include self-concept, coping and learning strategies, and achievement motivation and expectations, as well as a thirst for knowledge. For example, how willing a person might be to exhibit a talent depends on a basic level of expectation: A student who hopes for success is more likely to try than a student who fears failure. For individuals with learning disabilities, experiences in demand situations have often had mixed to poor results. These students have tempered their achievement motivation and expectations to be more consistent with their perceptions of their past experience and often have internalized poor outcomes as reflecting negatively on their self-worth. They may have a thirst for knowledge, but this interest is typically in a particular specialized area where they have experienced success. Students with learning disabilities have great difficulty stepping out of their comfort zone to explore new areas of knowledge. These students often need more emotional support to move to the next level in a particular area of study and profit from direct instruction on coping strategies for managing challenges and frustrations.

Moderator: Environmental factors. Heller (2004) also pointed to factors in the environment that have an impact on performance. Important factors included in this model are the role of the family as a support system for the student and the disruptive effects of stressful family circumstances. The impact of stress in the home is likely greater for students with disabilities due to the stress the family experiences in dealing with learning challenges in the student. Research on families with disabilities has found that family members experience greater stress and more physical problems due to the strain of interactions with the disabled student (Dyson, 1996). Seltzer et al. (2009) found that biological markers of stress were higher on days when parents of students with disabilities had the greatest interaction with the disabled child. Keep in mind that with gifted students with learning disabilities, it is most often the parents who are aware of the student's struggles with academic tasks and who likely provide support and attention at home to help their students compensate for learning challenges. These students are more likely to melt down in frustration at home after many challenging hours of school and homework. It is the parents' job to patch the student back together to make it through another day.

Another family factor that creates greater stress for families of learning disabled students is the higher probability that they have other family members with a learning disability. Studies have found that dyslexia, autism, and ADHD all cluster in families (Freitag, 2007; Thomson & Raskind, 2003; Wallis, Russell, & Muenke, 2008). Adults with learning disabilities often struggle with the management of daily tasks and routines due to weak executive skills. Families with a learning disabled child have a more complex situation to manage and may have fewer skills to manage the challenges effectively. Case management is very important for these families to help them cope more effectively.

The Munich Model also points to other environmental factors important to the expression of talent, particularly the school climate and its ability to flexibly meet the needs of diverse students. These factors speak to the debilitating effects on bright students who have instruction pitched at the wrong level. This issue is particularly problematic for students with dyslexia, who may be forced to suffer with work at the level of their reading skills rather than their intellectual capacity. Similarly, students with language-based learning disabilities often are mired in classrooms where the teacher relies solely on lecturing and verbal expression. These students are much more successful with multisensory instruction that facilitates their coping with language challenges.

The issue of the match between instruction and the student's skills and needs cannot be overemphasized. Vygotsky's (1978) theory of the Zone of Proximal Development clearly articulates the interaction of these factors in learning. In his view, students learn best with a moderate level of challenge. When work is too easy, students are not engaged or motivated to do the work, but when it is too difficult they assume that they cannot be successful in the task and avoid failure by not attempting it. For students with learning challenges, maintaining a moderate level of challenge is particularly tricky, as they often have wide variability in their skills across subject domains or types of work tasks. Often, each of these individuals requires differentiated instruction to optimize their learning. Vygotsky's concept of scaffolding is important in identifying that teachers perform a modulating function in titrating the level of challenge by providing support and accommodation as the skills develop, always keeping the level of challenge at a manageable level.

Moderator: Information processing factors. Although the Munich Model highlights two important moderating factors in determining whether gifts and talents are manifest, a third moderator is important for gifted students with learning disabilities: information processing factors. Figure 2.2 illustrates the combined influence of information processing, environmental, and personality factors on the expression of talent.

For the mainstream gifted student, his or her information processing is generally adequate and therefore not a significant determinant of performance. However, students with learning disabilities face a range of information processing challenges that affect both their personalities and responses to their environment, as well as play a role in determining the final outcome for their gifts. These skills cluster in four domains: language and phonological processing, memory and learning, attention and executive functions, and visual motor integration.

Language and phonological processing. Language and phonological processing are important in the development of literacy and writing skills. As we found in Carolyn's case, these difficulties may respond to remediation, but the student may also continue to experience the impact of basic language difficulties into adulthood. As these students mature, their language difficulties may manifest in a slow reading rate, poor reading comprehension of complex texts, and unsophisticated written expression. Phonological processing involves learning to discriminate individual phonemes (letter sounds) and to have the capacity to blend and segment individual sounds. Accommodations such as text-to-voice software (e.g., Kurzweil 3000) can be helpful in allowing gifted students with learning disabilities to read more efficiently by eliminating the

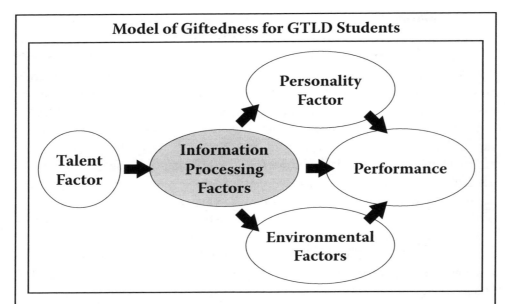

Model of Giftedness for GTLD Students

Figure 2.2. Model of giftedness for GTLD students. Adapted from "The Munich Model of Giftedness Designed to Identify and Promote Gifted Students" by K. A. Heller, C. Perleth, and T. K. Lim, in *Conceptions of Giftedness* (2nd ed., p. 149), by R. Sternberg and J. Davidson (Eds.), 2005, Cambridge UK: Cambridge University Press. Copyright 2005 by Cambridge University Press.

need for decoding and thereby improve their comprehension. Students with dyslexia or language disabilities typically struggle with foreign languages and may need reduced course requirements or adapted materials.

Memory and learning. In the areas of memory and learning, challenges often arise in the area of retrieval of information. Typically, students with learning disabilities have a solid fund of knowledge, but they often have difficulty accessing specific information on demand. These students have great difficulty with fill-in-the-blank tests and recalling specific dates of historical events. They are more successful with open-ended questions that have multiple response options or with multiple-choice questions that do not require retrieval. Often, retrieval difficulties reflect poor organization in the initial storage of information. Similar to a messy filing cabinet, students may have the information, but cannot find it quickly. Extended time accommodations are particularly important for these students because they need more time to find the information they need in their memory. These students also may have difficulty memorizing formulas in science and math and need a programmable calculator or lists of formulas for tests. Otherwise, tests are measuring their poor memory skills rather than their knowledge of science or mathematics.

Working memory challenges lie at the heart of many academic difficulties for students with learning disabilities. As we saw with Carolyn, these students have trouble coping with the flow of information in the moment. Their brains have difficulty taking in information and dispatching it to other brain functions. Often, details get lost in the shuffle, and they may not be able to hang on to information long enough to actually store it in memory. For individuals with dyslexia, poor working memory often interacts with slow reading speed to compromise reading comprehension: The student forgets the beginning of the passage by the time he or she has decoded the end. In Carolyn's case, she was able to compensate for losing information by filling it in from her comprehensive knowledge base using her strong reasoning skills. Students with poor working memory may not be able to compensate in this manner in the unfamiliar territory of a new subject area.

Working memory also helps with keeping track of procedures and remembering where one is in a sequence. Various academic tasks require completing a series of steps (e.g., the algorithm for long division), and GTLD students struggle to recall and order steps in these complex procedures. Often, students can be helped by visual lists or reminders of the steps in a process.

Nicolson and Fawcett (2008) proposed that a major difficulty for individuals with dyslexia is a deficit in procedural memory. These students have difficulty learning new procedures to the point of automaticity. Procedural memory difficulties create other learning challenges as well. When students are not able to advance to a level of automaticity in basic skills, they are prone to working memory overload because they are using inefficient procedures. These students also have difficulty with other rule-based learning beyond language and reading skills. They have difficulty mastering math facts and learning procedures for fractions and long division, as well as basic sequences like the months of the year. Students with poor procedural memory also have difficulty learning by observation and imitation and do better when given explicit skills instruction (Eide & Eide, 2011).

Attention and executive functioning. A third important area of neuropsychological functioning is in the area of attention and executive functioning. Mirsky, Anthony, Duncan, Ahearn, and Kellam (1991) have identified four important aspects of attention: the ability to focus, the ability for sustained concentration, the ability to encode (involving sequential memory and learning), and the ability to shift from one subject to another without undue stress. Each of these components can play a major role in school difficulties; in addition, weaknesses in these aspects of intelligence can interact in a synergistic manner.

Identifying the types of attentional challenge creating difficulty for a student does not necessarily clarify the causes of these issues. Whether a student has a biologically based attentional disorder or has difficulty attending because of poor language processing, he or she may struggle to focus on the appropriate information in the classroom. Students may also struggle to maintain their attention due to internal distractions. For example, students with autism spectrum disorders often have difficulty ignoring an inner monologue or the mental replay of video games or movies they have seen. Students with significant emotional challenges or obsessive anxious thoughts may also struggle to put aside these preoccupations to attend to instruction.

Executive functions refer to a range of skills that manage complex tasks. There are various models of executive functions but Adam Cox's (2008) Eight Pillars of Capability provides a useful starting point to understand these important brain processes. His eight pillars are: Initiation, Attention, Cognitive Flexibility, Working Memory, Organization, Planning, Self-Monitoring, and Emotional Control. Many students with weak executive skills struggle with task initiation; difficulty getting started on tasks is particularly problematic for gifted students who are often expected to complete advanced work in the form of independent projects. Although highly intelligent, gifted students with learning disabilities often struggle to understand the assignment and the expectations for the finished product. They may experience a task as overwhelming because they see the huge project before them and don't see how to break it down into manageable sections.

Students with various types of learning disabilities also struggle with cognitive flexibility. They often quickly leap to an answer and have difficulty seeing other options. Typically, they don't want to revisit their answer, as if their response was so effortful to begin with that they can't bear to change it—especially if the answer is in written form. These students can get stuck in thinking about a situation in one ineffective way and may continue to spin their wheels while ignoring feedback that indicates a change of course would be advisable. Power struggles often arise when cognitively rigid students interact with adults who also may have high expectations and strict standards.

Poor self-monitoring and emotional control also can present stumbling blocks in the classroom. Students with these executive skill weaknesses do a poor job of evaluating their progress toward a goal and whether they are still on the right course. They are vulnerable to following tangents that lead them away from the assigned task. Students with difficulties with emotional control may struggle to maintain an active, calm alertness; they may lack the physical or mental energy to activate higher order brain processes, or conversely, they may become so overexcited or upset so that they are not available to process information effectively.

Visual-motor integration. A fourth area of functioning important in academic output is visual-motor integration. Often, these difficulties begin in early childhood with mild delays in hand-eye coordination, such as difficulty learning to tie shoes or use scissors. The development of early handwriting skills can be problematic for GTLD students. For some, this may result in a simple delay in the development of handwriting skills; for others, handwriting struggles may persist. Gifted students often struggle in the early grades because their written output is so slow and laborious that they are too frustrated to try to express their complex ideas. They will verbalize a complex and detailed sentence and then proceed to write a five-word sentence with limited vocabulary. These students can be helped with handwriting instruction that minimizes the demands for motor movements, such as the Handwriting Without Tears program (http://www.hwtears.com).

Difficulties with complex visual-motor tasks, such as the Rey-Osterrieth Complex Figure Test, which requires students to copy a complex geometric line drawing, can indicate issues with a student's ability to organize and plan tasks. GTLD students may have difficulty taking a complex visual field and breaking it down into manageable chunks. Difficulties with visual complexity can be related to later difficulties in advanced math, including reading graphs and understanding geometric figures.

Conclusion

The complexity of information processing challenges for students with learning disabilities underscores the importance of using a multifaceted approach to understanding giftedness. Many current models of giftedness recognize that the manifestation of talent is not a given and that environmental and personality factors play important roles in the development of student strengths. For twice-exceptional students, both environmental and social-emotional issues can be more complex than for mainstream gifted students. In addition, information processing issues need to be recognized to provide appropriate intervention to foster the development of talent in twice-exceptional students.

chapter 3

Why Create a GTLD Program?

Twice-Exceptional Students Are at Risk for Underachievement

The National Council on Disability (NCD) produced a position paper in 2003 describing the state of postsecondary education for individuals with learning disabilities. It found that students with disabilities are less likely than their peers without disabilities to complete a full secondary school academic curriculum, especially in math and science curriculum areas, and are less likely to take advanced math and science courses in college. These students are also less likely to go to college and to qualify for admission to selective colleges. When ranked according to how qualified they were for college admission, students with disabilities were "much less likely to be even minimally qualified," based on an index score of grades, class rank, NELS composite test scores, and SAT/ACT scores (National Center for Educational Statistics, 1999, p. iv). The study found that young adults with disabilities in postsecondary education are less likely to persevere and complete a degree or certificate than peers without disabilities. On average, students with disabilities who finish postsecondary education take twice as long to complete their degree than do nondisabled peers. Eighty percent of youth with disabilities who attempt postsecondary education require some assistance to manage/coordinate their educational and related services.

Although gifted students with learning disabilities have some intellectual resources to compensate for their learning challenges and may find themselves admitted to challenging college programs, many twice-exceptional individuals do not perform at a level commensurate with their abilities. Pirozzo (1982) asserted that about half of the gifted children who score in the top 5% of intellectual ability on individualized IQ tests do not demonstrate comparable school achievement.

GTLD Programming Can Identify Skill Gaps

Provision of GTLD programming can help identify the skill gaps resulting from undiagnosed learning disabilities, particularly in the areas of executive function and working memory weaknesses. In addition to basic remediation, these students need training in specific compensatory strategies, self-advocacy, and executive functioning.

In a study of gifted college students with disabilities, Reis, McGuire, and Neu (2000) found that many of these students were not identified as either gifted or learning disabled prior to entering college. These students indicated that the metacognitive strategies that they learned at the college level were responsible for their academic success. Strategies they found helpful included memory skills (e.g., mnemonics), chunking of information, time management, note-taking skills, breaking down assignments into manageable units, and library skills. None of these students felt that these effective strategies were taught in their special education classrooms. Instead, classroom time was spent solely on remediating their areas of academic weakness, primarily in basic skills.

GTLD programming can provide students with the opportunity to learn these basic study survival skills. As indicated previously, these students may not demonstrate sufficient academic deficits to meet school system criteria to qualify for special education services, yet they clearly need additional support in the classroom. Development of GTLD programs provides the forum for students to receive more specialized training in metacognition without requiring an Individualized Education Program (IEP).

Programming for Twice-Exceptional Students Changes the School Culture and Increases Overall School Achievement

Recent analyses by the Thomas Fordham Institute using data from the National Assessment of Educational Progress (Duffett, Farkas, & Loveless, 2008) indicated that the general education approach is not working for high achievers in general. The NAEP data suggested that although the lowest-achieving students have made strides in academic achievement from implementation of the No Child Left Behind (2001) legislation, the performance of the highest achieving students has stagnated. Teacher surveys conducted in the Fordham report indicated that teachers found it difficult to implement differentiated instruction and spent a vast majority of their time interacting with low-achieving students. Although teachers believed all students were entitled to equal attention in meeting their needs, they found that the demands of accountability forced them to focus on the lower achieving students to the detriment of the higher achieving students. Various studies over the years have found that teachers have limited exposure to instructional methods for working with gifted students and do not typically provide instruction at their academic level. If the current approach to education is not working for mainstream high achievers, it certainly is not providing necessary components for gifted students with disabilities who are much more complex in their needs due to greater processing and social-emotional challenges.

GTLD Instruction Increases Rigor for All Students

Instructional methods appropriate for twice-exceptional students can provide the tools to apply greater rigor for all students. Kulik (1992) found that when students have been grouped according to ability with content appropriate to their capacity, all levels of students have been found to improve in academic attainment. Applying gifted strategies from Renzulli's Schoolwide Enrichment Model, Reis et al. (2007) assigned a heterogeneous group of students (including gifted students) to participate in the Schoolwide Enrichment Model in Reading (SEM-R) as compared to a traditional reading program. Students who participated in the SEM-R program showed improved oral reading fluency and comprehension, as well as more positive attitudes toward reading.

More generally, a large-scale research study using the National Assessment of Educational Progress found that classroom teaching practices associated with teaching higher order thinking skills, skills used in gifted programming, are associated with more advanced educational progress (Wenglinsky, 2000). In this study, *How Teaching Matters*, funded by the Milken Family Foundation and conducted under the auspices of the Educational Testing Service, Wenglinsky (2000) used statistical modeling to examine factors of teacher input (e.g., expertise in the field), student factors (e.g., socioeconomic status), and classroom practice factors (e.g., use of hands-on materials), and their relative contribution to student achievement in eighth-grade math and science. Because of statistical modeling, this study was able to compare the relative impact of factors leading to high achievement. Several interesting findings emerged. Higher achievement in mathematics was found in students whose teachers had received professional development in working with special populations and in teaching higher order thinking skills. Students whose teachers emphasized higher order thinking skills outperformed their peers by about 40% of a grade level. The overall findings of the report indicated that teachers with greater mastery of their subject and who received richer and more extensive professional development were better able to teach higher order thinking skills and used effective science instruction involving hands-on learning.

GTLD Programming Provides an Effective Model for Service Delivery

In addition to introducing more effective teaching strategies, the provision of GTLD services creates a model for effective intervention for all students. Twice-exceptional students benefit from a multidisciplinary team to provide services and monitor their educational progress. The team approach increases collaboration and cross-fertilization between staff members. Twice-exceptional students often need a close collaboration between home and school and benefit from a "case manager" model. Using this type of approach more broadly can provide benefits to other subgroups of the student population who also bring complicated interactions between home, school, and the community.

Twice-exceptional students typically do not fit a particular mold and often require considerable individualization in the approach to teaching and behavior management. Effective GTLD programming brings focus to a student's strengths *and* her weaknesses. Because these students frequently manage to hide both their strengths and weaknesses, seeing the whole child requires doing some detective work and can encourage teachers to be more evidence-based and to question assumptions. GTLD programs are child-centered in the sense that the program is focused on what works for a particular child.

Training in GTLD Identification Can Increase Sensitivity to Underserved Populations

The development of GTLD services can create a more inclusive and flexible mindset in identifying and understanding a more representative group of students overall. Teachers who are trained to identify and work with gifted students with learning disabilities are sensitized to individual behavioral and emotional responses to specific learning tasks. Many of these issues are present in other underserved gifted populations, including students of poverty and English language learners.

In 1996, the Texas State Board of Education (Slocumb & Olenchak, 2006) passed new regulations for the provision of gifted and talented services with the goal that the distribution of GT students should reflect the ethnic distribution of the total district. Evaluations of Texas GT programs indicated that there was a higher representation of middle class students than would be predicted and a much lower representation of children of poverty. Further underrepresentation was evident for English language learners. The Texas State Board of Education established a task force to examine inequity in GT services and to identify appropriate criteria for increasing the representativeness of the GT population served. The task force produced a very useful chart comparing qualities of traditional GT students with three groups of underrepresented students: students of poverty, English language learners in poverty, and special education students. Communalities were evident among these three underserved groups in comparison to traditional gifted students. The underserved groups struggled with aspects of language processing and expression, demonstrated stronger reasoning skills in real-world situations or situations where they held a personal interest, demonstrated strengths in nonacademic areas of interests, and needed modeling and support to grasp new concepts. On a personal level, these students were more likely to struggle with self-esteem issues and had difficulty seeing the future. They also worked better with some type of peer or adult support.

The task force (Slocumb & Olenchak, 2006) recommended that GT assessment measures be tailored to the specific population in a particular school and that differentiated measures be utilized that reflected local norms. For example, students of poverty might be identified as having advanced potential based on comparisons to their particular peer group rather than national or state norms. For example, a student who scored at the 80th percentile on a measure of achievement when her peer group typically scored at the 60th percentile might be viewed as having some exceptional ability.

The Texas findings provided a good illustration of how attention to particular underserved groups, such as twice-exceptional students, can lead to a better understanding of ways to identify other underserved groups for advanced programs. The communalities among underserved populations provide guidance for modifying programs to meet the learning styles of a broader range of students. Attention to these issues can stimulate greater creativity in gifted curriculum and program delivery.

GTLD Programming Can Prevent Some of the Social-Emotional Costs for Students Who Fall Between the Cracks

Unaddressed Challenges Lead to Avoidance Behavior

Bright youngsters entering school for the first time are typically eager to learn and hopeful about the future. The subset of students in this group who have dyslexia or other processing challenges learn fairly quickly that they are not achieving at the rate of their peers. Every first grader knows the pecking order of reading groups and the relative skills of members of the class despite adult efforts to disguise groupings with euphemistic names. Bright students who are struggling to master basic academic skills are also struggling to understand their situation. On the one hand, they think—or have been told—that they are smart, yet they can evaluate their skills and find them lacking. In our clinical experience, gifted students with learning disabilities typically cope with this dilemma by developing an attribution that they can't read or write because they are "stupid," or they may project their discomfort by blaming teachers and parents for "unfair" expectations. In both cases, to avoid painful feelings, these students shrink from academic challenges or engage in distracting behavior to disguise their avoidance. In addition, an unfortunate consequence of being identified as learning disabled, if the identification actually happens, is that students are pulled out for needed remedial work. These needed interventions have the consequence of confirming student attributions of being "stupid," because the work is necessarily at a lower level than their intellectual ability. Although inclusion instruction has limited the further ghettoization of students with learning disabilities, twice-exceptional students continue to struggle with the reality that they don't perform as well as their peers that they see as intellectual equals.

Students who engage in distraction and avoidance to hide their disabilities see confirmation in the lowered expectations that can occur due to their difficulties with basic academic skills. We have found that it is very difficult for classroom teachers to keep both the gifts and the deficits in mind in instruction, and there is a drift toward focusing on levels of current performance rather than potential.

In their classic longitudinal study of 1,500 gifted students, Terman and Oden (1947) found that gifted underachievers differed from academically successful gifted students in having low levels of self-confidence and feelings of inferiority, difficulty persevering, and difficulty establishing goals. Subsequent research (Rimm, 1995; Whitmore, 1987) has further identified factors in the home environment that interfere with student achievement in gifted underachievers.

Underachievement Syndrome

Sylvia Rimm (2008a) provided the most detailed analysis of what she calls "underachievement syndrome" in her four quadrant model. She pointed to the interaction of effort and outcome in the first part of the model: Students who see a connection between their efforts and positive results are likely to continue to pursue achievement. These students have traits seen in successful mainstream gifted students, namely they value learning for its own sake, attribute the positive outcome to their own efforts, and feel disappointed when they don't try and fail. For other students who either obtain easy success with limited effort or whose positive efforts do not lead to success, persistence in challenging tasks is more unlikely.

In the second part of her model, Rimm (2008a) indicated that some underachieving students make a positive effort but fail nevertheless. She noted that this situation is common for dyslexic students who are often faced with challenging reading tasks throughout the school day. For students with learning disabilities, this situation may occur because the assigned tasks are not within the student's skills. She pinpointed another poor fit in the classroom in the third section of the model—where students are successful without trying. This situation can be common with gifted students with learning disabilities who are so bright in the early grades that they are able to "fake it" and don't find the work particularly challenging. These students develop a vested interest in easy success and when demands increase in later grades, they may avoid challenges to save face and to hide a fear of inadequacy. Some of these students are able to compensate so well on basic primary tasks that more subtle but profound learning difficulties are not recognized. These students tend to go along with a string of disappointed parents and teachers who view them as lazy. The final part of Rimm's model represents students who have basically given up and feel hopeless; these students make little effort and expect the worst.

Rimm (2008a) identified several features of underachievement syndrome. These students lack a sense of internal control while also having skewed family dynamics in which parents have given them too much power at an early age, likely deceived by their precocity. They have intense conflict about competition and are intensely concerned about maintaining their status with peers. For students with hidden disabilities, there is intensified pressure to put up a front.

Underachievement in Gifted Students Is Related to Unaddressed Social-Emotional Concerns

Reis (1998) has suggested that gifted students who are not sufficiently challenged in school may actually be "dropping out with dignity" when they choose not to do work that is below their intellectual ability. A study by Reis, Hébert, Diaz, Maxfield, and Ratley (1995) found that gifted high school students of varying achievement levels reported significant boredom in lower grades. These students became more difficult to motivate in high school. Although the empirical data is limited, there is some evidence to suggest that successful programs to address underachievement in gifted students require attention to social and emotional factors, both in terms of managing the students' own emotional experiences and also in creating an environment that is flexible and attuned to the specific needs of individual students (Supplee, 1990; Whitmore, 1980). Additional factors were identified by Emerick (1992) in her qualitative study of the long-term trajectory of gifted underachievers into adulthood. Several factors appeared to be related to future academic success in these students, including the pursuit of personal interests outside of the school setting, support of parents and teachers, and a change in achievement motivation. Participants noted that a special relationship with a teacher was a major factor in reversing poor academic performance. Other studies have found that students who participate in extracurricular activities are less likely to be underachievers (Colangelo, Kerr, Christensen, & Maxey, 1993; Reis et al., 1995).

Pursuit of personal interests and a focus on student strengths has been found to increase achievement in underachieving gifted students. Research on the Renzulli Schoolwide Enrichment Model has found that the pursuit of student-selected projects was related to improved academic performance and classroom behavior (Renzulli, 1977; Renzulli & Reis, 1997). Baum, Renzulli, and Hébert (1995a, 1995b) suggested that flexible, student-centered enrichment approaches may help reverse underachievement in gifted students.

Compensatory Strategies Create Further Stress for GTLD Students

Other social and emotional costs for gifted and learning disabled students lie in the very nature of their compensatory strategies. Some of these students, such as Carolyn, work very hard to compensate, yet the level of self-monitoring and self-regulation required leads to significant restrictions in their personal interests and ability to observe the outside world. Students like Carolyn are constantly checking and revising their work and revisiting instructions and schedules because they know they make mistakes and have to be vigilant to avoid them. By high school, these students are worn down by the constant effort to function at an advanced level. They can appear humorless and mildly depressed. Often, their low-grade depression stems from a restriction in outlets to relieve stress—these students may spend so much time on homework that they don't have time to socialize, which can lead to impaired development in their social skills.

Providing programming for gifted students with learning disabilities can help these students learn ways to manage their affective experiences. Sometimes, simply the recognition that they are struggling with something that other people aren't coping with can be a huge relief. Even these fairly successful high school students may attribute their success to luck rather than effort despite their huge investment in energy. These students may have difficulty seeing the big picture due to their weak executive skills and may seem to be reacting based on superstition rather than an analysis that hard work leads to success. These students are always waiting for the next challenge that will lead to disaster and embarrassment. They are constantly scanning for the next failure experience, and as a result, they become avoidant of taking academic risks. Programming for twice-exceptional students can help them break out of their shells.

Conclusion

Twice-exceptional students face a number of risk factors that threaten their academic success. Because of their information processing challenges, they do not have the necessary skills to manage complex, higher order tasks and require explicit instruction to develop the necessary skills. In addition, many twice-exceptional students struggle to cope with the added emotional burden placed on them by their learning challenges. These students can benefit from targeted programming, as we will illustrate in our discussion of the best practices for programming. An added benefit of GTLD programming is its positive impact on teacher training in terms of providing child-centered, individualized instruction and increasing sensitivity to other at-risk student groups.

chapter 4

Characteristics of Twice-Exceptional Students

Prevalence of Gifted Students With Learning Disabilities

Ruban and Reis (2005) pointed to the difficulties in quantifying the prevalence of gifted students with learning disabilities due to the varying definitions of both giftedness and learning disabilities. As we have shown, definitions of learning disabilities and giftedness are often based on policy rather than research, and criteria differ across jurisdictions. An additional complication in determining the prevalence of twice-exceptional students is the fact that they are challenging to identify because of subtleties in their performance and their use of compensatory strategies. Research studies cited by Ruban and Reis, namely Silverman (1989) and Nielsen (2002), found that between 1% and 3% of gifted students have learning disabilities. Silverman examined testing data for a large group of gifted students to identify those who met criteria for learning disabilities and found a prevalence rate of 1.4%. Nielsen examined test data of a large group of students over a 7-year period who were diagnosed with specific learning disabilities and looked for evidence of giftedness. This study found a prevalence rate of 3.5% when teachers were educated regarding characteristics of gifted students with disabilities. These studies have more rigorous definitions of giftedness and learning disabilities than is common in the public school arena. The National Education Association (2006) estimated that the percent-

Table 4.1
Characteristics Shared by GTLD and Mainstream Gifted Students

Superior cognitive potential
Passionate about areas of interest
Strong motivation to learn (about topics of interest)
Intuitive, readily see the big picture
Have penetrating insights and unique points of view
Out-of-the-box thinkers
Creative and imaginative

age of twice-exceptional children probably mirrors that in the general population—around 6% of students. Generally about half of the twice-exceptional population falls in the domain of specific learning disabilities.

Gifted students with learning disabilities have a number of common characteristics, many of which they share with mainstream gifted students. These characteristics are listed in Table 4.1 and explained below in greater detail.

GTLD Students May Demonstrate Unique Cognitive Strengths

Although advanced cognitive ability is by definition a criterion of the GTLD concept, it can often be hard to recognize the superior intellectual abilities of twice-exceptional students. In this section, we will explore a different idea—that twice-exceptional students have different cognitive strengths than those of mainstream gifted students. Recent research has turned the focus of the information processing and performance differences in twice-exceptional individuals from a deficit perspective to a strength approach that identifies advantages to the particular information processing profiles in these disorders. In the area of specific learning disabilities, this approach has led to potential advantages in the visual-spatial processing of dyslexia. Similarly, visual-spatial strengths have been proposed in the processing approach of individuals with ADHD (e.g., Freed & Parsons, 1997) and autism spectrum disorders.

Dyslexia May Be Associated With Cognitive Strengths

The advanced cognitive ability of some gifted students with learning disabilities can be seen on standardized testing. For example, Nicolson and Fawcett (2008) suggested that students with dyslexia often do well with explicit declarative learning, the type of learning measured by intelligence tests, but actually have deficits in procedural learning that lead to their learning disabilities. Thus, they can have a split in test scores that results in a discrepancy between their overall IQ and their academic skills where the latter skills require competence in procedural learning.

However, the superior gifts of students with specific learning disabilities, such as dyslexia, may not fit the prototype of the typical verbally gifted student. In his book *In the Mind's Eye*, West (2009) described profiles of innovators in science, literature, business, and the arts who each appeared to have significant learning challenges, particularly in the area of reading and managing symbolic information. For example, Michael Faraday was well-known for his innovative conceptions of magnetic fields in physics, yet he was not able to explain his theories mathematically because he was unable to master the advanced calculation skills required. He developed his ideas based on visual modeling and conceptualization. West proposed that many individuals with dyslexia struggle with traditional text-based thinking but have sophisticated visual reasoning skills that will become particularly important in the 21st century where many computer-based innovations require sophisticated visual processing. In a review of research on dyslexia, however, Brown and Rice (2004) found that there was no evidence that individuals with dyslexia had more advanced visualization skills. Although some anatomical differences have been found between brains of persons with and without dyslexia, Brown and Rice suggested that these differences may be an outcome of different learning and brain development as a result of learning problems rather than a cause of the dyslexia.

Although the evidence of stronger visual skills in gifted individuals with specific learning disabilities is limited at present, there has been some research in considering dyslexia from a strength point of view. It is perhaps too early to tell whether the visual gifts of famously successful dyslexics apply to other dyslexic individuals as well. Some recent research cited by Eide and Eide (2011) suggested that there could be other ways to understand differences between dyslexic individuals and the mainstream population. In *The Dyslexia Advantage*, Eide and Eide suggested that the dyslexic brain does not simply have deficits in areas related to phonological processing; instead, the brains of individuals with dyslexia have a different organizing principle. In this perspective, reading difficulties are viewed as the flip side of a profile of strengths that account for the success of many dyslexic adults. Individuals with dyslexia tend to excel in four types of reasoning: visual-spatial reasoning, interconnected reasoning, narrative reasoning, and dynamic reasoning. Students with dyslexia have strengths in seeing the links between ideas, getting the gist of concepts, and seeing things from different perspectives. They are often highly able to reason well in situations where the facts are changing. Eide and Eide described the dichotomies between dyslexic and nondyslexic thinkers as trees to forest, fine to coarse grain distinctions, text to context, and parts to whole. Visual-spatial and global thinking skills are not typically measured in standardized testing and are more likely to be seen in a student's products, perhaps in personal pursuits not related to academic work.

Autistic Individuals May Excel in Specialized Visual-Spatial Skills

Temple Grandin (1996), a well-known person with autism and an animal scientist, has been a strong advocate of the idea that individuals on the autism spectrum have strengths in visual processing. According to Grandin, she doesn't assimilate information but stores it in individual pictures much like information is stored on a video storage device, such as a DVD. This information is then sequenced chronologically. Grandin hypothesized that all people with autism process information at a detail level first and then develop broader and more general concepts. In contrast, Grandin felt that neurotypical individuals rely more on generic general concepts from the start. In her 2006 update, Grandin expanded her view of specialized thinking processes in autism to include three types: visual thinkers like herself; music and math thinkers who think in patterns and excel in math, chess, and computer programming; and verbal logical thinkers who think in word details and excel in subjects such as history or foreign languages. Grandin indicated that all three types think in a detail-oriented manner that distinguishes them from neurotypical individuals. She also feels all three groups share a common difficulty with concept formation.

Although there are many anecdotal accounts of "savant" skills in individuals with autism, empirical research documenting cognitive strengths in autism is an emerging area of study. Howlin, Goode, Hutton, and Rutter (2009) investigated the rate and types of savant skills in a large group of adults with autism. A savant skill was defined as an exceptional cognitive ability or skill in comparison to the general population or compared to the individual's own general level of functioning. They found that 28.5% of adults with autism had a savant skill or exceptional cognitive ability. About half of this group scored highly on a block design measure and an equal number were rated as having exceptional achievement via parent report. Most savant talents involved prodigious memory, mathematical calculation skills, or musical skills (e.g., being able to perform complex compositions after hearing the piece once).

Research on specific cognitive processing strengths in autism has found enhanced perceptual skills in individuals with autism (Shah & Frith, 1993). Mottron, Dawson, Soulières, Hubert, and Burack (2006) proposed the Enhanced Perceptual Functioning model as a framework for understanding the perception of those with autism. In this view, superior functioning in persons with autism can be found in the perception of domain specific, low-level auditory and visual processing (e.g., in pattern recognition and feature detection). The model suggests that persons with autism have much stronger skills than typical individuals in their perception of localized, detailed information, but struggle to process and integrate complex information. Individuals with autism are more likely to maintain details that can be lost in the generalization of information. Aspects of poor social functioning in children with autism have been attributed to their hyperfocus on details of objects that prevents them from attending to important social information in their environment (Charwarska, Klin, & Volkmar, 2003).

In terms of reasoning skills, the literature on cognitive strengths in autism suggests that there are spikes in visual-spatial skills in the cognitive performance of those with high-functioning autism on intelligence tests. Michelle Dawson, a researcher in autism cognition who has autism, has criticized the interpretation of these visual-spatial spikes as "splinter" skills that often do not have a major real-life outcome and has pointed to the potential bias of the commonly used intelligence scales such as the Wechsler scales (see Woodford, 2006). Dawson, Soulières, Gernsbacher, and Mottron (2007) compared the performance of adults and children with high-functioning autism on the Wechsler intelligence scales and their performance on the Raven's Progressive Matrices test, a nonverbal test with limited motor demands that measures fluid reasoning and problem solving. Fluid reasoning refers to ability to reason and think logically in novel situations. In this study, individuals with autism scored on average 30 percentile points higher on the Raven's test than on the Wechsler scales. Dawson et al. cited these findings as indicating that there are important aspects of intelligence where individuals with autism excel that are not measured by traditional standardized tests.

In addition to specialized areas of strength that might not be measured in mainstream cognitive research, some studies have found differences between those with autism and neurotypical individuals in the coordination between traditional cognitive skills that could lead to unique strengths for persons with autism. For example, Goldstein et al. (2008) found that although individuals with autism had similar overall scores on a traditional intelligence test, their subtest scores did not cluster together into coherent domains in the manner seen in neurotypical individuals; rather, there was greater independence between individual subtests. Soulières, Dawson, Gernsbacher, and Mottron (2011) suggested that the independence of cognitive functions allows persons with autism to pursue simultaneous parallel cognitive processes resulting in increased creativity and novel problem solving. They suggested that the process of generalization required for the hierarchical organization of information in neurotypical brains results in a loss of detail that obscures possible new insights in the service of fitting information into prior structures.

Other research using brain imaging has found that there are differences in the use of cognitive resources in problem solving by individuals with autism and neurotypical peers (Sahyoun, Belliveau, Soulières, Schwartz, & Mody, 2010). In complex cognitive tasks, neurotypical individuals utilized more areas of the frontal lobe and language areas of the brain, while those with autism used more temporal lobe areas associated with visual processing. The overall performance of the two groups on the task did not differ. Whether individuals with autism have exceptional visual-spatial skills beyond that of their mainstream peers is not clear.

GTLD Students Are More Context-Dependent

In addition to the possibility of a preferred cognitive modality, twice-exceptional students also face some challenges in demonstrating their strong cognitive ability. Their performance can be more context-dependent or conditional than that of the traditionally gifted student. Although mainstream gifted students may be able to adapt to unexpected situations or to more open-ended task demands, many twice-exceptional learners can be thrown by surprises. GTLD students also show greater variability both within and between cognitive skill sets. They are more likely to struggle with easy tasks due to difficulties with executive functions or attention. The format in which a task is presented can be a huge stumbling block for learning disabled students. They often struggle to grasp task demands and may opt out of trying because of frustration. There is also greater day-to-day variability in their performance due to fluctuating motivation and effort. On some days they are "on," and on other days they struggle to just show up. However, it is important to keep in mind that these students have strong cognitive abilities in the right situation.

GTLD Students Have Passion and Motivation

Passions Drive the Effort to Compensate for Learning Challenges

Both mainstream gifted and twice-exceptional students can be passionate about areas of interest. In fact, passion is often the factor that keeps individuals with learning challenges willing to try and take risks to stretch their skills. In *In the Mind's Eye,* West (2009) described the severe learning difficulties of William

Butler Yeats, the acclaimed Irish poet and playwright, a writer well-known for his mastery of expressive language. Yeats had severe difficulties with spelling, punctuation, and oral expression that he was able to overcome through meticulous editing of his written work. According to West, Yeats described his engagement with his own thoughts (which provided him with inspiration), indicating that when he tried to do anything with his thoughts, "it was like trying to pack a balloon in a shed in high wind" (p. 211). Despite his extreme frustration with writing, Yeats nevertheless became one of the most gifted writers of his age.

Like Yeats, many gifted students with learning challenges have intense interests and are often willing to spend considerable energy to develop their expertise about a particular subject or talent. Because the structure of school is not geared to facilitate the expression of their gifts, these students often engage in intense intellectual activity on their own time. Parents frequently describe the phenomenal skills that their twice-exceptional children have developed without prompting or guidance from anyone. A recent documentary produced by RTE Irish television in 2005 (see http://www.autism-central.com/aspergers-syndrome-documentary-david-jordan/997; Autism Central, 2012) featured David Jordan, a graduate student pursuing a doctorate in geology who had been recently diagnosed with Asperger's syndrome (AS). Although he expressed painful awareness of social problems caused by his disorder, David also indicated that features of AS gave him the intense, single-minded focus to develop a comprehensive understanding of rock crystals, which led him to pursue graduate training. David's experiences with collaborative research led him to have enough success socially that he chose to work on his social skills and founded a social skills group at his university.

GTLD Students Need Encouragement to Leave Their Comfort Zones

Although some twice-exceptional students find a way to pursue their passions on their own terms, for others, their challenges can hold them back. For these students, negative experiences in performance situations have led them to stay in their comfort zones. Later in this book, we will discuss strategies to help students pursue areas of personal interest to develop their strengths. Social support is often important; West (2009) pointed out that many successful persons with dyslexia throughout history had supportive parents who were creative in accommodating their children's challenges in a world that did not recognize their difficulties or their strengths.

Like many people on the autism spectrum, David Jordan (Autism Central, 2012) described using his interests to help him cope with other challenges in his life. For students with autism spectrum disorders, intellectual pursuits can serve a self-soothing function; they may find reading about or contemplating chosen intellectual topics to be a source of comfort or a means of self-calming. For these students, their passion is a protective shield that they may have an investment in maintaining. They require considerable emotional support to broaden their focus to related topics or to move into new areas in a given topic.

Another challenge for some twice-exceptional students lies in their ability to shift away from their focus on their passion. They can go too deep into a topic to the exclusion of other interests or experiences. Particularly, students on the autism spectrum can become "little professors" who give others too much information and do not process nonverbal cues that indicate they should move on to another topic of conversation. These students can become internally distracted by their preferred topics and may not pay adequate attention to the ongoing world around them.

Both mainstream and twice-exceptional learners can be highly motivated. For mainstream gifted students this is likely to be in a variety of areas; they have varied talents that they pursue with dedication. Developing talent in one domain often leads to the development of more general skills that can be applied to other endeavors. For example, learning to play a musical instrument well can create the development of work habits that lead to advanced academic achievement.

GTLD Students Often Need Support and Scaffolding to Complete Complex Tasks

However, GTLD students often need more support to remain motivated in complex tasks and are likely to be sidetracked by difficulties prioritizing, coping with frustration, and staying on task. In other words, their weak information processing skills affect their efficiency in mastering content, even when they are highly motivated. Because of their learning challenges, they objectively have more things to be frustrated about, and their learning experience is more complicated because of their need to fill in or compensate for weaknesses. To fully develop their talents, these students need to be given more specific instructions in strategies to approach advanced tasks. A further challenge for twice-exceptional students is the difficulty they can have in generalizing skills. Because of poor processing, these students don't always categorize situations in the way that mainstream students do and might not spontaneously grasp that skills in one domain could apply in another situation. Providing GTLD students with learning supports can help them to more effectively maintain their motivation in the face of complex learning challenges.

Intuition, Insight, Creativity, and Out-of-the-Box Thinking

In his book, West (2009) presented case studies of famous innovators in science, literature, and the arts who all appear to have had dyslexia and all were creative, out-of-the-box thinkers. West attributed their creativity to advanced visual conceptualization skills. In *The Dyslexic Advantage*, Eide and Eide (2011) attributed higher creative potential to aspects of reasoning that they see in individuals with dyslexia. In their view, people with dyslexia have strengths in interconnected reasoning. They are able to see likenesses or causal relationships between more distantly related concepts and have the capacity to shift perspectives. Dyslexics often see the "gist" rather than being bogged down by details. Eide and Eide also attributed a form of dynamic reasoning to people with dyslexia. These individuals often excel in reasoning in fluid circumstances where the facts are changing.

Eide and Eide (2011) also indicated that features of brain development may provide the opportunity for increased capacity for creativity in individuals with dyslexia. Research by Turkeltaub, Gareau, Flowers, Zeffiro, and Eden (2003) on hemispheric dominance found that most readers begin reading with a mixture of right- and left-brain functions. As typical readers become more competent, they shift to using the left hemisphere to process written text. This progression is typical in learning new tasks: mixed dominance during early phases of learning followed by a move to left hemispheric dominance. This shift increases efficiency by the pruning of unnecessary neural pathways. For dyslexics, the shift to left dominance does not occur, leaving many more neural connections. Eide and Eide indicated that the impact of this pattern is an increased capacity to make distant connections and inferences, as well as to deal with ambiguities. These skills are often associated with creativity. This area of research is developing; Yale University recently started the Yale Center for Dyslexia & Creativity staffed by Sally and Bennett Shaywitz, well-known dyslexia researchers, to consider such ideas (see http://www.dyslexia.yale.edu).

An association between creativity and ADHD has also been proposed. Studies of thinking style have found that individuals with ADHD have stronger divergent thinking skills and struggle with convergent thinking (White & Shah, 2006). Divergent thinking refers to the capacity to identify multiple ideas or possible solutions whereas convergent thinking refers to the ability to focus on a logical train of thought toward a particular end. White and Shah (2011) indicated that individuals with ADHD are thought to be less influenced by contextual constraints when engaged in creative activities and, therefore, may have enhanced creativity. They suggested that the low levels of inhibition that characterize ADHD may actually lead to divergent thinking because multiple concepts and ideas are more likely to be retained in working memory.

In a study of creativity in real-world situations, White and Shah (2011) found that college students with ADHD had more real-world creative achievement than those in control groups. The ADHD group had greater achievement as measured by training and formal recognition in all areas measured including the arts, writing, invention, and science. The study also looked at preferences in the process of creative problem solving (problem identification, idea generation, solution development, and solution implementation) and found that ADHD students showed a preference for idea generation, a style that has been found to predict entrepreneurship and an orientation to jobs that require expressiveness and flexibility (Brophy, 2001).

Conclusion

As research has moved into a focus on strengths associated with learning challenges such as dyslexia, autism spectrum disorders, and ADHD, new information suggests that the information processing challenges associated with each set of symptoms also may lead to increased competence in specialized areas of cognition or may be associated with increased creativity and ingenuity. Twice-exceptional students often have the passion and motivation to overcome their challenges but profit from a supportive environment.

chapter 5

Additional Exceptionalities in Gifted Students

Gifted students can face other learning challenges beyond specific learning disabilities that lead to the characterization of twice-exceptionality. For example, gifted students with ADHD and autism spectrum disorders can face particular challenges in the classroom and in gifted programming.

Attention Deficit/Hyperactivity Disorder

ADHD and Overexcitability

Over the years, controversy has emerged over the potential overdiagnosis of ADHD in gifted students (e.g., Baum, Olenchak, & Owen, 1998; Cramond, 1995). These researchers claim that there are features of giftedness that are often mistaken for symptoms of ADHD. In a monograph from The National Research Center on the Gifted and Talented, Kaufmann, Kalbfleisch, and Castellanos (2000) indicated that they found no empirical support for this claim. The bone of contention lies in the theory of overexcitabilities proposed by Dabrowski and Piechowski (1977) who suggested that gifted individuals are more sensitive and have more extreme reactions to both sensory and emotional situations that can result in what is called *flow*, or persisting in an activity with intense focus. Kaufmann et al. suggested that it is counterproductive to juxtapose ADHD and gifted features as mutually exclusive, but rather, finer distinctions should be drawn to see how students could be both gifted and have ADHD. In their view, the issue is not whether there are similar behaviors in both conditions but the degree to which the ADHD symptoms impair the functioning of the student.

Gifted Students With ADHD Have Greater Social and Emotional Challenges

In a literature review of 20 years of research on ADHD and giftedness, Foley Nicpon, Allmon, Sieck, and Stinson (2010) found only 17 empirical studies, many of which were case studies. The one extensive longitudinal study, the Massachusetts General Hospital Longitudinal Family Studies of ADHD (Antshel et al., 2007), found that there were significant differences between gifted students with ADHD and mainstream gifted students. Standard diagnostic procedures were used to identify ADHD. In comparison to mainstream gifted students, gifted students with ADHD were found to have greater academic difficulty, more comorbid psychopathology (mood, anxiety, and disruptive behavior disorders), and greater social and family impairment that extended into adulthood. These more troubling outcomes are consistent with longitudinal studies of ADHD in the general population that have found a high rate of psychopathology and poor functioning in adult outcomes for ADHD. Moon, Zentall, Grskovic, Hall, and Stormont-Spurgin (2001) examined three gifted boys with ADHD in a profile analysis in comparison to gifted boys and boys of average ability with ADHD. They found that the gifted boys with ADHD experienced greater emotional intensity and distress than either the ADHD-only group or the gifted-only group.

Gifted Students With ADHD Struggle With Managing Tasks

Kaufmann et al. (2000) used the concepts of *flow* (gifted) and *hyperfocus* (ADHD) to draw some subtle distinctions. Kalbfleisch (2000) found that gifted students with ADHD are predisposed to engage in flow or hyperfocus. These students can show intense task commitment and motivation when their interests are engaged. The challenge for these students is being able to move on or switch to a different activity after an intense period of focusing on a particular topic (Moon et al., 2001). Because individuals with ADHD have a strong initial response to reinforcement, which fades more quickly than for mainstream peers, they may struggle with longer term projects that delay gratification. These students are those last-minute procrastinators pulling an all-nighter to finish a paper. The deadline pressure helps them mobilize their motivation and receive more immediate feedback.

As we indicated earlier, attention researchers such as Mirsky et al. (1991) have broken attention down into four components. Among the deficits in ADHD is difficulty sustaining attention. Kaufmann et al. (2000) pointed out that individuals with ADHD can sustain attention at times, as indicated by hyperfocus, but the problem is that they have difficulty maintaining attention when the task is not sufficiently engaging or if it requires effort. The constantly rewarding experience of playing video or computer games facilitates the child's ability to pay attention. Kaufmann et al. (2000) pointed out that because gifted individuals have more abilities, they encounter fewer tasks that require effort. Therefore, it may not be as apparent that a student actually has an underlying attentional issue. These subtle difficulties tend to become more apparent as the student gradually encounters more challenging work that puts his skills to the test.

In our experience, the nature of the sustained focus can be somewhat different in gifted individuals with ADHD than mainstream gifted students due to working memory and executive functioning weaknesses. They may persist at a task with intensity, but often with a certain amount of inefficiency. Weak working memory makes it difficult to keep track of a process, and individuals with ADHD can be constantly trying to regain their place. Additionally, weak executive skills make it difficult to prioritize, and students may invest a large amount of energy on aspects of a project that are more peripheral without seeing the main goal. For these students, the structure provided through a GTLD program would help them develop stronger executive skills to focus their energy more effectively.

Are Aspects of Creativity Misdiagnosed as ADHD in Gifted Students?

In addition to intense focus, Cramond (1995) has pointed to symptoms of inattention in gifted students as indicative of creativity rather than ADHD. Cramond shared examples of creative artists who are often leaving half-finished projects or may have multiple projects going at once. Again, there are subtle differences in the role of inattention for gifted students with ADHD. When a creative artist moves from one topic to the next, there is often a logical connection or flow of associations that leads the mind in new directions. The artist is able to come back to his or her incomplete projects and pick up where he or she left off. With the inattention of ADHD, the issue is one of being pulled from one thing by immediate contingencies that are not connected to the original project. Working memory challenges make it difficult to pick up where the project was left off, and multitasking can be challenging.

Cramond (1995) also posited that the preoccupation that creative artists have with their own mental life is often viewed as a symptom of ADHD. Again, there are subtle distinctions here. Internal distraction in ADHD is also often not purposeful in the way that the creative mind follows the flow of thoughts. Creative students with ADHD can become frustrated with their tendency to get off task and lose their train of thought.

Gifted Students With ADHD Have a Neurodevelopmental Lag

Along with the specific symptoms of ADHD, there are additional developmental factors that play into the challenges for gifted students with ADHD. As indicated previously, one feature of gifted students is asynchronous development, where students may have accelerated development in areas of intellectual capacity, but may function more like age peers in social and emotional areas, resulting in difficulty managing sophisticated knowledge of world events. Kinsbourne (1973) pointed out that, similar to students with learning disabilities, students with ADHD can have a neurodevelopmental lag and may actually be 2–3 years behind age peers in social development (Kaufmann & Castellanos, 2000). This lag appears to be fairly consistent over time, but becomes less prominent as students gain greater control over their environment (Mannuzza, Klein, Bessler, Malloy, & LaPadula, 1998). The social immaturity of gifted students with ADHD contrasts sharply with the more typical advanced social maturity of the mainstream gifted student.

Although gifted ADHD students may have strong intuitions and brilliant insights about relationships at times, they are more likely to have these insights about other people or in abstract situations. In their own social relationships, they tend to be impulsive and to have poor self-monitoring skills, resulting in difficulty seeing how their behavior is viewed by others and in actually evaluating the success of their social interactions. In particular, girls with the more active forms of ADHD struggle socially because of their constant talking and difficulty negotiating the subtle interactions of female friendships. They tend to be emotionally expressive and volatile and can be viewed as "high maintenance." Girls with inattentive ADHD, on the other hand, may totally miss the boat socially. They tend to be withdrawn and dreamy, oblivious to what is going on around them.

ADHD and Specific Learning Disabilities Are Often Comorbid Conditions

The picture for many of these students is further complicated by the comorbidity of ADHD with other conditions. For example, Yoshimasu et al. (2010, 2011) looked at the co-occurrence of ADHD and specific learning disabilities in a large-scale community-based sample. They found that the cumulative incidence of reading disorders by age 19 was much higher for both boys and girls who had ADHD than for children without this disorder. Fifty-one percent of ADHD boys and 46% of ADHD girls had reading disorders, as opposed to 14.5% of boys and 7.7% of girls without ADHD. Similarly, they found that the prevalence of writing disorders was even higher with both boys and girls with ADHD—64% for boys and 57% for girls. Interestingly, the study found that the onset of writing disabilities was much later than for reading disabilities. The authors suggested that children with ADHD were particularly vulnerable to writing disorders due to the high prevalence of visual-motor integration difficulties in this group, as well as difficulties with executive functioning and poor working memory. The high comorbidity of learning disorders and ADHD indicates that many gifted students with ADHD are actually considerably more complicated than the term twice-exceptional might suggest.

Case Study: ADHD in a Gifted Student

Jessica is a lively, opinionated middle school student who has a vast range of knowledge and strong desire for leadership. She tends to process her experience through talking, often going into elaborate explanations of her experiences and opinions on a range of topics. In addition to her superior verbal intelligence, she has strong artistic ability and a good sense of design. Besides being a gifted student, Jessica has both ADHD, Combined Type and specific learning disabilities in both reading and written expression due to underlying phonological processing and visual-motor integration difficulties.

Jessica has a good heart and is highly attuned to the feelings of others. She is ready to offer assistance and advice, at times not perceiving how her gestures are being received by others. She often comes up with ideas more quickly than her peers and can be perceived as "bossy." She reacts strongly to emotions and becomes overly active and impulsive to distract people from their distress. Jessica strongly desires friendships, but can get into conflicts because of her difficulty listening to the opinions of others and her unwillingness to compromise. She is a bit of a tomboy, yet is also interested in the intense world of middle school relationships.

Jessica is both perfectionistic and impulsive. She wants her output to be perfect and struggles to execute her elaborate ideas, yet she also rushes through tasks because she cannot tolerate the frustration of compensating for her visually based challenges. At times, her frustration is the result of the mismatch of her rapid cognitive processing with her symbolic processing difficulties resulting from dyslexia. Jessica can go from working cheerfully on a task that she is excited about to melting down into tears quite rapidly. Once she becomes upset about her progress on a task, she struggles to calm down and to revise her approach. Although she has had extensive remedial intervention, Jessica is still not reading with the level of fluency that would be expected in a youngster with superior verbal ability. She also struggles with written expression, both in terms of writing mechanics and expressing her ideas with appropriate grammar. She has difficulty organizing her ideas in writing. Nevertheless, Jessica has gradually become quite persistent with challenging tasks and often is able to tolerate considerable frustration.

In her GTLD program, Jessica has been working on a Rube Goldberg machine. Initially, she had difficulty grasping the concept of such a creation and began with an overly complex idea. She had some trouble understanding reading material on the project, but as her teacher guided her through the concept, Jessica quickly grasped the idea and was able to make connections to come up with an elaborate creation. Jessica had difficulty with the steps of a multistep project, but with structure was able to follow through.

Jessica is the typical ADHD female who is overactive and somewhat impulsive in her social relationships. Her weak executive skills make it challenging for her to tackle complex projects clearly within her intellectual ability.

Autism Spectrum Disorders (ASD)

Many Students With ASD Features Fall in a "Gray Area"

Gifted children with ASD form another group of twice-exceptional learners. These students experience delays in communication, social skills, and some cognitive processes. The complexity of their issues makes specific diagnoses challenging, hence the designation of autism spectrum disorder, which implies that there is a range of behavior under one umbrella. At this time, gifted students can receive one of several diagnoses, depending on their level of social relatedness and limited range of interests: Asperger's syndrome, high-functioning autism, or Pervasive Developmental Disorder–Not Otherwise Specified (PDD–NOS). The latter category is reserved for individuals who have significant impairment in social skills, but who may not meet full diagnostic criteria for autism or Asperger's syndrome. In our experience, there is also a group of students who fall in the gray area—these students have some features of autism, but do not have sufficient impairment to warrant a diagnosis. Some of these students with more ambiguous symptoms may receive a diagnosis of Nonverbal Learning Disorder. This diagnostic category is not included in the DSM-IV, but is used by clinicians for students who have social awkwardness and significant visual-motor difficulties. These students are often highly verbal and their difficulties can be masked by a type of "pseudosophistication" resulting from their advanced verbal skills.

With the advent of the new DSM-V (the upcoming fifth edition of the diagnostic manual of the American Psychiatric Association), significant changes have been made to the categorization of autistic behaviors. Under the new guidelines, the subcategories mentioned above have been eliminated and more restrictive criteria need to be met for a diagnosis of ASD. One of the consequences of this change is that the gray area group of students who have some features of autistic behavior, but who do not fully meet the criteria, will become a much larger portion of the school population. Categorization schemes of school systems do not rigidly follow the DSM, but the category of autism typically requires a formal diagnosis from a professional. Eventually, school definitions will come into alignment with the new DSM-V criteria for autism spectrum. One potential advantage of the Response to Intervention model is the focus on performance rather than labels. Students who have deficits in social and adaptive skills should be provided with appropriate interventions and accommodations, even without a formal diagnosis.

Gifted Students With ASD Have Cognitive, Academic, and Adaptive Challenges

Empirical research on gifted students with autism spectrum disorders is very limited. In a 20-year literature review, Foley Nicpon, Allmon, et al. (2010) found only five empirical studies of gifted students with ASD, most of which were part of the Iowa Twice-Exceptional Project, a Javits grant-funded program through the Iowa Department of Education and the Connie Belin and Jacqueline N. Blank International Center for Gifted Education and Talent Development. In the Iowa project, 37 gifted students with ASD were identified (Foley Nicpon, Doobay, & Assouline, 2010). Almost half (46%) were diagnosed with Asperger's syndrome, 35% with Autistic Disorder, and 19% with Pervasive Developmental Disorder. Boys outnumbered girls five to one. One third of these students had never been previously evaluated and had not been identified for gifted and talented services.

In terms of challenges, there were very large discrepancies in the students' cognitive, academic, and adaptive functioning, with about half also having significant difficulties with visual-motor integration. Assouline, Foley Nicpon, Colangelo, and O'Brien (2008) found a subgroup of 18 students in the Iowa Project that had the advanced verbal and nonverbal reasoning skills typically found in gifted students, but also had more age-appropriate working memory and processing speed skills. A similar pattern emerged in their academic performance, with strong skills in conceptual areas and relative difficulty with timed measures of academic fluency.

In addition to cognitive issues, about two thirds of the group had significant attention problems. Parents and teachers indicated significant difficulties in socialization and adaptation. Interestingly, no teacher indicated learning problems. In contrast to parent and teacher ratings, the vast majority of the students with ASD indicated that they did not have interpersonal concerns, felt self-reliant, and reported high self-esteem. About one third indicated significant symptoms of anxiety.

Students With ASD Often Have Multiple Exceptionalities

To return to the theme of multiple exceptionalities, note that about two thirds of the students with ASD in the Iowa Project had significant attentional issues and one third reported symptoms of anxiety. In our experience, distraction is a significant problem for students with ASD. This type of difficulty focusing is more typically due to internal distraction rather than the external distraction found in ADHD. These students can have great difficulty leaving behind more repetitive thoughts or preoccupations. They may get into a loop, repeating phrases or words they find pleasurable, or they may replay movie dialogue or computer games in their heads. For many students with ASD, the internal distraction is a constant that they have to choose to ignore to focus on the world around them—the movie is always running in the background. When stressful circumstances occur, retreating into this familiar and predictable world is a coping strategy that protects students with ASD from the bewildering experience of feeling that they don't know what people are getting at or how they are supposed to act.

ASD Symptoms Must Be Addressed When Providing Gifted Programming

Allowing students with ASD to engage in gifted projects in areas of personal interest is an important way to draw them out of their internal world and to develop their skills. Although students with ASD often have some areas of advanced knowledge, their information tends to be fact oriented and they may have trouble making connections or drawing conclusions. They also can get easily sidetracked by something that connects with their preoccupations when engaging in research on a topic. Students with ASD can cling to their current knowledge base and may take any opportunity to share their copious knowledge without awareness of the interest level of their audience. They enjoy being the expert, possibly due to many other experiences where they feel lost and befuddled about how to manage situations with peers and adults. These students typically need friendly structure from an adult who appreciates their expert status, but also gently pushes them to go beyond their comfort zone to see their topic from a different perspective.

One particular challenge for students with ASD lies in their lack of perspective-taking skills and poor theory of mind. Theory of mind refers the ability to understand things from another's point of view and to predict how another person will react based on known information about that person and their behavior. Students on the autism spectrum tend to use self-reference as a basis for making inferences about the motivations and actions of others. In gifted programming, this issue can become problematic as students develop projects to present their knowledge to others. ASD students have great difficulty with the idea of an "audience" and what they need to include to inform the audience about their topic. They tend to be self-referential and perceive giving basic information as too obvious because they know it. They have very limited motivation to show their process once they have reached an endpoint.

Sensory integration issues also need to be considered in understanding gifted students with ASD, as well as many of the students who have ASD characteristics but do not meet the formal criteria for a diagnosis. When students' sensory experiences are not well coordinated, they can have extreme reactions to commonplace events in the classroom. Particular smells or sounds can be almost painful in their intensity to students with sensory challenges. These students may be over- or underaroused compared to their mainstream peers in particular situations and may cope with their difficulties managing their sensory experiences in ways that can be disruptive to the classroom routine. For example, students may need to pace or may repeat phrases or words over and over. Many students with sensory difficulties have difficulty with some of the hallmark enrichment activities for gifted programming. For example, many of these students struggle on field trips, in assemblies, or with hands-on activities. Often, preparing these students by talking them through what will happen in advance or troubleshooting ways they could let their teacher know that they are in distress can help ASD students be more successful in these enrichment experiences. Having a procedure for handling the uncomfortable experiences can help students feel more in control. These students may also struggle with group activities, which are more varied and unpredictable than a teacher-led activity. The expectations for these children may need to be adjusted; if both the activity content is highly challenging and the social format is challenging, then students with ASD may become overwhelmed. It may be helpful to unlink intellectual and social demands—when a teacher could push intellectual stimulation with individual assignments (rather than group work) until the student has developed greater group competency.

Case Study: Gifted Student With an Autism Spectrum Disorder

Michael is an 8-year-old boy whose development has always been of some concern to his parents. Although they could not specifically pinpoint what seemed to be wrong, they had a sense from an early age that Michael's development was somewhat atypical. He displayed limited interest in observing and interacting with peers and was content to follow his solo concerns as a toddler. At times, he had strong reactions to events that other children take in stride; for example, he hated hearing the song "Happy Birthday" and frequently melted down at birthday parties (including his own) when it was time for cake. Michael could be attracted to unusual aspects of situations; for example, he might play with the hose by the swimming pool rather than show an interest in the pool itself. Once he was upset about a kite festival because he was afraid that the airborne kites would fall on him. Michael can also be inattentive and preoccupied with dialogue from his favorite video or computer game. His parents have to limit his conversation about his favorite *Star Wars* characters.

Like many children with autism spectrum disorders, Michael was a late walker and a somewhat late talker, although currently he is quite verbal. In fact, he interprets many experiences primarily through language and often struggles to notice visually based information. Michael can talk at length about his favorite character in the Harry Potter series (he has read all of the books) and with adults often seems "mature." Although his gifted intellect is obvious, there are some subtle issues in his comprehension and expression of complex ideas despite his strong knowledge base. Michael can speak eloquently about his preferred topics, but he has considerable difficulty mustering a response to demands placed on him by others. At these times, he becomes easily frustrated and may give vague or tangential replies that don't really answer the question. Similar issues are evident in his writing, which typically does not reflect the advanced cognitive potential that is apparent in his conversations.

Michael has a close and warm relationship with his parents, yet experiences considerable difficulty in developing friendships with peers. Somewhat surprisingly, although he is highly verbal in many situations, he is at a loss in attempting to engage his peers in play or conversation. He is more likely to poke or push a peer to gain his or her attention than to introduce an interesting topic of conversation. He does not usually think to ask about the other person or what he or she is doing, so he has difficulty coming up with something to say. Michael can be irritating to other children because he quickly becomes annoying or rigid in his conversation. Although they give him nonverbal feedback by avoiding eye contact and turning their bodies away, Michael is oblivious and keeps saying or doing the same thing. He is also likely to clown around because he is uncomfortable and runs out of ideas to discuss.

Michael loves rules and will cheerfully comply with directives framed as rules. He also feels that other children should abide by the rules and can become highly incensed when he feels that others are not following expectations. Like many gifted children, he has a strong sense of justice and will argue his point endlessly to win the day. Michael can be quite rigid in his thinking and can "dig himself into a hole" when a preferred strategy is not working. Rather than try something else, he keeps repeating the same ineffective strategy until he begins to cry in frustration. Michael has some awareness of this problem but this insight does not prevent him from continuing to get stuck.

Conclusion

Perhaps it is apparent from the discussion of ADHD and ASD that gifted students with learning challenges have a complex set of learning needs that require specialized intervention to address both their learning challenges and their intellectual gifts. In subsequent sections of the book, we will talk about how to identify these students and what types of programming are most effective to promote their academic development.

chapter 6

Why Are Twice-Exceptional Students So Hard to Recognize?

Twice-exceptional students often fall through the cracks in school because their competing strengths and deficits have a way of making their needs very hard to recognize and understand. Next, we will describe challenges and best practices in the identification and assessment of these unique learners.

Although these two terms—identification and assessment—are often used interchangeably, in this section we will be using them in a very specific way. *Identification* is a selection procedure that determines who will qualify for particular educational resources (e.g., gifted programming, LD supports). It is a multitiered process that includes qualitative and quantitative data from a variety of sources (e.g., teacher impressions, parent feedback, standardized test scores, grades). Identification tends to be dependent on many factors unrelated to the actual testing process, including school budgets and philosophical beliefs. In contrast, we define an *assessment* as an individualized psychoeducational evaluation. Assessments are often included as a component of identification; they are frequently used to determine whether students should be identified for school-based services. However, an assessment serves its own purpose as well; a well-done psychoeducational evaluation provides a wealth of information about a student's strengths, weaknesses, and learning style that can be used to help guide instruction. A well-conducted assessment can also help families better understand a student's learning needs—an important tool for advocacy and self-advocacy.

Gifted students with learning disabilities are frequently overlooked in the classroom. At best, these students may be seen as capable—though unremarkable—students who often are able to perform at an age-appropriate level. At worst, they frustrate teachers and parents and are viewed as students who could succeed academically if they just wanted to—if they simply put in the effort. In both cases, their gifts often go unrecognized and their learning difficulties unaddressed. Brody and Mills (1997) described three groups of GTLD students, which will be discussed below and illustrated with case studies. Each of these types of students presents a unique challenge to identification.

Challenge 1: Gifts Obscure Disabilities

Some gifted students are viewed as bright by teachers and parents, but their learning struggles are not readily apparent or do not appear to be the result of a clear learning disability. For these students, their gifts hide their disabilities. This group of twice-exceptional learners can be further subdivided by the way they respond to learning challenges. Some students, the classic underachievers, are viewed as not putting effort into academic tasks, while others—the "super compensators," put in excessive effort (typically completed in long hours at home) that allows them to achieve at a reasonable level, but takes its toll on their overall well-being.

Classic Underachievers

For classic underachievers, teachers and parents recognize the disparity between their ability and their output in the classroom, and their poor academic performance is often attributed to lack of motivation or even laziness. In the classroom, these students often present as verbally gifted, creative, and quick to grasp concepts, but their grades are impacted by failure to turn in homework, lack of attention to detail in assignments, minimal output on written tasks, and "careless"[1] mistakes. Often, these students have weak executive skills that contribute to difficulties managing homework, organizing materials, and planning time. Academically, they frequently struggle with written language output.

Case study: The classic underachiever. Alex's parents requested an evaluation at the end of his seventh-grade year due to a significant dip in his grades from the prior year. Alex's parents described him as a clever, verbally precocious

---

1 The word *careless* is misleading. Careless implies that the mistakes stem from lack of care, which is usually *not* the case. Most twice-exceptional students care deeply about their performance but are vulnerable to small errors due to the effects of their learning disability.

young man with an excellent sense of humor. They also reported that Alex was very intellectually curious and read "anything he could get his hands on"—from nonfiction books about politics and science to classical fiction. Likely because of this passion for reading, Alex demonstrated a broad knowledge base in a wide range of areas. Alex's mother shared a story of how, as a 9-year-old, he carried on a lengthy discussion with a museum tour guide about early space missions.

In elementary school, Alex performed well academically. Teachers occasionally complained about Alex's messy desk, his tendency to make careless mistakes, and his poor handwriting, but his verbal abilities and enthusiasm for learning endeared him to most school staff.

When Alex entered seventh grade, he began to struggle. For the first time, he had multiple teachers, was required to change classes, and had to manage a locker. Although Alex performed well on most tests, his grades started to slip because of difficulties with homework. In most classes, he failed to turn in assignments. Alex typically did his homework, if he realized he had it. Even when he finished homework, though, Alex would often fail to turn it in to his teachers. When homework was turned in, Alex sometimes lost points because he missed details. For example, he once failed a homework assignment on estimation because he worked all of the problems out rather than estimating them.

Writing was another area of difficulty for Alex. Although he could be verbose when talking about areas of interest, Alex's written work was typically brief; teachers described him as doing the "bare minimum" on assignments. Alex's writing was often riddled with small errors, such as missed commas and misspellings of simple words. Sometimes, he would spell the same word different ways in the same paragraph.

By the end of seventh grade, Alex's teachers were quite frustrated with the discrepancy between his enthusiastic class participation and verbal precocity and the quality of his work on written assignments. Many felt he could "do better if he wanted to," citing his inconsistent performance. Alex's parents were equally frustrated, and were confused about how to help Alex work to the level of his potential. They requested an evaluation to better understand the reasons for his inconsistent performance.

Results of cognitive testing demonstrated that Alex had a broad knowledge base and outstanding verbal and nonverbal reasoning abilities. His WISC-IV (Wechsler Intelligence Scale for Children, Fourth Edition) Verbal Comprehension score was 143 (above the 99th percentile), while his Perceptual Reasoning score was 130 (98th percentile). Alex was interested in and engaged on the subtests that comprise each of these areas. On verbal tasks in particular, he often provided much more information than was necessary to receive full credit for an item.

In contrast, Alex performed less well in the area of Working Memory (WMI = 100, 50th percentile). Alex's performance on the Working Memory subtests was inconsistent; he performed quite well on the Arithmetic subtest but struggled on the two core subtests, Digit Span and Letter-Number Sequencing. These two core tasks tested his ability to recite strings of numbers and letters in a specified order. Although Alex seemed engaged by the challenge of the Arithmetic subtest, he appeared to lose focus on the other two subtests and made small errors that affected his score. In addition, across all of the Working Memory subtests, Alex tended to make mistakes on easier items, only to get more challenging items correct.

Alex also struggled in the area of Processing Speed (PSI = 88, 21st percentile). On these subtests, his inconsistent style was once again evident. On one of the core subtests, Coding, Alex worked quite slowly. Rather than working steadily, he frequently paused and appeared to be lost in thought. Occasionally, he talked to the examiner as he worked. Although he did not make any errors on this subtest, his slow work pace resulted in a below average score. In contrast, Alex worked rather quickly on the other Processing Speed subtests, but made a number of errors.

Alex's scores on measures of academic achievement were also inconsistent. He excelled in reading; both his reading fluency and comprehension were well above average for his age. In math, Alex performed quite well on a test evaluating his problem-solving skills, demonstrating a strong conceptual understanding of math and a remarkable ability to calculate problems mentally, even those that were quite complex. On paper-based calculations, however, Alex's work showed numerous errors, nearly all of which were minor calculation mistakes. He rarely showed all of the steps in his work, which sometimes contributed to errors on more difficult problems.

Alex's performance in the area of written language was a more significant weakness. Although he generally performed quite well on subtests testing basic skills, he had greater difficulty when asked to write a passage. At the beginning of a timed passage-writing test, Alex sat for several minutes, insisting he was not sure what to say. With encouragement, he eventually started writing, but at the end of the 25-minute writing period, the content of Alex's written output was very brief and did not reflect his strong oral verbal abilities. In addition, what Alex had written was not well-organized and did not completely address the demands of the prompt. Alex's written work also had a number of minor errors (e.g., missed periods, misspellings of simple words).

Alex's inconsistent performance in school and on the tests administered in the evaluation was determined to stem from significant deficits in executive function. Alex's history and overall presentation was also consistent with a diagnosis of ADHD, Predominately Inattentive Type. Alex began to work regularly with a tutor outside of school, focusing on developing his organization and study skills and improving his writing. At home, Alex's parents worked with him to set up an organized study area in the family dining room, which allowed them to more easily structure and monitor his study time. Alex also met with his pediatrician and started a trial of stimulant medication.

In school, his parents obtained a 504 Plan that established some accommodations to help Alex's performance. One particularly effective accommodation was a "check-in" at the end of each day with the resource room teacher. This teacher reviewed Alex's assignments with him to help make sure that he had all of the needed materials before leaving for the day. Another very helpful accommodation for Alex was provided in his math class. Previously, Alex had consistently been graded down for failing to show his work, even when he ultimately answered the problems correctly. Alex and his teacher worked out a compromise that allowed Alex to get credit for problems he answered correctly without showing his work, so long as he showed his work correctly on two items selected by his teacher.

Super Compensators

In contrast to the classic underachievers, the super compensators hide their learning struggles by a combination of determination, hard work, and parent support. These students may show subtle signs of learning problems in the classroom. For example, they may be quiet in class discussions because of difficulties with expressive language, and/or they may have trouble completing timed tasks. Typically, these students are well-behaved and cooperative and work hard. As a result, teachers usually like them and may be generous in grading their work, allowing extra credit assignments or giving extra points on homework or tests for strong effort. At home, these students work exceptionally hard on assignments, often with the help of their parents. Homework frequently takes much longer than it should, and these students may experience stress and anxiety because of the amount of effort they must put in to their work relative to peers. Because of their determination and the support they receive at home and school, the overall grades of these students usually do not reflect the extent of their struggles.

Case study: A super compensator. Jack was a seventh-grade student in a rigorous independent school who was a star pupil in humanities classes. He was a voracious reader and a talented writer; his teachers had commented that his essays were "models for the class." Jack's enthusiasm for learning, intellectual curiosity, and good attitude endeared him to teachers, and he nearly always made A's in his classes.

Jack's parents requested an evaluation because of concerns about his performance in math. Jack's relative difficulty in this subject resulted in his being placed in the slowest-paced math group in his grade. At first, this affected Jack's placement in all of his classes, as his school tracked students based on their math performance. Ultimately, though, Jack's parents were able to advocate for a waiver of this rule for him so that he could be placed in the more challenging language arts courses. In addition to his difficulties in math, Jack struggled with physical organization (e.g., managing materials, keeping a lab notebook). He also had difficulties with peers; he was somewhat awkward socially and had been a target of teasing. In class, Jack could be impatient with students with whom he did not see eye-to-eye or those who did not grasp concepts as quickly as he did. His lack of diplomacy in these situations contributed to some of his difficulties with peers.

In the evaluation, Jack initially presented as shy, but gradually became more relaxed and comfortable. Throughout testing, he worked very hard, even on tasks that were clearly very difficult for him. Jack's frustration on certain subtests was evident, although subtle—he frequently sighed on particularly difficult tasks or made comments like, "I'm not going to get this." At other times, though, he gave himself verbal encouragement, saying, "That looks right" or "I *can* do this." Although he was frustrated, Jack was persistent and careful on challenging tasks.

Jack's performance on the WISC-III was extremely discrepant; he excelled on verbal tasks and struggled on visual ones. His verbal abilities were in the very superior range (Verbal IQ = 137, 99th percentile), while his nonverbal/visual-spatial abilities were significantly below average (Performance IQ = 68, 2nd percentile). Jack's performance on achievement testing mirrored his profile on cognitive testing; he generally excelled on tasks that tapped his strong verbal abilities (e.g., reading comprehension, written language) and had greater difficulty on those tasks tapping his visual abilities, like math.

Jack's testing profile and history of difficulties were determined to be consistent with a Nonverbal Learning Disorder (NLD). First identified in the 1980s (Rourke, 1989), NLD is a dysfunction of the right hemisphere of the brain (the part of the brain that processes nonverbal information). Individuals with NLD frequently struggle in three major areas: motor skills (e.g., difficulties with coordination, impaired fine motor skills), spatial awareness (e.g., trouble with physical organization, poor sense of direction, difficulties with spatial concepts in math), and social skills (e.g., missing social cues, difficulty understanding nonverbal communication). For many years, Jack had hidden the effects of his disability on his academic performance because he was so adept at compensating for his visual processing deficits. Most notably, Jack used his outstanding verbal abilities to talk himself through visual tasks. He also had considerable support from his parents at home. Because of Jack's ability to compensate for his weaknesses, he had been able to hold his own in a challenging school environment throughout elementary school. Although Jack's difficulties with math and organization were beginning to become more evident in middle school, they had still not risen to a level of significant concern for his teachers.

Jack's parents pursued a school change for high school because of his ongoing peer difficulties at his old school. In this new environment, Jack received additional targeted and specific accommodations to support his learning (e.g., organizational support, use of a computer for written assignments, double time on tests). His parents provided additional interventions, such as math tutoring and a social skills group. He also attended a summer program for gifted students where he connected with some other "quirky" kids. Getting a fresh start at a new school was also tremendously helpful. Although he was not highly social in the new school, Jack made several good acquaintances and was no longer subjected to teasing.

Ultimately, Jack attended a highly selective liberal arts college. Although math and science courses continued to be more difficult for him, he was able to excel in his interdisciplinary humanities major and graduated with honors. Negotiating social relationships continued to be a bit of a challenge for Jack, and he lived in a single room all 4 years of college. However, he did make friends and managed to find his niche. Currently, Jack works as a consultant in the information technology field.

Challenge 2: Disabilities Hide Gifts

Some students who have been diagnosed with significant learning challenges also have gifts that have gone unrecognized. Often, these students have language-based learning disabilities that make oral and written expression difficult and impact performance in all classes. The gifts of these students are frequently in areas that are not always easy to recognize in the classroom. For instance, these children may be highly creative and very good at thinking outside of the box, or they may have tremendous visual-spatial ability. Identifying the gifts of these students is particularly challenging because they usually do not perform well on tests. In addition, their gifts are often in areas that are not frequently or easily evaluated by standard measures.

Case Study: Severe Dyslexia in a Gifted Student

Jenny was a student with significant learning challenges whose gifts had been mostly overlooked. Identified with a reading disability in second grade,

Jenny had an IEP and had worked with learning specialists in her school to build her reading and writing skills. Despite considerable intervention in school and tutorial support outside of school, Jenny continued to struggle with reading as an 10th grader and was reading well below grade level. She was frustrated and discouraged by her academic difficulties and had very low self-esteem. Although Jenny viewed herself as being "dumb," her parents remarked that she had outstanding artistic abilities and was an insightful, creative thinker. Jenny's gifts and talents were not recognized in school, however, in large part because her learning disabilities were so severe. In addition, Jenny's poor academic self-concept and low self-esteem helped mask her abilities. Jenny did not like to stand out and was very reluctant to try new things or take intellectual risks; she had a very strong fear of failure. In school, she often sat in the back of the classroom and rarely spoke up unless called on directly. Jenny did not view college as a reasonable option for her future and was not convinced that she would even finish high school.

In the evaluation, Jenny was pleasant and cooperative, but she was tense, lacked confidence, and appeared defeated. When Jenny encountered difficult tasks, she was quick to give up. At times, she seemed embarrassed by her struggles. With considerable encouragement, she would persist, and she seemed surprised when she was able to complete a task successfully. Over the course of the cognitive assessment, Jenny began to relax a little and even seemed to enjoy some of the hands-on activities. When faced with reading tasks, however, Jenny again seemed quite tense and was very reluctant to persist or to guess when she was unsure of an answer.

On the WISC-III, Jenny excelled in the area of nonverbal and visual-spatial processing (Perceptual Organization Index = 130, 98th percentile) and performed quite well on verbal tasks (Verbal Comprehension Index = 119, 90th percentile). Within the verbal area, Jenny performed best on subtests tapping her verbal reasoning; she had relative difficulty (although her scores were still in the average to slightly above average range) on measures of verbal knowledge. At times, Jenny struggled to retrieve information from memory, which she found quite frustrating and embarrassing.

Although Jenny had received considerable intervention and support over the years to remediate her learning disability, she performed poorly on all assessments of reading and writing. Indeed, her scores on measures of word recognition, decoding, spelling, and fluency were all at or below the fifth percentile for her age. Jenny's comprehension skills were somewhat stronger, though still slightly below average for her age. As Jenny worked on comprehension questions, it was clear she was using her strong reasoning skills to make educated guesses, even when she had substantial difficulty reading the text.

Jenny's disability was not in question—the results of the evaluation were clearly consistent with a diagnosis of severe dyslexia—and the need for further intensive remediation and support for her learning disability was emphasized. A major focus of the feedback session with Jenny and her family, however, was an issue that had not been fully addressed before: Jenny's giftedness. Because of her severe learning disability, Jenny's needs as a gifted child had not been a priority. In addition to her academic difficulties, Jenny's social and emotional struggles had led to low self-esteem and a lack of confidence that affected her ability to succeed in other life pursuits. Of course, it was necessary to continue to address Jenny's severe dyslexia; intensive remediation both in and out of school was recommended to help her gain functional reading and writing skills by the end of high school. However, recognition of Jenny's gifts in visual-spatial and artistic skills needed to be nurtured. Jenny's school allowed her to take part in a graphic arts course, and her parents pursued summer programs that would allow Jenny to explore her visual-spatial talents.

Challenge 3: Gifts and Disabilities Mask Each Other

The most elusive group of twice-exceptional students are those children whose gifts and disabilities mask each other. These children are bright enough to compensate for their learning struggles, but their areas of weakness affect the expression of their gifts. As a result, in the classroom, these students often appear to be of average ability, and their academic performance on standardized tests is typically on grade level. Although their classroom performance may show signs of their learning difficulty (e.g., reduced output on written assignments, spelling mistakes, slow work pace), their performance is not bad enough to indicate a significant problem. Often, these students are quiet members of their classroom community; they may be hesitant to speak out in class unless called upon.

In contrast to their school presentation, the gifts and struggles of these students are often more evident at home. They may demonstrate an encyclopedic knowledge of a preferred topic or show an ability to comprehend higher level math concepts (although they may struggle with computational aspects of math). However, homework frequently takes an excessive amount of time, and the child may express anxiety about assignments or frustration about her abilities.

The concept of masking is controversial on several fronts. First, there are philosophical concerns with the concept of identifying an average performer as having a learning disability. Although providing services for the *clearly* gifted underachiever can be a hard sell, at least these students may be demonstrating glimmers of brilliance and discrepant performance that suggests that they have potential that is not being realized. Those students whose gifts and disabilities mask each other, however, simply appear to be unremarkable, solidly average, grade-level students. They do not obviously demonstrate discrepant performance, so the need for encouraging strengths and remediating weaknesses is not as clear. Many writers have questioned the appropriateness of identifying average-level performers as having a disability, citing the ADA's "average person" standard: Individuals can be qualified as disabled only if they suffer from a "substantial impairment in a major life activity" (Gordon, Lewandowski, & Keiser, 1999, p. 491). There are also concerns that underperformance in a gifted student may be due to factors other than a disability. McCoach, Kehle, Bray, and Siegle (2001), for example, noted that the average performance of a gifted student could be due to any number of factors, including motivation, interest in the topic, and self-efficacy. Gordon et al. (1999) concurred, noting that "superior intelligence is not necessarily a ticket to superior achievement" (p. 487).

We take a more nuanced view that "masking" is actually the product of a misfit between a student's learning profile and/or needs and the classroom environment. Many times, students whose gifts and disabilities mask each other in the early grades go on to have their gifts and/or their disabilities become more evident as they progress through school. For example, the gifts of a student who has subtle language processing issues but strong visual-spatial talents may become more obvious in high school when there are the opportunities to take electives that tap into her strong spatial abilities. More commonly, a disability in a gifted student becomes more evident as he or she progresses through school and encounters more difficult material. At some point in time—it may be as late as college or even graduate school—a student is unable to continue to use his or her gifts to compensate for the disability. Often, these students have experienced considerable frustration and stress over the years due to the effects of their subtle disability.

Gordon and colleagues (1999) were correct in asserting that not all underachievement stems from a learning disability; there are many gifted individuals who underachieve for reasons that are completely unrelated to any sort of learning problem. However, this does not mean that it is not important to try and understand the reason behind a student's underachievement—whether it relates to a learning disability, an emotional concern, motivational issues, or a combination of these or other factors. Careful and informed assessment can help to tease apart the reasons why a student may not be living up to his or her potential.

There are also concerns about the concept of masking from a policy and logistical point of view. For example, it can be difficult to justify the allocation of limited financial resources for LD services for students who are technically functioning on grade level (Gordon et al., 1999). In addition, there is the practical problem of identifying students who are so easily hidden in the classroom. Screening all average-performing students to look for possible learning disabilities is not a realistic option for schools (McCoach et al., 2001). However, astute and well-informed teachers can serve as a first line of identification for twice-exceptional students. Teachers who are alert to the possibility of twice-exceptionality and who encourage open dialogue with parents are more likely to "catch" these students in the classroom. The next section provides some red flags to alert teachers to the possibility that a student's abilities and disabilities may be masked.

Although it is usually difficult to identify masked students from their classroom performance, their gifts and disabilities can be identified through thoughtful and thorough assessment. Despite their average academic performance in the classroom, their pattern of performance in diagnostic evaluations is typically marked by considerable scatter (i.e., significant strengths and weaknesses). In addition, careful observation of the student across a range of testing tasks often reveals signs of struggle and/or frustration that may not be reflected in the test scores. These motivated and determined students are very adept at compensating for their deficits. Although the final product of their work may be acceptable, the amount of struggle and effort it took to get there is often striking.

Case Study: Mild Dyslexia Masks a Child's Gifts

Mark was an enthusiastic and hardworking second grader who had a passion for science. In kindergarten, he was identified through teacher recommendations as a child who would benefit from additional enrichment and challenge. Mark excelled in a weekly enrichment program, which provided hands-on learning opportunities and outlets for his creativity. Mark expressed a love of school and spoke enthusiastically about the projects and activities that were part of the enrichment program.

In first and second grade, concerns arose about Mark's academic performance. Ultimately, Mark's school decided that he could not continue in the enrichment program because his scores on recent standardized testing were inconsistent with those of the other participants. In addition, Mark's classroom teacher believed that he could benefit from time in class to build his reading skills. Although Mark's scores on reading assessments demonstrated that he was reading on grade level, his teacher felt that he needed to work on his reading fluency. Mark's parents also had concerns about his reading; he seemed reluctant to read independently, although he loved having his parents read to him. Mark's parents requested that the school's reading specialist evaluate Mark on two separate occasions. After the evaluations, the reading specialist reported that although Mark showed some relative weaknesses in fluency, his overall performance in reading was on grade level and he was not eligible for any formal reading supports through his school.

Mark's parents were concerned that the school viewed Mark as an average student with a minor weakness in reading fluency while ignoring his insightfulness, creativity, and passion for science. They also worried that removing him from the enrichment program would be a blow to his academic self-concept and that he would miss having the opportunity for critical thinking and hands-on learning that the enrichment program provided. At the same time, they felt that the school was minimizing Mark's difficulties with reading, and worried that his struggles in this area were beginning to make him feel somewhat anxious about school. Because of these concerns, they sought a psychoeducational evaluation to learn more about Mark's abilities and needs.

Mark presented as a friendly, engaging child who was extremely cooperative, focused, and hardworking. On many challenging tasks—particularly during cognitive testing and on the math evaluation—Mark was persistent and often used unique strategies to work through problems. In contrast, on reading and writing tasks, Mark sometimes appeared mildly frustrated. Although he was still determined and persistent, he sometimes sighed or made frustrated comments under his breath like, "I probably won't be able to do this."

On the WISC-IV, Mark demonstrated outstanding verbal abilities. His Verbal Comprehension score was 132, at the 99th percentile for his age. Mark performed in the high average range for his age on both the Perceptual Reasoning and Working Memory composites of the WISC-IV. In contrast, he struggled on the WISC-IV Processing Speed composite, scoring in the below average range at the 14th percentile. Mark worked slowly on the Processing Speed subtests; he appeared to have difficulty quickly tracking visual material, making visual discriminations, and attending to visual detail. Mark's difficulties with aspects of visual processing were evident on other cognitive tests where he was asked to process visual material with speed and accuracy. He also worked very slowly on rapid naming exercises, which tapped his ability to quickly identify and process visual symbols. Students who struggle on rapid naming tasks often have weak reading fluency.

Educational testing results confirmed that Mark had weaknesses in reading fluency. The speed and accuracy of his reading of sentences and passages was consistently in the lower end of the average range for his age. Though technically on grade level, this level of performance was significantly discrepant from his outstanding verbal ability. Observations of Mark's reading suggested that he struggled with the visual aspects of reading; he tended to make errors such as skipping or adding in words, skipping lines, or substituting a visually similar word. When Mark encountered unfamiliar words, he slowly and methodically sounded them out. His frequent pauses for laborious decoding slowed his reading speed considerably. Mark's reading comprehension was more solidly average but was discrepant from his highly developed oral comprehension skills. At times, it appeared that Mark was using his strong verbal reasoning ability to make educated guesses rather than relying on his recall of the reading passages.

Further assessment of Mark's information processing skills indicated that his reading difficulties resulted from a specific subtype of dyslexia. Orthographic dyslexia has its roots in visual processing and encoding; individuals with this type of dyslexia have trouble storing mental images of words, which affects their ability to quickly recognize and read most words by sight. As a result, they tend to be slow and dysfluent readers. Mark's phonological awareness and decoding skills were sound, and he relied on them heavily when he came to words he did not know. Because he had trouble retaining sight words, however, his reading fluency was weak.

Because he was able to compensate for his relatively mild learning disability, Mark was not provided with special services for students with learning challenges. However, his reading difficulties negatively affected his performance in all areas of academics as the classroom expectations increasingly focused on the application of reading skills rather than the acquisition of basic skills. Further, Mark's reading disability affected his scores on standardized tests sufficiently to call into question the appropriateness of his placement in the gifted program.

With the results of the evaluation, Mark's parents were able to obtain a 504 Plan for Mark at school. Accommodations provided for Mark included additional time on tests, use of technological aids to support his reading, and the opportunity to demonstrate his knowledge in alternative ways that played to his strengths and did not require reading or writing. Because Mark was reading on grade level, he was not given an IEP and was not considered eligible for remedial reading programs in his school. His parents were, however, able to find a tutor to work with him twice a week after school. Perhaps most importantly, it was agreed that Mark should continue to be identified as a gifted student and participate in programs for advanced learners with accommodations in place to foster his success. Being allowed to continue to participate in gifted programming provided a tremendous boost to Mark's self-esteem that helped to energize him to tackle his learning challenges.

Conclusion

In summary, the complex interaction of gifts and disabilities in GTLD learners make these students very difficult to recognize. For some children, gifts may hide disabilities; for others, disabilities may obscure gifts. A third group of students is particularly hard to identify—those students whose gifts and disabilities mask each other. The intelligence of these students enables them to compensate—to a point—for their learning challenges, while their disabilities impede the expression of their gifts. As a result, they often appear to be solid, adequate classroom performers, but may be struggling behind the scenes. Information and insights from sensitive and observant teachers can help to catch these students who might otherwise fall through the cracks. In the next chapter, we discuss some classroom red flags that can help to identify GTLD students.

chapter 7

Red Flags That Can Help Identify GTLD Students in the Classroom

As the case studies in Chapter 6 illustrated, twice-exceptional students can be difficult to recognize for a variety of reasons. Teachers can play a critical role in identifying gifted children with learning disabilities; when they tap into their observations and gut feelings, they can help to identify gifted students who might otherwise fall through the cracks. Indeed, a prerequisite to creating effective educational programs for twice-exceptional students is increased faculty and staff awareness that gifted students with learning disabilities *do* exist. Because of the complexity of GTLD students and the ways in which their gifts and learning challenges interact, it can be easy to miss—or to misunderstand—these students in the classroom. It is critical to help staff know what these students might look like.

In the following sections, we describe some common characteristics of GTLD students that can help school staff to recognize children who might be twice-exceptional. It is important to note that this is not an all-inclusive list: Not every twice-exceptional learner will show all of these characteristics. However, most will show at least one or two.

Gifted Students With Learning Difficulties Are Consistently Inconsistent

This inconsistency may manifest in a number of ways. First, there are twice-exceptional students who excel in classroom activities, but have difficulty on tests and assignments. These children often participate readily in class discussion, demonstrate incredible critical thinking skills, and view concepts and topics in a unique and insightful way. Their talents shine in interactive and discussion-based activities, but they struggle to show their knowledge on tests, homework, and written assignments. They may have trouble with completing tasks, and their written output may be sparse and fail to demonstrate their strong oral language skills. These students are classic underachievers, and their performance inconsistencies are particularly frustrating to their parents and teachers.

Occasionally, one may see the opposite pattern—students may demonstrate their knowledge effectively on tests and assignments, but struggle with group work and class discussions. Language processing, working memory, and/or attention difficulties can cause some students to have difficulty following lectures and understanding oral instructions; these students may seemed disengaged, inattentive, or even confused. Other students may have difficulty with the social demands of in-class assignments. Although they may perform well on individual tasks, they may struggle with group work because they are disengaged in their interactions with others and/or have trouble interacting effectively with peers. Alternatively, they may have difficulties reading social cues and understanding the unwritten rules of social interactions, which can cause them to monopolize class discussions and take too much control of projects.

Students' inconsistencies may also manifest in specific subject areas. For example, a student might excel in one academic area but perform less well in another (e.g., the math wiz who struggles with writing). Sometimes, inconsistencies may be seen across time in one subject area (e.g., a student who achieves near-perfect scores on a particular math test, only to perform poorly on another assignment covering the same material).

Finally, other students simply demonstrate inconsistent performance from one day to the next. On some days, they are "on"—eager, enthusiastic, and clearly showing their abilities; on other days they seem disengaged, disinterested, or confused. These students can be particularly frustrating to parents and teachers, because it is difficult to understand why they can excel on some occasions but not others. Day-to-day inconsistency can stem from a number of causes. For some students, memory challenges affect their performance; they may be able to demonstrate mastery of a concept one day but be completely confused about the same concept a few days (and sometimes even a few hours) later. A number of students struggle with waxing and waning mental energy and effort; they may be engaged and excel in some tasks and activities only to appear disengaged and unmotivated at other times. Variability in energy and effort may result from a number of causes: attention challenges, fatigue from the effort they are putting forth to compensate for their weaknesses, frustration and discouragement at their struggles, and so forth. Some students may develop a defeatist attitude: "I'm not going to do well at this, so why try?" For these students, a skilled teacher or a captivating subject may help them reengage with the learning process.

Twice-Exceptional Students Are Seen as Lazy

The inconsistent performance of twice-exceptional students often results in them being seen as lazy. When a teacher finds himself frustrated by a student who "could just do well if he *wanted* to," the possibility of twice-exceptionality should be considered.

Twice-exceptional students who are viewed as lazy tend to share several characteristics. For instance, they are often gifted with oral language and can be active and engaged participants in class discussion. They may demonstrate an insightfulness and curiosity that is unusual for their age. Typically, these students are passionate about topics of interest and may demonstrate a mature and deep understanding of complex material. A parent of a twice-exceptional student recently shared how her fifth-grade son—who was struggling in school because of organizational challenges, writing struggles, and missed work—independently engaged in intensive study of ancient history:

> Completely on his own he found . . . an old Cliff Notes on mythology from the 1970s. It's nearly 200 pages and is a dry, difficult read. He was enthralled and didn't put it down until he finished. Then he read 300 pages of the *Iliad* and 100 of the *Odyssey* and loved and understood it. This was all in one week [and] all on his own, merely because he was interested.

This student's information processing deficits—weaknesses in executive function—caused many school staff members to view him as being unmotivated and lazy. However, this example illustrates that this child is very far from lazy! When his interests are engaged, he is a passionate and eager learner.

Students viewed as lazy are also usually global thinkers, readily seeing and understanding big picture concepts. In contrast, these students often struggle with details. For example, they may readily grasp complex mathematical concepts but make numerous detail errors in mathematical computations. Tasks that require a sequential approach often challenge these students—they tend to skip steps and "miss the trees for the forest." Often, what seems to elude these children is not cognitively difficult—in the words of one parent, for these students, "what is hard is easy, and what is easy is hard." It is for this reason that they are frequently viewed as lazy—it is difficult for teachers and parents to understand why a student who can tackle difficult concepts with ease can struggle with the simplest of tasks.

For gifted students with weaknesses in attention and executive function, the struggle to initiate and sustain effort on tasks contributes to the appearance of laziness. As Levine and Reed (2001) indicated, for these students, "work is too much work (p. 24)." They struggle to harness mental energy and effort to get started on a task, as well as to sustain their effort to complete it. Less structured activities are particularly challenging for these students. When they are overwhelmed by the open-ended nature of an assignment, they may get stuck and have trouble generating any sort of output. Frequently, they are procrastinators. Once they do get started on a task, these students often have trouble regulating their focus and effort to produce a quality product. As a result, their output may be brief or simplistic. The contrast between the poor quantity and/or quality of their work on some assignments and their passion around topics of interest often causes them to be misperceived as lazy or oppositional.

Twice-Exceptional Students Are "Absent-Minded Professors"

Organization difficulties are particularly common in gifted students with learning challenges. For example, many twice-exceptional students have great difficulty keeping track of their belongings and managing homework. They may fail to write down assignments, assuming they can simply remember the homework requirements. Even when students actually do their homework, they may forget to turn it in or misplace it in their backpack or locker. These students are often susceptible to losing materials other than homework; they frequently misplace their belongings, such as coats, musical instruments, eyeglasses, and wallets.

A twice-exceptional student's struggle with organization is not only limited to physical organization, however; these students often struggle with organizing their thoughts, planning their approach to tasks, and managing time. In conversations, they may appear scattered; their ideas may move from topic to topic in a nonlinear fashion. Often, their ideas are exceptionally creative and the links and the connections they make between concepts may be perceptive and insightful, but the roundabout way in which they present their ideas may be hard to follow. Similar issues may be seen in writing; their ideas may come out on the page in a stream-of-consciousness fashion.

Deficits in the area of working memory can also contribute to a student being perceived as scattered. Critical to most academic tasks, working memory is the ability to hold, manipulate, and manage information in the mind in order to complete tasks. Students with weaknesses in working memory can seem disorganized, inattentive, and "spacey." They often have trouble following multistep directions and may appear forgetful. Students with working memory deficits can also have specific struggles in academic subjects. In math, working memory helps students keep their place as they execute multiple steps of a problem. In reading comprehension, working memory enables students to hold key story elements in memory as they read further in the text. A student with working memory deficits can also have trouble juggling various aspects of the writing process. As a child writes, he or she must retrieve ideas, facts, and vocabulary; plan what to say; organize thoughts effectively; retrieve and apply rules of grammar and mechanics; and attend to the details of spelling and punctuation. If a student puts energy and effort into one area of his or her written work—say, coming up with ideas—other aspects of the work may not be polished. For example, a child's written work may have numerous minor errors in spelling—a child may spell the same word incorrectly in different ways in the same paragraph.

Writing Problems Are Very Common in Twice-Exceptional Students

Many gifted students struggle with poor executive skills, both due to learning disabilities and ADHD. Written language tasks place significant demands on the executive functions. Students with weaknesses in this area may struggle with initiating the writing process—brainstorming and coming up with ideas—and may have difficulty organizing their thoughts. They may also be prone to detail errors (e.g., minor mistakes in spelling and writing mechanics) and may resist or have trouble checking their work for these sorts of mistakes. Many students with weaknesses in executive function also have difficulty persisting on writing; their written output is often quite short.

Other gifted students with learning challenges may have subtle weaknesses in cognitive processing that affect many subjects, but are most noticeable in their written output. Language processing problems, working memory weaknesses, and even difficulties with social skills can all have an impact on writing.

In short, writing is an activity that places demands on many different areas of cognitive functioning, and students must integrate these multiple skills at once. Deficits in any one area or areas may lead to problems in another. For example, a student with fine motor problems who has to expend significant mental energy and effort attending to the quality of her handwriting may be more likely to make small errors in writing mechanics.

For many gifted children, a disparity between strong oral language skills and limited written output is a first sign of academic struggles. In addition to organization and initiation problems associated with weak executive skills and poor working memory, these students may also have relative delays in fine motor skills. For many students, weak handwriting skills make the process of writing tiring and frustrating. For bright students with big ideas, the frustration when their hands cannot keep pace with their thoughts may lead to the avoidance of writing altogether. Frequently, gifted students who struggle with written language cope with their frustration by doing the bare minimum on written assignments. What appears to be laziness is often an ineffective means of coping with a complex challenge.

Twice-Exceptional Students Often Work Slowly on Tasks

It is not unusual for mainstream gifted students to take a methodical and contemplative approach to tasks. They often need to delve deeply into a topic and consider all of the angles before moving forward. However, for other students who work slowly, their work pace reflects slow and inefficient information processing. Rather than working through a rich flow of ideas, these students are struggling to get the basics down on paper. These gifted and slow processing students can be distinguished from their intellectually average peers in two ways: (a) they often demonstrate greater sophistication and fluency in class discussion and in active, hands-on activities; and (b) they can give a stronger performance when allowed additional time to complete a task.

Processing speed deficits in a gifted student can manifest in a number of different ways. Some students may work slowly on a specific academic activity—they may, for example, be slow readers or have trouble completing math tests and worksheets in a timely manner. Other students show more global weaknesses in processing speed and have trouble completing most tasks within a time limit. For others, the level of structure provided determines their processing efficiency. These students may be able to complete structured, in-class exercises in a reasonable time frame, but spend inordinate amounts of time in the more unstructured homework setting or when given more open-ended assignments.

The causes of a processing speed deficit can vary, but typically relate to a "glitch" in some aspect of cognitive processing (e.g., attention control, language processing, memory, visual processing). The distractibility and inconsistent engagement of students with attention problems, for example, can result in them working more slowly on timed tasks. Many gifted students are particularly vulnerable to internal distractions—they have a multitude of ideas and are highly divergent thinkers. As a result, a test question or discussion point in class may cause their ideas to go off in many different directions. Difficulty keeping their ideas focused on the task slows their rate of output. Other students who work slowly struggle with language processing and take longer to process verbal information. For example, they may be slow readers who need to read and reread text multiple times to grasp its meaning, or it may take longer than normal for them to generate ideas for writing. Memory retrieval difficulties can also affect processing speed. Rapid retrieval of specific information is frequently challenging for many twice-exceptional students. They may struggle with word retrieval or have difficulty recalling math facts quickly. In sum, the roots of a processing speed deficit can be quite varied. Comprehensive and thoughtful psychological assessment can help to understand the reasons behind a child's slow rate of output.

Twice-Exceptional Students May Struggle Socially

Research in the area of learning disabilities suggests that students with learning disabilities generally have more social difficulties than students without learning problems (King, 2005). Although one might expect that giftedness might mitigate the social challenges that can come with learning disabilities, research has suggested that GTLD students are vulnerable to difficulties with peers (Moon & Dillon, 1995; Vespi & Yewchuk, 1992).

Silverman (2002) remarked that the juxtaposition of intellectual gifts and academic struggles often contributes to social and emotional stress and difficulties with adjustment. The experience of being gifted while also having academic difficulties is confusing; a student may struggle to understand why she breezes through some tasks but needs help with others. This confusion can make a child question where she really fits (King, 2005). Academic struggles may make these students feel alienated from other gifted students, while at the same time they may struggle to find age peers who share their intellectual interests.

Often, twice-exceptional students have social challenges that relate directly to their cognitive style and processing weaknesses. Research has shown that executive functions are very important in social relationships (Beauchamp & Anderson, 2010; Ganesalingam et al., 2011; Walker, 2011). Twice-exceptional students with executive weaknesses may have specific kinds of difficulty with peers. For example, it is not unusual for twice-exceptional students to have trouble thinking flexibly; they can be rigid and have trouble seeing things from different perspectives. Difficulty seeing things from others' viewpoints can lead to problems reading social cues. Another aspect of executive function that is critical for social relationships is self-monitoring (i.e., the ability to accurately evaluate the effectiveness of one's behavior and make changes when necessary). Difficulties with self-monitoring may result in a twice-exceptional student correcting a teacher in an undiplomatic way or behaving in a manner that is irritating to his peers without recognizing it.

As discussed earlier in this text, autism spectrum disorders are not uncommon in gifted students. These students may have more extreme and pervasive social difficulties; they struggle with reading social cues, taking the perspective of others, and mastering the social "give and take." In some situations, the social and behavioral struggles of the student may be so significant that they become the primary focus of programming and intervention, with his needs as a gifted child taking a back seat. At other times, the social quirks of a gifted student on the autism spectrum may be attributed to solely to her giftedness, resulting in a child not receiving needed supports and interventions for the disability (Neihart, 2000).

Twice-Exceptional Students May Experience Emotional Challenges

For most twice-exceptional students, school can be quite stressful. The "balancing act" (Olenchak & Reis, 2002) necessary for GTLD students to cultivate their talents while also compensating for their deficits is difficult and frustrating for these students (Brody & Mills, 1997; Moon & Dillon, 1995). In working with students, teachers should be aware that a child's emotional reactions, particularly around her academic performance, may be another red flag that can suggest a hidden learning disability.

GTLD students may show their frustration at their academic difficulties in a variety of ways. Some students externalize their frustration through strong emotional reactions. For example, some may show their frustration through angry outbursts at relatively small mistakes or challenges (e.g., the student who breaks a pencil out of frustration when misspelling a word) or through abrupt mood shifts (e.g., the student who enthusiastically discusses a book in class but quickly turns irritable and resistant when asked to work on a writing assignment.) Other twice-exceptional learners tend to internalize their frustration and may appear quiet, passive, and/or apathetic. Lacking confidence, they may be hesitant to take intellectual risks and may appear anxious. Some may become overdependent on a teacher for guidance and support.

Perfectionism can be particularly challenging for twice-exceptional students. Like many gifted students, a GTLD student can set unreasonably high expectations for performance, and may become very frustrated when she cannot achieve those goals. That frustration may be exacerbated if the student becomes aware that she is having difficulty relative to peers due to the effects of the learning disability. Perfectionism in twice-exceptional students can often be seen in their response to the writing process. Many students have incredible difficulty initiating effort on a written assignment. Although trouble getting started may relate to struggles with executive function, perfectionism can also play a role; many students write, edit, and rewrite multiple times in their head before ever putting pen to paper.

Conclusion

Students who are frustrating to teachers and parents because of their inconsistent performance and/or laziness may actually be struggling with an undiagnosed learning disability. Observant and insightful teachers who are aware of the concept of GTLD are invaluable, as they can prevent these students from falling through the cracks. When a teacher has concerns that a student might be twice-exceptional, a thorough assessment can help to identify the student's strengths, learning challenges, and overall educational needs. In the next chapter, we discuss the important role of assessment in understanding the needs of the GTLD student.

chapter 8

Assessment as a Tool for Understanding Twice-Exceptional Students

Recognizing the red flags that suggest that a student might be twice-exceptional is a critical first step. Once a parent or teacher believes that a gifted student has a learning disability, a comprehensive and thoughtful assessment is critical. A good assessment (a) can help to identify a child for programs and services; (b) provides information about a student's strengths, weaknesses, and learning style that helps inform instruction; and (c) is a tool for self-understanding.

Commonly, a psychoeducational evaluation is seen as the means to an end: a tool to determine whether a child is eligible for a specific program, qualifies for certain services, or meets the criteria for a diagnosis that may provide the basis for other supports or interventions. Assessment is indeed a useful tool for identifying students for programs, services, and other interventions, but these benefits form only the tip of the iceberg. The most important function of assessment is the detailed profile of cognitive, academic, and social-emotional strengths and weaknesses that leads to the understanding of the learning needs and potential internal resources of a specific student.

Diagnosis of a learning problem is not a stopping point, as students with the same diagnosis may, in fact, be incredibly different from one another—both in their presentation and in the types of interventions and strategies that may be most useful for them. For example, on paper, Alan and Mark appear very similar: Both are gifted eighth graders with a diagnosis of ADHD, Inattentive Type. The similarities between the two students stop there, however. Alan is outgoing and verbally precocious; he has the "gift of gab" and enjoys making his classmates laugh. He struggles with aspects of attention control and executive function; Alan has difficulty initiating tasks, has poor time management, and has poor task completion due to his tendency to rush through assignments with careless mistakes. Writing is particularly challenging for him; the work he turns in is often brief and does not reflect his strong verbal ability. Mark, in contrast, is a shy, contemplative daydreamer. He does not speak much in class, and when called on, he has some difficulty organizing his ideas in a fluid manner. Mark also works very slowly; his work pace itself is quite methodical, but the rate of his output is also affected by what he calls "mind blips"—he easily gets lost in his thoughts and can lose track of what is going on around him. Mark is frustrated by his extreme disorganization. He has a strong desire to do well at school, but difficulties managing assignments have significantly affected his performance. Although both Alan and Mark have ADHD, their strengths, weaknesses, and needs are very different.

The real value of a comprehensive assessment, then, is the understanding it provides of just who the student is as a learner. One piece of the puzzle is the clarification of the specific nature of the child's learning disability, but a good evaluation should include a broader assessment of a student's strengths, weaknesses (those related to the learning challenge as well as those not), overall learning style, and social-emotional adjustment. In short, the assessment should be designed to ask: How does this student learn best? What strengths does the child have that he or she can employ to help work around areas of weakness? What social and emotional strengths and/or challenges does the student have? In the example above, although Alan and Mark had the same diagnosis, their comprehensive assessments provided important information that differentiated their learning styles and appropriate instructional strategies and supports in and out of the classroom. Although classroom assessments provide much useful information about a student's learning profile, formal diagnostic testing reveals important information about underlying issues that may not be obvious to the observer and can tease out competing hypotheses about factors that led to a particular educational outcome.

A thorough evaluation of a twice-exceptional student should take into consideration important factors associated with giftedness, in addition to a thorough assessment of learning disabilities. The Munich Model of Giftedness provides guidance in identifying important variables that impact a student's ability to demonstrate his or her gifts. An assessment should consider the child's gifts and talents, personality and learning style characteristics, environmental factors, and information processing. In many ways, there is nothing magical about an assessment to uncover potential learning problems in a gifted student. In short, a good GTLD assessment is simply a good assessment. Skilled and astute examiners who take a holistic approach to assessment will consider the interplay of a student's strengths and weaknesses in a thorough assessment of information processing issues and careful observation of a student's behavior during testing, placed in the context of the student's developmental history and current contextual factors.

An important, and often overlooked, component of an assessment is the dissemination of the findings. When teachers and parents better understand factors contributing to their underlying feeling that something doesn't add up in a particular student's performance, they can be even better observers and supporters of the student. It is important for the student to receive feedback about the diagnostic findings as well. Many twice-exceptional students are frustrated and misunderstood. They may have been labeled as lazy or unmotivated, and/or their gifts may have gone unrecognized. The opportunity to understand why they learn the way they do can be incredibly fulfilling and empowering for twice-exceptional students. Levine (2002a) described the process of sharing assessment feedback with a family as *demystification*. It involves a detailed but understandable explanation of the child's learning problem, and includes a delineation of a child's strengths, as well as his or her learning challenges. Information is presented in real-world language, and concrete examples are shared to help the child understand his or her learning style and needs. Through the process of demystification, parents, school professionals, and the child are seen as working together to discover solutions.

The importance of assessment as a tool for understanding cannot be overemphasized. First, understanding the nature of a child's learning problem can help dispel the notion that a child is lazy, unmotivated, or resistant. Having parents and teachers recognize and acknowledge the real nature of the learning problem can bolster a student's self-esteem. In addition, specific knowledge of the nature of the learning challenges can help teachers better understand the types of supports and instructional styles that will work best with the student. To return to the example of Alan and Mark—Mark benefited from having a teacher check in with him, to help draw his attention back to the task at hand and organize his thoughts. These sorts of check-ins would have been frustrating for Alan, due to his outgoing style and quick mental pace. More effective strategies for Alan included specific instruction on time management strategies and reminders to review his work for errors. Although both students had the same diagnosis, many of the accommodations and supports they needed were quite different.

Highlighting the strengths of twice-exceptional students provides an important avenue of intervention for student learning challenges. Many of these students are able to use areas of strength to compensate for their learning challenges. In fact, many of these students have been effectively hiding their deficits for years by using stronger skills to disguise underlying learning disabilities. However, the homegrown strategies students use are often inefficient and some efforts are designed more to save face than to improve performance. These students may feel guilty or embarrassed about their tactics to manage challenging academic tasks. Bringing the issue of compensation into the open can lend legitimacy to a student's efforts to work around his or her problems. In addition, an assessment may identify more effective and efficient compensatory strategies than those students develop on their own through trial and error. For example, a highly visual-spatial student with organizational challenges could be taught to employ visual strategies for physical organization or webbing strategies for organizing his thoughts for writing.

Challenges in the Assessment of the Twice-Exceptional Student

A good psychoeducational evaluation is an amazing tool that can lead to the understanding of the complex needs of the twice-exceptional student. There are, however, a number of specific assessment challenges that arise when assessing gifted students with learning problems. Awareness of and attention to these issues will increase the effectiveness of the psychoeducational evaluation in identifying the needs of a twice-exceptional student.

Composite Scores Can Be Misleading

Gifted students with learning disabilities typically have considerable scatter—highs and lows—in their testing profile. Evaluating and interpreting this scatter is a critical piece in understanding a student's information processing, but the presence of the scatter also makes composite scores misleading. In most cases, the Full Scale IQ score will *not* be the best way to summarize a GTLD student's overall abilities.

For many gifted students (including those without learning disabilities), scores on the WISC-IV assessing working memory and processing speed are typically lower than those for verbal comprehension and perceptual reasoning. Indeed, in the sample of students identified as gifted in the *WISC-IV Technical and Interpretive Manual* (Wechsler, 2003), gifted students had an average Verbal Comprehension score and Perceptual Reasoning score of 124.7 and 120.4, respectively, while their Working Memory and Processing Speed scores were 112.5 and 110.6. For most gifted students with learning disabilities, this discrepancy is usually even greater due to the impact of their information processing challenges on their performance on tasks evaluating their automaticity, speed, and working memory. The WISC General Ability Index, or GAI (Raiford, Weiss, Rolfhus, & Coalson, 2005), was developed to provide a summary score less affected by working memory and processing speed than the WISC Full Scale IQ. The GAI can be useful in all learning disability evaluations, but is critical in the assessment of twice-exceptional children; with it, the gifts of twice-exceptional students are more readily identified (Rowe, Kingsley, & Thompson, 2010). The GAI should be reported whenever there is a significant discrepancy between the Verbal Comprehension/Perceptual Organization and Working Memory/Processing Speed indexes.

Although inclusion of the GAI is very important for evaluating a student's higher order thinking skills, the disparity between these skills and measures of working memory and processing speed should not be glossed over. Measures of cognitive efficiency, such as working memory and processing speed, provide critical insights into glitches in information processing and their impact on student learning. Effectively managing the input and output of information has a major impact on academic performance. For example, Rowe et al. (2010) found that scores on the WISC-IV Working Memory Index actually had a higher correlation with a child's reading and math scores than either the Verbal Comprehension Index or the Perceptual Reasoning Index.

Although the GAI is often a very useful estimate of intellectual potential in GTLD students, there are situations where a student's cognitive performance is sufficiently complex to require further fine-grained analysis. Although overall discrepancies between higher order thinking and cognitive efficiency are the most common profile in twice-exceptional students, other patterns of performance can occur. In the case of Jack, the "super compensator," his Verbal IQ score fell at the 99th percentile, yet his Performance IQ score fell at the 2nd percentile. If someone chose to look only at Jack's Full Scale IQ—or even his GAI—he would look like a student of average abilities. Indeed, Jack's Full Scale IQ was exactly 103, at the 58th percentile. Clearly, the composite score provided absolutely no useful information about Jack, either from the perspective of his strengths or his weaknesses. Although Jack's case is an extreme example, it emphasizes the importance of using composite scores (including the GAI) with caution when evaluating twice-exceptional students.

Individual index scores (e.g., the Verbal Comprehension, Perceptual Reasoning, Working Memory, and Processing Speed indexes of the WISC-IV) can provide a more detailed view of a student's strengths and weaknesses, but they too are summary scores and can sometimes be misleading. For example, Marianne, a teen with dyslexia, scored in the average range on the Verbal Comprehension Index on the WISC-IV. However, her performance on the individual subtests that comprise the index ranged from the low end of the average range to the very superior range. Marianne performed best on subtests that tapped her reasoning skills and allowed her to elaborate her thoughts in her own way and her own time. Tasks that placed demands on her ability to recall specific information from memory were much more difficult for her. In addition, because Marianne tended to avoid reading, her verbal knowledge base was a relative weakness for her. Simply focusing on the Verbal Comprehension score in describing Marianne's performance missed important clues to the nature of her learning difficulties and her learning needs.

Although the problems with IQ score composites are particularly noteworthy, it is important to note that the same principles hold true with other tests. Take, for instance, the Gray Oral Reading Test (GORT; Wiederholt & Bryant, 2012). The GORT consists of two subscales evaluating reading fluency and comprehension. It is quite common for a twice-exceptional student to score well on measures of comprehension but to struggle on measures of fluency. Simply looking at the GORT Oral Reading Quotient—the overall score on the test—may provide misleading information about a student's reading skills.

Most Standardized Achievement Tests Do Not Fully Assess the Learning Challenges of Twice-Exceptional Students

The learning difficulties of many twice-exceptional students may not be evident on achievement tests focusing on basic academic skills. Broad-based achievement batteries, such as the Woodcock-Johnson Tests of Achievement-III (WJ III; Woodcock, McGrew, & Mather, 2001) and the Wechsler Individual Achievement Test-III (WIAT-III; Wechsler, 2009) are important tools in evaluating academic ability, but for some students, using these measures in isolation may miss signs of learning difficulties. For instance, gifted students with reading disabilities may be able to compensate for their weaknesses and perform in a capable manner on untimed tests of single word reading (e.g., Letter-Word Identification on the Woodcock-Johnson Tests of Achievement) or sentence reading (e.g., Woodcock-Johnson Passage Comprehension subtest). Although a student's performance on these sorts of tests provides important information, her struggles may be more evident on timed reading tests, direct assessments of reading fluency, or measures of complex passage comprehension.

To further complicate the situation, some gifted students are also able to compensate for their learning difficulties on more sophisticated standardized achievement measures. These students may be able to use their "smarts" to outwit the test. For example, Coleman, Lindstrom, Nelson, Lindstrom, and Gregg (2010) administered the Nelson-Denny Reading Test to groups of academically at risk and typically performing university students. For this test, students are asked to read passages that are several paragraphs in length and answer multiple-choice comprehension questions in a format similar to that used in scholastic aptitude tests. To determine whether intelligent guessing could affect their score, students were given a "passageless" format test—in other words, they were asked to answer the questions without access to or experience with the reading passages themselves. The success of all students in guessing the correct answer on the passageless items exceeded chance. Passage-independent questions have been found on a number of other reading comprehension measures as well (Coleman et al., 2010; Keenan & Betjemann, 2006).

It is very difficult to design a reading test that accurately reflects the demands of advanced high school and college course requirements. Often, students can power through for the 20 minutes of a standardized reading measure, but have true difficulty sustaining their efforts to read a chapter in a novel or textbook. In addition, many standardized reading tests do not adequately assess inferential reading comprehension, often a major source of academic challenge for GTLD students. The multiple-choice format used in most reading measures allows students to make intelligent guesses without true comprehension of the reading content.

To accurately assess the reading skills of bright students, it is helpful to look for evidence of early reading difficulties in their history and to collect information about reading performance from teachers and parents who have the opportunity to observe the student under real-life conditions. Students themselves also usually provide accurate descriptions of their reading challenges. Within the reading measures themselves, additional information can be gleaned relevant to underlying reading inefficiencies. Comparisons of timed and extended time performance can be useful, as well as considering the accuracy rate of a student's performance. For example, a high school student may work more quickly, and possibly impulsively, than age peers resulting in an average number of correct responses, yet he also may have answered a fair number of items incorrectly. This student could obtain an average Nelson-Denny score with an accuracy rate of 70%. Obviously, in a real-world situation, such as a classroom test, this level of performance would not be considered adequate.

Although writing challenges are common for gifted students with learning disabilities, these issues are also difficult to assess via standardized diagnostic tests. Writing is a subject that has a variety of potential breakdown points. Students may struggle with handwriting, mechanics, spelling, grammar and syntax, word retrieval and idea generation, organization, initiation and persistence, and any combination of the above. Twice-exceptional students who have difficulty with basic writing mechanics can be more easily identified with standard assessment measures. However, many gifted students with writing problems have a solid command of the basics of writing—and struggle, instead, with the higher level aspects of written language, such as generating ideas, organizing content, and communicating thoughts clearly. Even the best norm-referenced assessment tools available for use in a psychoeducational evaluation cannot adequately capture the demands and expectations inherent in a term paper or lab report. A gifted student who struggles with writing in school may nevertheless be able to compose a completely adequate brief writing sample along the lines required by most standardized writing tests. The fact that many of the commonly used writing tests require creative output is also problematic; many gifted students find it easier to generate a creative writing sample, where they have more control over the content, than an essay or term paper that is more structured and places greater demands on organization. Again, it is important to collect information from parents and teachers to gain perspective on how the student performs on writing tasks in real-world situations. Collecting samples of written work is also a good way to assess real-world competence.

Compensatory Strategies of Twice-Exceptional Students Influence Their Performance on Diagnostic Tests

Gifted students with learning disabilities are often very adept at compensating for their learning challenges. This ability to compensate does not stop at the evaluation room door; indeed, in most cases an observant examiner will have many opportunities to watch the twice-exceptional student use his or her gifts to work around weaknesses. Careful observation of the student in the assessment setting is critical. It is not uncommon for a child to perform adequately on a task, purely from a score perspective. However, observation of the child's approach to the task tells a very different story.

Caleb's story illustrates how careful observations can uncover the use of compensation strategies that may be bolstering a twice-exceptional student's performance on tests. Caleb was a high school student who was referred for an assessment because of his parents' concerns with the amount of time he had to spend completing homework. Caleb was a successful student—in fact, his mother acknowledged that his teachers would "think she was crazy" if they knew she was bringing Caleb for an evaluation. On cognitive testing, Caleb had very superior verbal and nonverbal abilities, with significant weaknesses in working memory. In the educational assessment, Caleb's performance on simple measures of reading (word and sentence reading) was above average across the board. In contrast, his performance on a more challenging passage-reading task was lower, though within the average range for his age. On this task, Caleb had a high accuracy rate (percent correct) but was not able to finish the test. Although his score might suggest there was nothing to be concerned about, observations of Caleb's process for completing the reading task told a different story, revealing Caleb's struggle to achieve this average level of performance. The text of the stories he was given to read was covered with notes, outlines, and diagrams; he also underlined and circled key parts of the text. Caleb's strategy of marking up the text was a way to compensate for his working memory deficits. Although using these strategies definitely aided his reading comprehension, their time-consuming nature made it difficult for Caleb to finish his reading efficiently. From a score perspective, Caleb's strategic approach to compensate for his working memory deficits to some degree masked the impact of his working memory problems on his reading performance.

For other twice-exceptional learners, the effects of the disability can impact the expression of their gifts. Students with language processing disabilities, for example, may have trouble adequately showing their verbal knowledge on tests with high expressive language demands. Again, observations of a child's struggles are incredibly informative and should lead the examiner to introduce alternative assessments that may enable the student to demonstrate his abilities more readily.

Kathryn's story provides an example of how a child's disability can mask gifts in an assessment. Kathryn was referred for testing because of concerns about attention and her difficulties with writing. Cognitive testing demonstrated that Kathryn had very superior nonverbal abilities with average verbal abilities. Her verbal subtest scores, however, showed some scatter; Kathryn performed better on subtests where she could answer in one or a few words than on subtests that required greater verbal elaboration. Observations of Kathryn's performance on the verbal subtests showed that she had difficulty organizing her thoughts, finding words, and fluidly explaining her ideas. Although word-finding difficulties were also evident on subtests where Kathryn could answer in just a few words, the untimed nature of the tasks enabled Kathryn to ultimately get to the correct answer. The more complex demands of the other verbal subtests tapped her language processing problems more directly, resulting in decreased verbal output and a weaker performance on the subtests.

Because observations of Kathryn's performance were suggestive of language processing problems, she was also given a receptive vocabulary assessment. When the expressive language demands were taken out of the equation, Kathryn's verbal knowledge was able to shine; her score on the receptive language task was above the 99th percentile.

Kathryn and Caleb's stories illustrate how critical observations are in the evaluation of the twice-exceptional student. For all children—but particularly for GTLD students—test scores themselves tell only a small part of the story.

Gifts, Learning Difficulties, and/or Social-Emotional Adjustment May Interact and Contribute to Inconsistent Performance That Is Difficult to Interpret

As mentioned earlier in this text, gifted students with learning disabilities are often consistently inconsistent. Executive functioning weaknesses are a common cause of this inconsistency and can lead to confusing or misleading evaluation results. Students may show variable performance from one task to another, depending on their interest or engagement. "Swiss cheese" performance, where a child misses both easy and difficult items throughout a subtest, can suggest inconsistent focus. Sometimes, twice-exceptional students may actually perform less well on easier items; because they feel confident the tasks are within their grasp, they may rush and pay less attention to detail. GTLD students can also show variable performance from one day to another. It is not uncommon, for example, for a gifted student to "pull out all of the stops" and compensate very well the first day of an evaluation. On the subsequent day(s) of testing, a child may relax and be more likely to demonstrate the issues that lead to the assessment referral. Conducting an evaluation over more than one assessment session often provides important insights to a child's learning needs.

Social-emotional factors can also lead to inconsistent performance. Gifted students who face learning challenges are typically highly aware of—and sensitive about—their weaknesses. When faced with test items they view as difficult, they may give up quickly or say they don't know an answer rather than risk being wrong. In an assessment setting, one may see more perfectionism and hesitancy in risk-taking at the beginning of the assessment, when the child is less comfortable, than at the end.

The Assessment Profile of Many Twice-Exceptional Students Does Not Meet the Criteria for Specific Learning Disabilities

IDEA (2004) uses a categorical definition for learning disabilities: Students must meet criteria for a specific learning disability in a particular subject (i.e., math or reading). However, many twice-exceptional students show inconsistent performance that makes a specific learning disability difficult to document. These students often have more general weaknesses that have a global, rather than specific, impact on their academics. For these students, their learning disabilities are often based on weak executive functions, slow processing speed, or poor working memory that affect academics across the board, albeit to a milder degree than might be seen in a specific learning disability. For these students the most appropriate diagnosis is Learning Disorder, Not Otherwise Specified (LD NOS) with a qualifier specifying particular functional deficits.

The lack of specificity of a diagnosis like LD NOS can be somewhat unsettling and is unfamiliar to many school staff more attuned to IDEA categories for specific learning disabilities. To some, it might seem to be a desperate attempt to gain a diagnosis when the scores may not clearly indicate a problem. However, factors that produce these global but low-grade deficits are insidious. A student with a specific reading disorder may improve drastically with effective remediation and may go on to a successful academic career functioning pretty much as her peers do. In contrast, a student with LD NOS will face his very real processing challenges in every academic subject and will likely need to continue to use strategies to compensate throughout his school career. The diagnosis of LD NOS is more consistent with the definition of disability provided through the Americans with Disabilities Act that focuses on a "functional impairment."

Case Study: LD NOS. Kostya came for evaluation as a high school junior. Although his grades were generally A's and B's, his family was concerned about his poor attention, hyperactivity, and difficulty completing schoolwork within expected time frames. Kostya reported that he was a slow reader, had difficulty maintaining his focus while reading and writing, and sometimes struggled to comprehend what he had just read. Despite his difficulties, Kostya was highly motivated and put forth tremendous effort to complete his work. He had recently been diagnosed with ADHD by his pediatrician.

Kostya immigrated to the United States from Russia in first grade. He spoke no English at the time and attended English language learner classes but was mainstreamed by the end of first grade. Throughout elementary school, he alternated years living with his grandmother in Russia with years of schooling in the United States. Kostya continued to struggle with his reading rate, writing, and mastery of English grammar, but generally found the public school program "not demanding." However, he began to have academic difficulties in seventh grade at his highly selective college preparatory school where he struggled with reading comprehension, written expression, and the application of advanced math concepts.

Kostya's family described him as an independent and ambitious young man who loved his family and was understanding of others. He had high social competence, was a good communicator, and a "great observer" of others' behavior. He excelled in music and sports and also enjoyed playing the virtual stock exchange.

Kostya's performance on the WAIS-III demonstrated a wide split between his very superior Verbal IQ score of 143 (above the 99th percentile) and his low average Performance IQ score of 85 (16th percentile). This level of disparity between scores occurs in 1% of the population. At the level of index scores,

Kostya scored very superior for both verbal comprehension and working memory. In contrast, he scored in the low average range on measures of perceptual reasoning and low average on processing speed. Kostya demonstrated exceptional ability in his vocabulary knowledge, fund of information, and abstract verbal reasoning. In the area of nonverbal reasoning, Kostya scored solidly in the average range on an untimed measure of visual pattern completion, but his scores were barely average when he was expected to attend to detail and when asked to complete block patterns and puzzles under time pressure. Kostya scored below average on timed paper-and-pencil measures of visual processing speed.

Neuropsychological testing further demonstrated the impact of poor visual processing. Kostya had difficulty on tasks that required him to make figure ground distinctions and to identify matching figures that were distorted in some manner. He worked very slowly on a task requiring him to connect a series of numbered circles in numerical order. He also had difficulty accurately producing designs and quickly marking target shapes. Consistent with his low reading fluency, Kostya had difficulty with rapid retrieval of letters and names of objects. His executive functioning and memory were otherwise average.

The results of Kostya's achievement testing illustrate some of the difficulties in evaluating learning disabilities for very bright young adults. Kostya and his family reported that he had significant reading difficulties in advanced coursework, a report substantiated by the fact that a hard-working student with exceptional verbal ability was only making mediocre grades. Yet his reading scores generally fell in the average range. A few scores still showed the impact of underlying reading issues. As mentioned previously, he continued to struggle with rapid retrieval of basic information, and a timed measure of sight word reading was below average. He had difficulty with spelling pseudo-words that used common phonetic patterns. Kostya was able to use his strong intelligence to compensate sufficiently to score at an average level on the Nelson-Denny test, possibly aided by the multiple-choice format that allowed intelligent guessing. He was not able to finish the test, however, and his accuracy was a mere 80%. He was observed to engage in frequent rereading of the passages before answering test questions.

On tests of mathematics, Kostya did significantly better on untimed measures of calculation and applied math concepts than on timed math measures. In writing, when asked to write sentences meeting specific criteria, he scored in the superior range, yet when asked to compose a story about a series of pictures, he used simplistic language and misspelled many words. His spelling mistakes included "severly" for severely, "ganitor" for janitor, and "mourning" for morning.

Like many learning disabled young adults, Kostya's current learning difficulties reflected inefficiency for the most part, and he did not meet the criteria for a specific learning disability in reading, math, or writing. However, his underlying slow retrieval and poor visual processing affected his efficiency across the board, making LD NOS the appropriate diagnosis. Kostya received accommodations including extended time, notetaker support, and tutoring. He went on to a successful college career at a selective university and graduated with a major in international relations and history.

One issue to consider in the case of Kostya is the role of second language acquisition. For many of his formative educational years, he was shuttling back and forth between the English and Cyrillic alphabets and had to learn phonemic patterns in two languages. It is likely that his severe visual processing difficulties further compounded the challenge of managing two such different language systems. However, Kostya developed considerable fluency and comprehension in his spoken English that was not evident in his reading fluency and comprehension of English text.

Conclusion

In summary, a good psychoeducational evaluation is an important tool for fully understanding the strengths, weaknesses, and educational needs of the twice-exceptional student. Information from the assessment can help to understand a student's overall learning style and can be used to inform effective interventions to help the student achieve academic success. Assessment of the GTLD student can be difficult, however, and individuals conducting evaluations of twice-exceptional learners should be well-informed about the challenges inherent in evaluating these students. In the next chapter, we discuss several best practices to guide individuals who will be assessing GTLD students.

chapter 9

Best Practices in Assessing Twice-Exceptional Students

Twice-exceptional learners can be very challenging—but also exceptionally rewarding—students to evaluate. The following three principles outline best practices in assessing these students.

An Evaluation of a Twice-Exceptional Student Should Adopt a Neuropsychological Approach to Identify Processing Deficits That Are Affecting Performance

Brody and Mills (1997) emphasized the importance of identifying processing deficits when assessing a GTLD student. They noted that finding a processing deficit is important because it can help to distinguish students who are underachieving due to the effects of a learning disability from those who are underperforming due to other factors (e.g., being placed in an academic setting that is insufficiently challenging, emotional problems). In addition, identifying underlying processing problems helps to inform the strategies that are most likely to be effective in addressing the student's learning problems and improving his or her performance. An evaluation utilizing a neuropsychological approach provides the best information to fully understand students' processing challenges.

By *neuropsychological*, we mean an approach that assesses important information processing domains that affect learning. This type of assessment does not require a neuropsychologist; many evaluators who provide excellent diagnostic evaluations are not officially neuropsychologists. Often, equivalent evaluations are called *neuropsychological evaluations* or *psychoeducational evaluations*. However, not all psychoeducational evaluations include the important information processing measures that guide a strong evaluation. It is worth the money to seek out an evaluation that includes neuropsychological testing, whatever the report may be called. A neuropsychological approach looks at the student through the lens of brain processes that affect learning. Assessments should be designed to evaluate specific neuropsychological processes (e.g., memory, executive function, visual-spatial processing, phonological awareness, visual-motor integration), focusing on areas that seem likely to be problematic for the specific child, given the referral question.

The identification of a processing deficit using a neuropsychological approach is key in the evaluation of a twice-exceptional student for two major reasons. First, it provides evidence of the presence of a learning struggle. Because these students can use their abilities to compensate for their weaknesses, their disabilities may not show up in an obvious, consistent way in the classroom or on standardized tests. Using assessment measures that pinpoint specific learning processes can demonstrate the challenges that the student is experiencing. Second, identifying the specific processing deficit also provides information that can be used to develop specific interventions and supports that can help the student be more successful. A child who is struggling with math because of issues related to executive function, for example, will need different interventions than a child who struggles with math due to memory problems.

Key to identifying a processing deficit is the use of profile analysis, which is the examination of the pattern of test scores across a variety of tests. Profile analysis includes the evaluation of the pattern of composite scores across a test or tests, as well as the examination of the pattern of certain subtest scores (which can also be known as *scatter analysis*). Evaluation of subtest scores is particularly important in situations when there is considerable scatter in the scores. As mentioned in the previous chapter, test composite scores are very misleading and should not be relied upon for decision making when there are considerable highs and lows in a student's profile of test scores.

The use of profile and scatter analysis is not without its critics. Lovett and Lewandowski (2006), for example, noted that scatter in WISC-IV profiles, specifically, is not uncommon, and, in fact, is frequently seen among students with high abilities. They also had psychometric concerns about the use of profile analysis, noting that subtest scores have lower reliability coefficients than the total test scores. As a result, it is uncertain whether a student's test score profile on a given day would be consistent over time. Lovett and Lewandowski also implied that clinicians who rely on scatter and profile analysis tend to misinterpret the pattern of high and low scores. For example, they cite Gordon et al. (1999) who asked, "Why is someone who is average in spelling but outstanding in reading comprehension and math considered disabled in spelling—why is he or she not just considered to be unusually good at math and reading comprehension?" (p. 488).

The research of Assouline et al. (2010) attempted to evaluate the effectiveness of profile analysis in understanding a sample of gifted students with writing disabilities. The researchers identified patterns in these students' cognitive ability profiles, including (a) students' verbal abilities being higher than nonverbal abilities, (b) students' working memory and processing speed being discrepant from their verbal abilities and in the average range for their age, and (c) students' visual-motor integration being in the low average to average range, suggesting fine motor challenges. Regarding the working memory and processing speed weaknesses specifically, Assouline et al. (2010) commented that although weaker working memory and processing speed skills are not uncommon among gifted students, the size of the score discrepancies in their sample was greater than those reported for gifted students without learning problems. Assouline et al. (2010) concluded that the results of their study demonstrated that (a) twice-exceptional students do exist; (b) a comprehensive evaluation can help to describe an individual student's ability, achievement, and learning needs; and (c) using this information can help with talent identification and development in gifted students with specific learning disabilities.

Lovett (2011) responded to the Assouline et al. (2010) article, proposing alternative explanations for the discrepancy between the ability scores and written language achievement scores of the students in Assouline et al.'s (2010) sample: motivation, prior learning experiences, and measurement error in the assessment itself. Assouline, Foley Nicpon, and Whiteman (2011), in turn, responded to each of Lovett's (2011) criticisms, ruling out the possibility of measurement error and stressing that the clinical interview screened for the possible effects of motivation and/or prior learning experiences on the performance of the students.

Although the debate around this issue remains unresolved, it does highlight two major issues that need to be considered in twice-exceptional assessment. First, it is indeed important to consider psychometric variables and typical patterns of performance on psychological tests to ensure that profile analysis and the examination of ability-achievement discrepancies are not overinterpreted.

No child is expected to have a completely "flat" assessment profile—variability in assessment scores, both across subtests and across composites is common. Although lower scores on the WISC-IV Working Memory and Processing Speed indexes are frequently seen in children with learning problems, they are also evident (though usually to a lesser degree) in gifted students without disabilities (Wechsler, 2003).

Second, a good assessment involves much, much more than reviewing test scores. It is critical to take into account the pattern of a student's subtest and composite score performance in the context of (a) his educational and psychosocial history; (b) reports from parents, teachers, and the student himself about academic performance; and (c) observations from the diagnostician of the student's performance on the subtests. The diagnosis of learning disabilities is not formulaic, relying only on test scores. Clinical judgment is key in assimilating the results of a variety of assessment measures, which includes interview data, historical information, and observations, in addition to the test results themselves. Astute examiners will use clinical judgment to rule out factors such as motivation, past learning experiences, and even emotional issues as possible contributors to a gifted student's underachievement.

One challenge in adopting a neuropsychological approach to assessment is that psychologists working in schools often do not have the time and resources to conduct lengthy batteries, using multiple measures to examine every aspect of a child's learning strengths and weaknesses. Although it is ideal to incorporate some neuropsychological assessment measures into the GTLD evaluation, one can adopt a neuropsychological mindset to the assessment even when giving only an intelligence test and an achievement test. The philosophical approach to the evaluation is what is most critical—the idea that the purpose of the assessment is to understand who the child is as a learner, rather than just determining if he or she meets the criteria for a diagnosis, program, or service. In the situation where it is only possible to administer the WISC-IV and the Woodcock-Johnson III, for example, a psychologist can still glean a wealth of data by examining the child's pattern of subtest performance and considering this information in the context of the behavioral observations, the child's history, and relevant data from teachers and parents. For example, each of the WISC-IV subtests can capture different aspects of a child's learning processes. An astute examiner can evaluate a child's pattern of performance on the WISC-IV and at least come with some tentative conclusions as to what might be the specific learning breakdown points for a particular child.

Although one can adopt a neuropsychological mindset to a basic intelligence and achievement assessment, in an ideal situation, additional cognitive/neuropsychological measures would be incorporated into an evaluation to get a more comprehensive picture of a student's learning profile. Assessment batteries should be tailored to the specific referral question to maximize efficiency. Included in Table 9.1 are some examples of assessment measures that can be useful in understanding the underlying processing deficits in gifted students with specific learning challenges. Many of the measures could be included in a short battery that includes an intelligence test and a few other brief measures.

Achievement Testing Should Incorporate Timed Assessments; Provide Challenging, In-Depth Measures of Specific Skills; and Include a Review of Real-Life Work Samples

Well-planned and executed achievement testing can also provide a wealth of data about a child's learning processes and where the breakdowns in learning may be occurring. One challenge with achievement measures, however, is that some of the most commonly used assessments are not particularly sensitive to the types of learning challenges that most twice-exceptional students face. In the area of reading, for example, weaknesses in reading comprehension may not be evident on brief assessments (e.g., cloze exercises where a student reads one sentence and provides a missing word that will complete the sentence correctly). Multiple-choice subtests may also be less likely to emphasize the reading comprehension difficulties of a GTLD student. In both of these cases, gifted students can use their strong reasoning abilities to make an educated guess at the answer, even if they did not truly understand the passage. In the area of writing, evaluations that are very structured (e.g., assessments where a student is asked to write a sentence in response to a specific prompt) are much easier for gifted students with writing challenges than open-ended assignments that require the student to plan, organize, and retrieve information and place considerable demands on working memory. Incorporating GTLD-sensitive approaches to the educational assessment can increase the likelihood that the evaluation will capture the types of learning challenges twice-exceptional students have.

First, to adequately evaluate twice-exceptional students, it is critical to include timed assessment measures. Processing speed challenges and a slow work pace on academic tasks are extremely common in gifted students with learning disabilities. Achievement measures that tap quick retrieval of information and require students to "output" information at a rapid pace are very informative. Timed assessments that require students to quickly attend to details can

Table 9.1

Tests Useful in Evaluating Processing Deficits in GTLD Students

Reading	Math
Phonological Awareness	*Memory Retrieval*
<ul><li>CTOPP: Phonological Awareness subtests</li><li>WJ III Achievement: Sound Awareness</li><li>WJ III Cognitive: Sound Blending</li><li>WJ III Cognitive: Incomplete Words</li><li>Woodcock Reading Mastery Test-III: Phonological Awareness subtests</li></ul>	<ul><li>WJ III Cognitive: Rapid Picture Naming</li><li>WJ III Cognitive: Retrieval Fluency</li><li>WJ III Achievement: Math Fluency</li></ul>
Orthographic Processing	*Visual Processing*
<ul><li>PAL-2 Receptive & Expressive Coding</li><li>CTOPP: Rapid Naming subtests</li><li>Woodcock Reading Mastery Test-III: Rapid Naming subtests</li></ul>	<ul><li>WJ III Cognitive: Visual Matching</li><li>WJ III Cognitive: Spatial Relations</li><li>WISC-IV Perceptual Reasoning subtests</li></ul>
Working Memory	*Working Memory*
<ul><li>WISC-IV Working Memory subtests</li><li>WJ III Cognitive: Auditory Working Memory</li><li>WJ III Cognitive: Numbers Reversed</li></ul>	<ul><li>WISC-IV Working Memory Index</li><li>WJ III Cognitive: Auditory Working Memory</li><li>WJ III Cognitive: Numbers Reversed</li></ul>
Language Processing	*Visual-Motor*
<ul><li>WISC-IV Verbal Comprehension subtests</li><li>WJ III Achievement: Oral Comprehension</li><li>WJ III Achievement: Understanding Directions</li><li>Woodcock Reading Mastery Test-III: Word Comprehension subtests</li><li>Woodcock Reading Mastery Test-III: Listening Comprehension</li></ul>	<ul><li>Beery-Buktenica Test of Visual-Motor Integration</li><li>Bender Gestalt</li><li>PAL-2 Handwriting subtests</li></ul>
Writing	**General Underachievement**
Visual-Motor	*Executive Function*
<ul><li>Beery-Buktenica Test of Visual-Motor Integration</li><li>Bender Gestalt</li><li>PAL-2 Handwriting subtests</li></ul>	<ul><li>Delis-Kaplan Executive Function System</li><li>WJ III Cognitive: Concept Formation</li><li>WJ III Cognitive: Pair Cancellation</li><li>Behavior Rating Inventory of Executive Function (checklist)</li></ul>
Memory Retrieval	*Emotional*
<ul><li>WJ III Cognitive: Rapid Picture Naming</li><li>WJ III Cognitive: Retrieval Fluency</li></ul>	<ul><li>Behavior Assessement System for Children-2 (Checklist)</li></ul>
Working Memory	*Language Processing*
<ul><li>WISC-IV Working Memory Index</li><li>WJ III Cognitive: Auditory Working Memory</li><li>WJ III Cognitive: Numbers Reversed</li></ul>	<ul><li>WISC-IV Verbal Comprehension subtests</li><li>WJ III Achievement: Oral Comprehension</li><li>WJ III Achievement: Understanding Directions</li><li>Woodcock Reading Mastery Test-III: Word Comprehension subtests</li><li>Woodcock Reading Mastery Test-III: Listening Comprehension</li></ul>

also be very useful. The Academic Fluency cluster of the Woodcock-Johnson III Tests of Achievement is particularly useful in evaluating many twice-exceptional students. This cluster consists of three subtests: Reading Fluency, where a child reads a series of simple sentences and decides whether each is true or false; Math Fluency, where a student quickly solves single-digit addition, subtraction, and multiplication problems; and Writing Fluency, where a child writes sentences incorporating three specific words. Although the tasks on their face are quite simple, students with learning disabilities frequently have trouble executing them with speed and accuracy. In addition to these basic fluency measures, it is also very helpful to evaluate a child's performance on longer timed measures (i.e., writing a story in 15 minutes or reading a series of passages and responding to questions about them in a 20-minute timeframe).

Second, because brief measures of achievement are often not very sensitive to the challenges of GTLD students, it is important, whenever possible, to incorporate lengthier and more demanding measures of academic skills. For example, a reading assessment should include a passage-based comprehension assessment, such as the Gray Silent Reading Tests or the Nelson-Denny Reading Test, in addition to sentence-based measures of reading comprehension. In a math evaluation, it is important to make sure that there is a sufficient number and range of problems administered to capture the nature of the child's learning struggle. On a relatively brief assessment of computation skills, a GTLD student may be able to reason out the answer to some test items that in actuality she does not solidly understand. Administering a lengthier math assessment with a wider variety of items can provide a clearer understanding of how the student may be struggling. Finally, in writing, assessments that require a student to plan and execute a lengthy passage will test the skills of the twice-exceptional student much more effectively than assessments that require them only to write words, phrases, or sentences.

Even when one incorporates longer and harder academic skill measures, it may be difficult to capture an accurate picture of the types of difficulties a GTLD student may be having in the classroom. This is, in large part, because of the role executive dysfunction often plays in the learning profile of these students. The assessment setting is a relatively ideal one for students with challenges in executive function: It is highly regulated, structured, novel, and has considerable variety. In addition, the assessment tasks generally do not require any real long-term planning or significant physical organization—areas that are common challenges for twice-exceptional students.

Difficulties with written language in a gifted student, in particular, are challenging to fully and accurately evaluate. Even when one incorporates true passage composition measures (where a student is given a time limit and asked to write a story or article in response to a specific prompt), these assessments do not capture how most students are expected to write in the classroom. Writing a research paper, for example—where a child has to do independent research and organize and integrate her ideas into a cohesive report—places demands on a student that are difficult to evaluate in the assessment setting. For this reason, it is important, as much as possible, to gain information about a student's academic performance outside the testing room. This sort of information can be gathered through classroom observations, conversations with teachers and parents, and evaluation of work samples. Using this sort of qualitative information together with the norm-referenced data that is gleaned through traditional assessments provides a fuller and more accurate picture of the challenges and the strengths of the twice-exceptional student.

Diagnosticians Working With Twice-Exceptional Students Should Have Keen Observational Skills and Be Good Detectives

For the reasons discussed above, raw assessment data often provides a limited view of the struggles, challenges, and abilities of the twice-exceptional learner. Rounding out the "numerical view" of a student with data from parents and teachers, classroom observations, and careful assessment observations provides a much broader and more accurate understanding of the challenges the student faces, the compensation strategies and coping resources the child employs, and the real day-to-day needs of the student.

Assessment observations, in particular, are critical. As mentioned earlier, two students can arrive at the same numerical score on a subtest for entirely different reasons. A student may perform poorly on a math computation subtest, for example, because of difficulties grasping the concepts or due to small computational mistakes and clerical errors (e.g., missing signs). Carefully observing a student as she works and documenting her approach to the task is a necessary first step. In many cases, it is extremely helpful to test the limits of a child's ability after he or she has completed the standardized assessment. For example, on a test of math computation, one could ask a student to work a missed problem again, talking aloud to herself as she works. On a measure of silent reading comprehension, one might ask the student to read the passage aloud to himself and then work through the questions orally so that it is possible to observe his thinking process. These sort of careful, interactive observations and explorations of a child's learning process provide information that is invaluable in understanding the learning needs of the twice-exceptional student.

Case Study: The Importance of Thoughtful Assessment

As has been discussed, assessing gifted students with learning disabilities is challenging because of the complex interplay of their strengths and weaknesses. Their performance in an evaluation can be inconsistent and confusing. Even the most experienced of diagnosticians may be left scratching their heads. Complicating matters further, a twice-exceptional learner can look very different from one assessment to another. These students' ability to compensate, together with the changing demands of school as they grow older, can make it particularly difficult to evaluate and understand their strengths, weaknesses, and needs over multiple evaluations. Flexibility, an open mind and investigative spirit, and willingness to collaborate and consult with colleagues are tremendously important in working with these students.

Andrew's story provides a wonderful example of the ways a twice-exceptional student can compensate for weaknesses and hide academic struggles, as well as the way the symptom picture of these learners can change over time. Andrew's parents first brought him for an evaluation when he was 8 years old. Verbally precocious and extremely imaginative, Andrew seemed to be the type of student who would have been very successful in school, but he had had trouble adjusting to kindergarten. The social experiences in kindergarten were stressful for Andrew; he became tense and frustrated when in large groups of children, and generally seemed unhappy about going to school. Because of these difficulties, Andrew's parents decided to homeschool him in first grade. Although homeschooling was initially a positive experience, over time Andrew began to demonstrate some academic struggles in math and writing, and he became frustrated and resistant. Andrew's parents hoped that the evaluation would help them to better understand Andrew's needs, both from a social and academic perspective. They also hoped to receive guidance about what sort of educational setting would be best for Andrew, as they eventually hoped to stop homeschooling and move him into a regular school environment.

Andrew presented as a very outgoing and talkative child who was extremely articulate and verbally expressive. Although he was occasionally a bit distractible, he engaged well with the examiner and put forth good effort throughout the evaluation. Andrew's performance on the WISC-III showed extreme variability: His verbal abilities were very strong, in the superior range and at the 95th percentile for his age, while his nonverbal and visual-spatial skills were considerably weaker (low average range, 12th percentile). Andrew also had significant weaknesses in working memory (low average range, 14th percentile) and processing speed (borderline range, 6th percentile). Further cognitive testing provided additional evidence of significant deficits in processing speed, as well as extremely poor visual-motor and handwriting skills. Academic testing showed above-average skills in reading, but significantly below average skills in written language (borderline range, 3rd percentile). In math, Andrew's performance was in the lower end of the average range (34th percentile). Conversations with Andrew's parents confirmed his ongoing struggles with math and writing. They also described how Andrew continued to have social difficulties, particularly in large group settings. He also tended to worry a lot and felt unhappy quite frequently.

Andrew's profile of strengths and weaknesses was determined to be consistent with a diagnosis of nonverbal learning disability and dysgraphia. His significantly weak visual-spatial skills were determined to play a role in his trouble with math, as well as the social struggles he was having. Recommendations were made regarding appropriate educational settings for Andrew, as well as what sorts of supports and accommodations would assist him both in and out of school. Andrew's parents were also encouraged to help him use his verbal strengths to compensate for his weaknesses in other areas (e.g., Andrew was encouraged to talk himself through tasks, particularly those that had visual components or tapped his working memory).

Andrew returned for a reevaluation 4 years later and had made considerable progress, particularly in the social realm. After the prior evaluation, Andrew's parents had made their top priority helping Andrew to build his social skills and self-confidence. They selected a school that was known for its small class size, warm social environment, and flexible teaching approach, and it was an excellent fit for Andrew's needs. By the end of his time there, his social difficulties had completely disappeared; he was well-liked and sought after by peers. His teachers were also quite fond of him, remarking that he had outstanding reasoning abilities, was exceptionally curious, and was very creative.

Andrew had made academic progress as well since the prior assessment, but continued to struggle in both math and writing. He had received some academic supports and interventions in school, such as occupational therapy and time with a learning support teacher to work on math. He was also allowed to use a computer to work on lengthy writing assignments. His parents hoped that an updated evaluation might more clearly delineate Andrew's academic needs.

Consistent with the prior evaluation, Andrew's performance on cognitive testing again showed extreme variability in his performance across subtests. His verbal abilities were in the very superior range (99th percentile), while his performance on measures of nonverbal/visual-spatial abilities, working memory, and processing speed were in the low average to well below average range.

The most surprising finding in this reevaluation had to do with Andrew's performance in reading. Because Andrew did not have any obvious difficulties with reading, either from reports from parents and teachers or in his performance on the prior evaluation, the examiner initially administered an untimed, multiple-choice assessment of silent reading comprehension just as a quick check up of his skills. Andrew performed well on this assessment, scoring at the 98th percentile. In the writing evaluation, Andrew performed quite poorly on a dictated spelling task (16th percentile). The examiner surmised that Andrew's trouble with spelling was most likely due to his poor visual memory, and set out to demonstrate this by administering a spelling test of nonwords that are spelled exactly as they sound. Surprisingly, Andrew also performed poorly on this assessment, suggesting something other than poor visual memory was at the root of his spelling difficulties. To further explore Andrew's difficulties, the examiner administered a measure of phonological awareness—the understanding of how sounds fit together to make words, which is a key cognitive ability underlying reading and writing. Andrew also struggled on this measure, scoring at the 21st percentile. With this new data, the examiner decided to take a second look at Andrew's reading, and found that he had poor word attack skills. In addition, when Andrew was asked to read aloud, his struggles with reading became much more evident—he read slowly and with numerous errors.

The results of this second evaluation demonstrated that Andrew also had dyslexia. Andrew's dyslexia had been masked by the fact that he had not yet encountered significant reading demands in school and had been able to use his strong verbal abilities to compensate for his deficits in phonological awareness and his poor word attack skills. Although Andrew did have a long history of problems with written language, they had been attributed to his poor visual-motor skills and weak working memory. However, the updated evaluation demonstrated that poor phonological awareness also was a factor underlying Andrew's difficulty with writing, and spelling in particular.

The examiner evaluated Andrew two subsequent times, and his strong ability to compensate for his weaknesses continued to shine. Although aspects of Andrew's writing continued to be a struggle (e.g., spelling and handwriting), the content of his writing was outstanding, and Andrew started to think about incorporating writing into his future career plans. He also continued to enjoy reading for pleasure, although his fluency on highly academic texts could be slow.

Conclusion

The take-home message of Andrew's story is the importance of thoughtful assessment and a constant questioning approach when assessing these students. In working with GTLD students, it is critical to adopt a neuropsychological perspective that identifies the processing problems that are interfering with a student's performance. It is also important to incorporate achievement tests into the evaluation that are likely to highlight the types of difficulties that are most common in GTLD students. Finally, and perhaps most importantly, the observations of the examiner are key to a good GTLD assessment, as one can learn a volume of information about a student's struggles and compensation strategies by watching how he tackles tasks.

chapter 10

Best Practices for Identifying Twice-Exceptional Students for Gifted Programs

Because of the complicated nature of GTLD students and the difficulties they can have with consistently showing their abilities on tests and in the classroom, it can be very easy to overlook twice-exceptional students for gifted programs. It is possible, however, to create gifted identification procedures that are GTLD-friendly.

The National Association for Gifted Children (NAGC; 2008) posted a position paper on its website on the best practices for identification of gifted students that outlines some nonnegotiable practices in the assessment of students for giftedness. Although its recommendations address gifted students more broadly, following these suggestions would help maximize the possibility of identifying giftedness in a twice-exceptional student. The following best practices are particularly critical points in identifying twice-exceptional students for gifted programs.

Assessments Used to Identify Students for Gifted Programs Should Match the Skill(s) Needed for Success in the Program

It is important to consider the aspects that are critical to the success of a gifted program, whether it be a specific academic skill, creativity, reasoning ability, motivation, or interest, and identify measures that accurately evaluate those constructs. Many twice-exceptional students would benefit from and excel in enrichment-style gifted programs emphasizing creativity and project-based learning. However, there is the potential that they may be prevented from entering such a program if the measures used to identify students for the programs emphasize strong performance on measures of academic skill that may not be critical to program success.

Even in the case of programs that are related more closely to academic skill (e.g., an accelerative math program), consideration should be given to students who may have the ability and interest needed to be successful in the program, but may not show their abilities effectively on qualification tests because of the effects of their learning challenges. A student may ultimately be able to shine in a program for gifted math students because of her strong reasoning ability and passion for numbers. However, her performance on a standardized test used to identify students for the program may more clearly demonstrate her struggles with attention to detail, following instructions, and processing speed than her quantitative ability.

Individuals Who Administer, Score, and Evaluate Assessments for Gifted Programs Should Be Aware of Common Patterns of Performance Seen in Twice-Exceptional Students

Gifted students with learning challenges often show a recognizable pattern of performance on standardized tests, as outlined in Table 10.1. First, they may make errors throughout a test that do not seem to relate to difficulty level. These errors typically do not relate to difficulty with item content, but instead reflect fluctuations in attention, missed details, misunderstanding of directions, and so forth. This pattern of responding is sometimes known as a Swiss cheese profile because of the seemingly random nature of the missed items. In addition to making apparently random errors, twice-exceptional learners may tend to correctly answer difficult items while missing less challenging questions. Because the students recognize easier questions as being within their grasp, they tend to let their guard down and are more vulnerable to small mistakes, such as missing directions, misreading arithmetic signs, or copying an answer down incorrectly. When faced with more challenging material, they become more engaged and are often less vulnerable to the effects of small errors. Speaking of small errors,

Table 10.1
Patterns of Test Performance Common in Twice-Exceptional Students

Making seemingly random errors throughout a test
Correctly answering difficult questions while missing easier items
Making an abundance of careless errors
Skipping items
Correctly answering attempted items but failing to finish the test

an abundance of careless mistakes are commonly seen in the test performance of twice-exceptional students—both content errors such as minor calculation mistakes and format errors like skipping items or misrecording answers on an answer sheet. Finally, many twice-exceptional students have deficits in processing speed and therefore struggle to complete tests within a time limit. Often, though, these students will answer most or all of the items that they attempted correctly—weaker performance on the test is due only to their difficulty working quickly.

Multimodal Evaluations Give Students Many Ways to Demonstrate Their Gifts and Provide a More Comprehensive View of a Student

Ideally, assessment for gifted programs should test a variety of academic and nonacademic skills in addition to incorporating qualitative assessments of student performance such as parent and teacher ratings. In addition, the formalized tests should also offer a variety of formats (e.g., performance evaluations vs. a paper test). Multimodal evaluations are critical in the assessment of giftedness in a twice-exceptional student, as they give the student the opportunity to show his abilities in multiple ways. Take, for example, the assessment of mathematical ability in a gifted student. Assessments that require a child to complete written calculations and show his work may be less likely to capture the abilities of a twice-exceptional student than a quantitative reasoning measure that relies less on rote computation skills.

When Possible, Performance Assessments Should Be Used in Identifying Students for Gifted Programs

Performance assessments are particularly useful because they may be more sensitive to the abilities of the twice-exceptional learner. These assessments directly measure a specific construct or ability and can allow GTLD students to emphasize their strengths. Performance evaluations tend to be more open-ended and subjective. For example, students may be asked to demonstrate their verbal knowledge by debating a topic or show their reasoning ability by completing a science project. Portfolios can allow a student to demonstrate her knowledge and ability in an area of interest. Although performance assessments can provide a way to enable twice-exceptional students to demonstrate their abilities with reduced interference from their processing challenges, the process to evaluate the assessments are more subjective. The NAGC (2008) position paper recommended that two raters be used to evaluate these sorts of assessments. In addition, sufficient training must be given to enable evaluators to achieve an acceptable interrater agreement of 80%.

Conclusion

Appropriate identification and assessment strategies are integral to serving the complex needs of twice-exceptional learners. Having teachers who are aware that gifted students can have learning disabilities and are able to recognize the characteristics that suggest a student may be twice-exceptional is a key first step. Next, it is important to implement assessments designed to identify students' strengths, as well as the processing deficits that are impacting their performance. Having this information helps to identify the students' educational needs and guides educators on strategies that can be implemented to help improve student performance. Next, we focus on some of these strategies by identifying best practices for GTLD programming.

chapter 11

The Paradoxical Nature of the GTLD Experience

With current economic constraints and the pressure on schools to increase the academic performance of the most at-risk students, we approach the issue of programming with the understanding that there are limited resources available for programming for gifted children of any sort and hope to point to ways that various settings could introduce modest changes more beneficial to twice-exceptional students. For many school districts, it is likely not realistic to establish separate GTLD programs, and schools will need to address the needs of twice-exceptional students in a more creative manner. Twice-exceptional students can be served in a variety of settings, including general education, gifted programs, and special education programs. The best fit for a given student will depend on the relative complexity and severity of his learning disabilities. In later sections of the book, we will present ongoing efforts to meet the needs of twice-exceptional students in a variety of settings, with the hope of encouraging schools to make the effort to meet the needs of these students.

Effective programming for twice-exceptional learners requires a fundamental shift in teaching style to address the complexity of these students. Although there are teachers who naturally work well with complex students, most will require training to develop the skill sets in classroom management and curriculum delivery that are needed to address both learning challenges and giftedness. General educators often have limited training in strategies for teaching learning disabled students or gifted students. Similarly, special education teachers generally learn remediation strategies and have few opportunities to learn about teaching higher order thinking skills. Gifted teachers have little exposure to strategies to accommodate and adapt instruction for students with learning disabilities. Professional development regarding best practices for twice-exceptional students is likely to enrich the entire school teaching staff. As research (Wenglinsky, 2000) has shown, professional development with special populations has been found to improve teacher success overall. However, it is important for administrators to realize that a fundamental shift in teaching orientation requires significant investment in staff development over a period of years and likely requires more structure than a few in-service training sessions.

GTLD Students Are Defined by Extremes

Successful teachers are typically good managers—organized and focused on specific goals for instruction. They run a tight ship and provide authoritative leadership in the classroom. However, twice-exceptional learners can throw a wrench in the works due to their inconsistency in skills across tasks and over time. These students are defined by extremes. They are often very perceptive in some ways and may be oblivious in others. They can catch on almost instantaneously to some concepts and lag far beyond their same-age peers on others. They know something one day and then seem to never have seen the material the next day. Twice-exceptional students may have enveloping passions at the expense of practical endeavors. Although students of all types have strengths and weaknesses, the pendulum swings the farthest for GTLD students. Their complex learning profile requires teachers to follow a moving target with good humor and a sense of adventure. Twice-exceptional students often have competing needs. Presenting a framework of their paradoxical characteristics can help teachers to conceptualize the duality of the needs of bright students who learn differently.

Twice-Exceptional Students Need Both Flexibility and Structure

Twice-exceptional students have competing needs in the domain of structure. Their information processing challenges can create a certain degree of rigidity in their thinking that can be further compounded by social and emotional issues. These students often have difficulty shifting gears and seeing situations from multiple points of view. Sometimes, they can have difficulty understanding the big picture. When frustrated, they can dig in and keep trying the same ineffectual strategies with little awareness that their approach is not working. Although many mainstream gifted students may have a preferred learning style, most can fairly readily accommodate to a teacher's demand to handle information in a nonpreferred way. However, twice-exceptional students are often not able to accommodate to a less favored method of learning because they actually do not learn well under these conditions. This problem is particularly common for visually gifted students who do not learn well in a highly verbal classroom. Unfortunately, many teachers' preferred teaching style is highly verbal and they may operate under the assumption that all gifted students are verbally precocious.

Teachers Need to Meet GTLD Students Where They Are

Twice-exceptional students need teachers to meet them where they are and to engage them in a preferred learning style where they can experience success. For teachers, this means that they must be flexible and willing to juggle multiple balls as students in their classes access the same material in a variety of ways. Success with this population means there is no one-size-fits-all solution. Expecting GTLD students to immediately and easily accommodate to teacher expectations is likely to lead to power struggles and/or to the student shutting down. A successful GTLD teacher needs to have a more sophisticated understanding of leadership and be able to see that choosing one's battles is an effective form of management and not a sign of weakness. Taking student resistance personally is ineffective; instead the resistance should be viewed as an emotional manifestation of the student's learning challenges. Although the student's preferred learning style should be accommodated initially, one of the goals in GTLD programming is to assist students in broadening their horizons. However, these students must be engaged first and must develop a sense of trust with the teacher in order to take risks and try new things.

Teachers may also need to develop a more flexible understanding of their role as a teacher to work with GTLD students. These students may have complex family circumstances that require the teacher to engage in greater case management than might be typical. Recognizing that the parents of twice-exceptional students may also have processing challenges, teachers may need to be more active in maintaining contact with families and should not assume that parents receive and actually read written communication. Teachers of GTLD students also need to be willing to share authority with other teaching staff and specialists and be willing to accept feedback about their teaching methods with particular students.

GTLD Students Need Clear Guidelines for Academic Work and Behavior

Although students need teachers to approach them flexibly, they also need teachers to provide structure. Many students with learning disabilities have significant executive functioning weaknesses that cause them to struggle to understand task demands, organize long-term projects, and initiate tasks. These students often feel at a loss when assigned an open-ended task. They do not always attend to what is going on around them and don't pick up on expectations or routines that might be obvious to their peers. These students are often not good at reading the teacher and understanding teacher preferences and classroom expectations for behavior. As Sprick (2009) pointed out, teachers should not assume that students know what is expected, but should explicitly teach students how they are expected to behave in particular situations in the classroom. Establishing clear routines and providing visual cues in the classroom can help twice-exceptional students, as well as other learning disabled students, be more successful in the classroom.

In academic tasks, teachers need to start with student interests and provide a problem-solving structure to help students see the steps to an end product. GTLD students often need the teacher to provide a model of how to approach a task and may need scaffolding to engage in the steps in a problem-solving process. Consistency in the use of a problem-solving approach can be helpful for these students. Once they learn a method, students can often learn to apply it independently.

Teachers Need Support From the School Administration

Teachers can be encouraged to be more flexible and to take a problem-solving approach when the school administration provides support and models flexibility and good problem solving. Teachers need a forum to explore issues that challenge them in the classroom and should be able to discuss these issues without fearing negative evaluation. Often, professional learning communities or consultation with master teachers who mentor newer teachers can provide needed support. Encouraging teachers to conduct action research also sets a tone that teachers are engaged in active experimentation and self-improvement. Teachers are likely to be more flexible when they feel that administrators recognize the complexity of what they are dealing with in the classroom and support their efforts to creatively address these challenges. Focusing solely on outcomes leads to a negative dynamic for both students and teachers that can create risk avoidance.

Case Study: The Importance of Balancing Structure and Flexibility

The difficulties twice-exceptional students can have with structure are particularly prevalent in advanced high school courses where they are expected to master a certain level of content within a specific time frame. In these high-demand settings, students with complex learning profiles struggle with work pace and have difficulty showing their mastery of the material. Sarah demonstrated a typical pattern for GTLD students, with exceptional verbal ability combined with very slow processing speed. She was very aware of her difficulties producing work commensurate with her ability and over time had developed considerable anxiety that exacerbated her problems. Sarah's difficulties came to a head in her advanced English class. She could demonstrate mastery of advanced content on tests and on structured, time-limited writing assignments; however, Sarah fell apart when expected to write longer and more open-ended papers. In addition to being a slow processor, Sarah had difficulty getting started and frequently experienced writer's block because of her extreme perfectionism. Her grades suffered because she often did not turn in these long-term assignments. This negative cycle resulted in failing grades in her English and social studies classes, despite the fact that she had earned very high marks on final exams. Sadly, Sarah ended up being placed in a much lower level English class and she began to refuse to go to school. Her attendance dropped, as well as all of the rest of her grades.

Although Sarah had a 504 Plan for accommodations, the teaching staff did not focus on the downward trajectory of her academic performance until her parents brought in an educational advocate. Once the multidisciplinary team met to work on addressing her needs, an effective intervention plan was developed. However, the teaching staff struggled to see how such a bright student could have such difficulty in completing assignments and were resistant to providing Sarah with more support because they felt she should not be coddled. Eventually, Sarah was assigned a teacher-mentor who worked with her on time and task management to plan long-term assignments. This teacher also served as an advocate for Sarah in working out difficulties with her teachers and helped her learn strategies for self-advocacy. Providing structure and flexibility was a key component for Sarah's success.

Twice-Exceptional Students Need Both High Expectations and Empathy for Challenges

Issues around expectations for twice-exceptional students can be a minefield, especially when students have high-achieving parents. Both parents and students are wrestling with frustration and disappointment when bright students do not seem to be able to produce work commensurate with their potential. Often, by the time these students are identified, the family has developed a sense of diminished expectations to avoid disappointment. Twice-exceptional students often have considerable drive and ambition, but as Rimm (2008a) pointed out, may have significant conflicts over issues of competition. They may refuse to try an assignment just to avoid painful feelings due to potential failure.

It is important to hold these students to high expectations: The GTLD student can and should be expected to do gifted work. Because of past experiences of failure and the resulting frustration, both parents and students may require persuasion that these high standards are realistic. Teachers need to have a clear understanding of what constitutes gifted work and should show patience in guiding students to their best work. When students have had a long history of limited expectations and assignments that did not stretch their skills, they are likely to have a negative reaction to new expectations. Their parents may also be wary about new challenges and may have become accustomed to focusing on their children as underachievers. Initially, it is important to focus on quality and not quantity and to recognize that twice-exceptional students may take longer and require greater scaffolding than mainstream gifted peers to produce gifted work. Parents may need more guidance in developing realistic expectations that students can meet. The GTLD teacher must keep an eye on the goal and believe in students' strengths—that they are diamonds in the rough.

Teachers Should Monitor Students' Emotional Reactions

In order to maintain student effort and progress toward meeting gifted expectations, teachers need to carefully monitor students' emotional reactions and use empathy to anticipate stumbling blocks that can derail the whole process. It is important for teachers to take the time to look at the students' work processes in detail and to appreciate how their information processing challenges hamper their efforts to show their strengths. Professional development on the possible information processing deficits of twice-exceptional learners and their impact on academic performance can enhance teachers' ability to see the students' challenges. Teachers who appreciate and admire the perseverance and pluck of students attempting to overcome significant challenges are likely to have greatest success in coaxing these students to rise to new heights.

Twice-Exceptional Students Seek Community, But Struggle With Individuality

Many gifted activities involve cooperative learning, and certainly, the ability to work effectively with others is critical in other educational settings (e.g., college) as well as in the work world. Teachers must help twice-exceptional students to engage with their peers, but also recognize that these interactions can be difficult and stressful. Because of their past learning and social experiences, many GTLD students are often quite ambivalent about group activities. They may desire friends, particularly those who might share their intellectual interests. Gifted programming provides them with the opportunity to socialize with like-minded peers. However, these students may struggle to manage the increased social and sensory demands of group work and may have received negative feedback from their peers in the past. As a result, group work may lead to heightened anxiety.

GTLD Students Need Explicit Role Identification and Behavioral Expectations for Group Work

Working in a group successfully requires students to be flexible and to be able to engage in perspective taking. Students need to be able to identify roles within the group and develop expectations for each role, and they must be able to respect the boundaries of their roles. Successful groups also require that each person follow through with his or her assignment. A perpetual complaint among school children is that some people in their group opt out of their assigned tasks and others wind up doing everything to fill in the gaps. Or a student takes over and dominates the group task, bossing around the other students in the group.

Twice-exceptional students, particularly those on the autism spectrum, may need group expectations spelled out for them. These students often have strong opinions and have difficulty listening to other perspectives. There is often a certain amount of chaos and ambiguity when students are expected to organize an open-ended group task. For students who have difficulty discerning structure in their environment and grasping task demands, this situation may be fraught with anxiety, which further compromises their social and coping skills. They are likely to need coaching to assist them in meeting role expectations in group work.

Twice-Exceptional Students Need to Accept Limitations and Become Aware of Strengths

As we have seen, it is often difficult for knowledgeable adults to recognize the strengths and weaknesses of twice-exceptional students, so it is no surprise that the students themselves struggle to grasp the contradictions of their learning profiles. They live with the frustrations of not being able to express their ideas and plans effectively on a daily basis. They compare themselves to others and often find their own performance wanting, and they may resent the extra effort required for them to complete their school tasks. It is important for teachers to appreciate that the issue of limitations is a sensitive topic, but it is one that must be addressed. Although it is tempting to cover these issues and provide informal accommodations to avoid making the student feel bad, in the long run, this strategy is not helpful for students who will need documentation and self-advocacy skills to receive needed accommodations in college. Although all students profit from greater self-awareness, twice-exceptional learners especially need to become comfortable in discussing their learning challenges.

On the other hand, GTLD students also have considerable ambivalence about their strengths. Even in areas of talent, they may experience inconsistent performance that creates considerable performance anxiety. They often struggle with demand situations, even when they may have the relevant knowledge or skill. Because of fragile self-esteem, they may bolster their self-image by exaggerating their talents, or they may be afraid to put their skills to the test in order to maintain a belief in their competence. Other twice-exceptional students may cope with their learning challenges by trying to fade into the background and avoid being noticed by teachers and peers.

GTLD teachers can play a crucial role in helping students become more aware of and comfortable with both strengths and weaknesses. Teachers who openly share their own struggles with learning (we all have some) and how they overcame them provide powerful role models for students. Teaching and encouraging students in the class to give and receive constructive feedback can also provide a real boost for GTLD students. They are more likely to believe positive feedback from peers than from adults. Creating an atmosphere of shared problems rather than competition can help students reach out to peers and help them see what they have to offer to the group.

Conclusion

Successful instruction of twice-exceptional students requires teachers to develop comfort with uncertainty and ambiguity. GTLD teachers need to be able to allow the needs of the student, which may change at the drop of a hat, to drive their approach to instruction. They need to be able to keep the big picture in mind while dealing with local turbulence. GTLD students need guidance, understanding, support, and encouragement toward greater independence and toward the capacity to work with others while also advocating for their own needs. Appreciating the complexity of the teaching endeavor will also help teachers respect the challenges faced by their twice-exceptional students on a daily basis.

chapter 12

Best Practice for GTLD Programming 1:
Focus on Student Strengths and Interests to Engage Students

Gifted programming can be provided in several ways in the general education setting, including embedding within differentiated instruction in a mainstream classroom, ability groupings, accelerated instruction, and pull-out programs with gifted curriculum content. At the high school level, students are offered honors courses and college-level curriculum. To develop our best practices, we conducted case studies of a variety of school settings with an eye toward the needs of twice-exceptional students from a neuropsychological perspective. We will provide examples from public and private settings from elementary to high school that we feel illustrate important principles that would lead to effective instruction of GTLD students. The next six chapters outline our best practices for GTLD programming.

The Challenge of Keeping Both Strengths and Weaknesses in Perspective

Because twice-exceptional learners can be perplexing—and sometimes even maddening—to their teachers and parents, it is all too easy to focus on their weaknesses and challenges instead of their strengths. For some students, an emphasis on weaknesses results from the severity of their learning difficulties; because of the degree to which their disabilities impair their functioning, the gifts may seem inconsequential in light of the larger challenges the students face. Even for gifted students with milder disabilities, frustration with the student's underachievement may draw attention away from her gifts. A belief that the student is lazy or that her struggles are the result of willful behavior (i.e., "if she wanted to put in the effort, she could . . .") can make school professionals question the appropriateness of allowing opportunities for intellectual challenge and enrichment. Add to the fact that some twice-exceptional students may question rote work in a rather undiplomatic manner (e.g., "This is baby work—why do I have to do this?") and an almost-punitive mindset can result: Why should these students participate in gifted programming when they can't be successful on the simplest of tasks? In addition, it can be easy to assume that the gifts will simply take care of themselves—that the student can and will engage in his or her passions and talents through extracurricular activities.

Focusing on deficits at the expense of strengths is ultimately counterproductive for twice-exceptional learners, however, as it reduces their motivation, increases the possibility of academic failure, and negatively affects their emotional well-being (Bianco, Carothers, & Smiley, 2009). Twice-exceptional students need learning opportunities that tap into their strengths and interests—not only to optimize achievement levels, but also to minimize emotional barriers they may have to learning. In short, "strength-based educational planning prevents students' disabilities from becoming an obstacle to their learning" (Bianco et al., 2009, p. 214).

GTLD Students Require Dual Differentiation

Baum, Cooper, and Neu (2001) stressed the importance of developing programs for GTLD students that encourage and develop their gifts while accommodating and supporting their weaknesses. This dual differentiation balances the remediation and accommodation of the learning disability with the nurturance and development of a child's strengths. A focus on students' strengths also provides opportunities for the students to recognize and develop compensatory strategies that will help them to work around weaknesses. A student with visual gifts, for example, could be encouraged to demonstrate his knowledge through a multimedia presentation or hands-on model rather than a written product. Alternatively, a student with creative and verbal strengths who struggles with math could be encouraged to make up a story that goes along with a math concept that she just learned.

Project High Hopes

A good example of how powerful strengths-based learning can be for twice-exceptional students can be found in the outcomes of the summer institute of Project High Hopes (Gentry & Neu, 1998). Project High Hopes was a 3-year federally funded program designed to identify and develop the talents and abilities of gifted students with disabilities. Students were evaluated and identified as having strengths in one of four areas: visual arts, performing arts, engineering, and life science. After the identification process was complete, students participated in programming during the school year as well as a one-week residential summer program. The purpose of the summer program was to provide the students with an authentic learning experience: one where they worked on solving real-world problems using methods that a professional in the field might use. Because these learning experiences focused on using practical, hands-on, real-life skills, basic academic abilities—such as reading text and recalling math facts—were not emphasized (Baum et al., 2001). As a result, the students could fully engage with the project using their strengths and talents.

In the Project High Hopes summer institute, students were divided into groups and asked to grapple with a real-world problem: On the grounds of the institute, a water feature had been created that was neither attractive nor environmentally sound. Students were asked to develop original and creative solutions that would improve the water feature. At the end of the institute, they presented their proposals to the school board. Within each group, students chose specific problems to solve based on their individual strengths. For example, a student with gifts in the visual arts focused on landscape design, while a student gifted in biology devised a plan to reintroduce fish to the pond. The groups also utilized their strengths in their presentations, sharing the data in a variety of ways that played to their individual abilities—visual techniques (e.g., creating a video tape, developing a mural), traditional business approaches (e.g., using flip charts, slides, and scale models), and artistic expression (e.g., performing a play; Gentry & Neu, 1998).

Having the opportunity to engage in activities using their strengths in this way was beneficial to the students' well-being; teacher-facilitators in the program noticed increased self-confidence and self-esteem in the students as they worked together over the course of the program. Follow-up with the students after completion of the program suggested that the improved self-confidence and self-efficacy that they experienced persisted into the following school year.

Prior to the summer institute, none of the 27 participants had taken part in programs that played to their strengths (e.g., Odyssey of the Mind, science fairs, art shows). In the next school year, a total of 26 of the students engaged in one of these activities (Gentry & Neu, 1998). These findings suggest that tapping into student strengths can have a lasting impact on students' self-concept and overall engagement with learning.

GTLD Students Have Strong Preferences

Students' strengths and interests often go hand-in-hand. Tapping into student interests is another important element for instructing GTLD students, as these students often have strong passions, as well as strong aversions to certain topics. Engaging student interests can provide a powerful way to harness the students' motivation and enthusiasm for learning, and may also provide a tool for helping students compensate for their weaknesses. Levine (2002b) described how student interests—or affinities, as he called them—can be used to actually teach skills. Take, for example, a student with a math learning disability who has a passion for baseball. A teacher could use the child's interest in baseball to increase his motivation for learning math concepts by teaching how math can be used to calculate sports statistics.

Finding and using an area of passion can be particularly useful in working with gifted students who are on the autism spectrum. One characteristic of students with Asperger's syndrome in particular is having an intense interest in a specific area (American Psychiatric Association, 2000). Winter-Messiers (2007) interviewed 23 students with AS and found that using this specialized interest in instruction can have powerful positive impacts for these children. First, Winter-Messiers found that the special interests are an integral part of the self-image of the AS student, as "children and youth with AS define themselves by their special interest area" (p. 148). As a result, using this special interest in instruction can be a powerful way to harness students' motivation, particularly when working on skills and tasks that may be challenging for them. For example, although fine motor skills are frequently an area of weakness for students with AS, Winter-Messiers found that when students engaged in fine motor tasks related to their special interest, they did so with persistence and patience. The author also found that the special interest could be a useful tool for managing the emotional and behavioral challenges that are often part of AS; students could use their special interest to help calm themselves and manage anxiety. In general, using the special interest in instruction had global benefits for the children in the study; the author observed that the deficits related to AS were less problematic when students were engaged in their interests. Identifying and using the special interest, then, can be beneficial for the student with AS on a variety of levels. Bianco et al. (2009) suggested that teachers working with a gifted student with AS create a concept map that can be used to highlight areas for further study around the student's interest. The concept map can then be used to create lessons and design independent projects that relate to the student's passion areas.

Mentoring Can Tap Into Student Strengths and Interests

Mentoring has long been seen as a powerful and beneficial way to encourage and support gifted students (Bianco et al., 2009; Little, Kearney, & Britner, 2010), but it can be a particularly useful and powerful way to meet the needs of twice-exceptional learners. Shevitz, Weinfeld, Jeweler, and Barnes-Robinson (2003) described a mentoring program—the Wings Mentor Program—specifically designed to provide support to twice-exceptional students. First developed in 1989, the Wings Mentor Program was initially used in a GTLD self-contained classroom. Over time, though, the program was expanded to meet the needs of gifted students who were underachieving in the general education classroom.

Shevitz et al. (2003) described four principles underlying the mentor program: (a) focusing on strengths, (b) maximizing the potential for success by working one-on-one with a mentor in an area of interest, (c) building self-confidence and self-esteem through student successes, and (d) setting the stage for future success. The Wings program pairs underachieving bright students with adult mentors who are experts in the students' area of interest. Students and mentors are carefully matched to ensure shared interests, enthusiasm, and authenticity. The students meet weekly with their mentors, designing and developing a product that has relevance in the field of interest and is an authentic project that has value and use. At the end of 8 weeks, the students present their projects at a final showcase. The Wings Mentor Program has been highly successful in maintaining persistence and task completion to help underachievers create projects that seem far beyond the capability of students their same chronological age.

Shevitz et al. (2003) noted that while the increased knowledge gained through the mentor program is important, it is the relationship between the student and the mentor that is the most valuable. Mentors are trained to be aware of the students' self-concept and to look for opportunities to strengthen the students' self-esteem. In short, "it is the mentor/student relationship that serves as a catalyst for improving the students' view of themselves, empowering them to be successful in the classroom" (Shevitz et al., 2003, p. 39).

Strength-Based Instruction Engages Students in Authentic Projects

It appears, then, that utilizing the strengths and interests of the twice-exceptional student in instruction has three benefits. First, engaging students in authentic (i.e., real-world) projects that capture their interests and invite them to use their strengths helps them to feel more engaged in and motivated by school. Many twice-exceptional learners have a strong need to know what the purpose of an activity is and a need to accept the validity of an assignment before they can become engaged in it. These students are often whole-to-part learners that need to see the big picture before being willing to embark on a task. When teachers are willing to attend to the question of "why" at the start of a unit or lesson, GTLD students are much more likely to buy into the learning experience. Tapping into students' strengths and interests through real-world learning often results in these students being more engaged and invested in the learning process. As a result, they may work to overcome their challenges—sometimes without even realizing it.

Strength-Based Instruction Guides Accommodation and Adaptation

Focusing on the strengths of a twice-exceptional student can also help school staff better understand how to help these students compensate for their learning disabilities. Providing opportunities for these students to use their strengths can be empowering, as it encourages them to utilize their abilities and to find ways to work around their deficits. Again, finding ways for these learners to engage in real-world, project-based activities can be particularly powerful, as those learning experiences allow the students to demonstrate and use their gifts in abstract thinking, problem solving, and creativity while circumventing weaknesses in basic academic skills. By observing students engaged with a project that taps into their strengths and interests, teachers can gain a fuller understanding of how the students learn best (Baum et al., 2001). These insights can inform strategies and techniques that can help the students grapple with the struggles they face as the result of their learning disabilities.

Strength-Based Instruction
Increases Student Self-Esteem

Finally, adopting a strengths-based approach to instructing GTLD students has a powerful positive impact on their self-confidence and self-esteem that may have far-reaching effects. As mentioned above, after participating in a strengths-based summer program, gifted students with disabilities increased their participation in other activities designed to develop their talents and abilities (Gentry & Neu, 1998). It appears that a focus on strengths and interests helps to instill a sense of hope in students: They start to think more in terms of what they *can* do, rather than focusing on their limitations. This sense of empowerment may help the students feel more motivated to work on their deficit areas—and more hopeful that hard work will result in improvements in their performance.

Case Study: The Johns Hopkins University Center for Talented Youth, Baltimore, MD

Founded in 1979 by Dr. Julian Stanley and Johns Hopkins University, the Center for Talented Youth (CTY) is a world leader in talent identification and development in students from kindergarten through 12th grade. CTY offers a variety of programs and services for gifted students, including an academic talent search, summer programs, distance education through the CTY*Online* program, and family learning opportunities through Family Academic Programs. CTY has a long history of understanding and supporting twice-exceptional students. In 1997, Linda Brody and Carol Mills, staff members at CTY, published the seminal article, "Gifted Students With Learning Disabilities: A Review of the Issues." Not long afterward, the CTY Diagnostic and Counseling Center was created; this clinic assesses gifted students with learning challenges and advises parents and teachers on how to work effectively with twice-exceptional students.

CTY staff members have worked for many years to accommodate students with disabilities, including providing testing accommodations for students participating in the CTY Talent Search and implementing a variety of supports and accommodations for students participating in all of CTY's academic programs. In 2010, CTY created a full-time disabilities support position. In her role as Disability Services Administrator, Melissa Kistler communicates and coordinates with parents and program staff to develop accommodation and/or support plans for students in CTY's programs.

Kistler reports that the majority of requests for learning supports come from students participating in CTY's summer programs. These programs, held on roughly 25 sites around the country and the world, are open to students in grades 2–12. Between 9,000 and 10,000 students attend the programs each year. According to CTY's website, the summer programs are designed to "offer eligible students . . . the opportunity to engage in challenging academic work in the company of peers who share their exceptional abilities and love of learning" (CTY, n.d.b, para. 1). Students take one course for a 3-week session. The academic experience is rigorous and intensive; for example, older students' courses cover roughly the amount of information covered in a semester-long college course in 3 weeks. In addition to the intensive and rigorous learning experience, the summer programs emphasize personal and social growth; structured activities and social opportunities are planned outside of class time.

CTY strongly encourages parents of students with all kinds of disabilities—learning, medical, and physical—to contact the Disability Services Office to share needs that their children may have. Kistler reports that in the summer of 2012, Disability Services received 128 formal requests from students with learning needs: 34 students with autism spectrum disorders, 50 with ADHD, and 44 with specific learning disabilities. Kistler corresponds with the parents of these students to discuss these needs and to plan how to support them in the summer programs. She also works closely with the academic counselor (an administrative staff role similar to that of a school counselor) at each summer program site to coordinate efforts to support students with disabilities.

CTY, as a part of Johns Hopkins University, acts under the Americans with Disabilities Act and Section 504 of the Rehabilitation Act of 1973 rather than IDEA. As discussed earlier, ADA prohibits discrimination and ensures the right of a student with a disability to have a level playing field. To this end, Kistler works to develop accommodation plans that provide students with disabilities equal access to CTY's programs. Common accommodations include extended time, use of a computer for word processing, and copies of class notes. In addition to these accommodation plans, students in CTY summer programs may also be given support plans. Supports provided to students are not required to provide equal access, but are given to help a student to be successful in the program. Examples of supports include help with study skills, assistance with organization, and support with social skills. Kistler noted that the line between an accommodation and a support is a fuzzy one and may vary depending on the individual needs of the student.

In CTY's residential programs, supports and accommodations also extend to residential life. Kistler described that students with autism spectrum disorders, in particular, benefit from this sort of assistance. Accommodations and supports provided may include allowing a single room, providing advanced warning of transitions, and permitting a student to sit out of social activities if needed.

Kistler shared one interesting and important observation about her experiences working with twice-exceptional students in CTY's summer programs: Often, the types of accommodations and interventions that are needed in school don't end up being necessary at CTY. Staff members work proactively to put the accommodation and/or support plans into place, but at the end of the summer, they frequently find that students performed well without utilizing the range of accommodations to which they were entitled. Kistler feels this is due in large part to the fact that students choose the course they will take in the summer program. As a result, they are immersed in a learning experience that fully engages their interests and utilizes their strengths. The fact that students are taking a course that they are passionate about has social benefits as well—something that is particularly meaningful for students on the autism spectrum. Kistler noted that the opportunity for these students to "be with other quirky, smart kids who share their interests is really powerful." Students find—often for the first time—other like-minded peers who can talk about concepts and issues in a similar way. For many students, this experience is so meaningful that they return to CTY year after year. For some, the positive social and academic experiences they encounter at CTY can help carry them through a school year that may be less positive.

Kistler also feels that the culture of the CTY summer programs contributes to the success of students—particularly those students who may have learning disabilities and/or difficulties with peers. The CTY summer programs have an honor code that students are expected to uphold from the first day. The honor code requires students to "uphold personal and academic integrity, respect the ideas and property of others, and ensure that those around them do the same" (CTY, n.d.a, para. 20). Respecting others—particularly those who may be different in some way—is central to the honor code. In addition, CTY has a zero indifference policy that states that staff must always intervene in negative social situations: name-calling, teasing, and roughhousing are simply not allowed, even among friends. The honor code, together with the zero indifference policy, builds a community of respect and trust that tends to make CTY a more comfortable and safe learning and social environment for students who often do not feel accepted in school.

Conclusion

The disabilities of twice-exceptional students often become a primary focus of teachers and parents, either because of the severity of the disabilities or because of a general frustration with a student's underachievement. It can be easy to place a student's strengths and interests on the back burner and focus instead on her daily struggles. Doing so, however, is counterproductive, as it tends to reduce the students' motivation and exacerbate their underachievement. Focusing on children's strengths and interests through dual differentiation or special activities like mentoring programs can harness the engagement of twice-exceptional learners and their increase self-esteem. In some cases, it may even help them become more effective at compensating for the effects of their learning challenges.

chapter 13

Best Practice for GTLD Programming 2: Encourage an Open and Communicative Culture

Researchers have noted that school culture is a key element in the design and implementation of school programs (Rhodes, Stevens, & Hemmings, 2011), and indeed, developing and fostering a positive school climate is a critical step in developing effective educational programs for twice-exceptional students. An open and communicative school community enables teachers, school staff, parents, and students to work together in a collaborative and effective manner—something that is extremely important when working with these perplexing and complex learners.

Effective Communication Increases Student Success

First and foremost, good communication is critical, as it fosters interpersonal trust and helps to set the foundation for a collaborative and accepting school community. Perhaps most importantly, there must be positive and constructive communication between teachers and students. Twice-exceptional students thrive in an atmosphere of challenge and intellectual stimulation; having teachers who set high expectations are essential for them. However, as mentioned earlier, because of the frustrating learning challenges these students face, empathy must balance the high expectations. Effective communication in the classroom can help to achieve an appropriate balance between high expectations and empathy. Twice-exceptional learners need teachers who are able to clearly articulate, both orally and in writing, their expectations for how to be successful academically. This can be in many forms. Basic classroom routines need to be posted, discussed, practiced, and reflected upon. Routine assignments need to be relevant, consistent, and understandable. Projects need to be broken down into components with written checklists, manageable chunks, and reasonable rubrics that clarify expectations and demystify the grading process. In addition to outlining clear expectations for twice-exceptional learners, teachers must also communicate empathy and a sense of genuine regard and concern for these students. As Shevitz et al. (2003) discovered in the Wings Mentor Program, for GTLD students, a positive and supportive relationship with an adult can be the "catalyst for improving the students' view of themselves, empowering them to be successful in the classroom" (p. 39). A teacher who clearly communicates high expectations and standards while also relaying empathy for a student's learning challenges and genuine regard for him or her as a person will get the best out of these complex learners.

Good Communication Fosters Self-Advocacy Skills in GTLD Students

Another important aspect of positive communication is encouraging the students to convey their thoughts about their own learning needs—which is a first step toward helping them develop good self-advocacy skills. Bright students should be encouraged to examine and analyze their learning style, behavior, and overall learning needs. With some guidance, many twice-exceptional learners are quite capable of developing metacognitive skills to target their own behavioral goals. They should be encouraged to play a major role in developing their own learning plans and are often a valuable source for monitoring their own plans and analyzing their progress.

Twice-exceptional learners may also need assistance to effectively stand up for their own perspective. Many gifted students think and speak quickly and are very competent at gaining the floor in discussion or conversation. GTLD students who need additional time to formulate and organize their ideas can be left behind in the conversation. These students can be hesitant to offer a perspective that challenges their more verbally precocious peers. On the other hand, some twice-exceptional students may monopolize the conversation and have a poor sense of how well they are connecting with their audience. GTLD teachers need to be sensitive to group dynamics and provide coaching to both twice-exceptional students and their peers who may not be sensitive to each person's right to participate.

Effective Communication Increases Parental Understanding and Support for GTLD Students

Effective communication between parents and teachers is another key component of a successful GTLD program. Parents of twice-exceptional students may be very frustrated and stymied by their child's learning challenges. Effective and meaningful communication between home and school is crucial; parents can greatly support teachers (and vice versa) only when they communicate openly and attempt to understand each other's perspectives. Successful communication between parents and teachers can lead to a richer understanding of the needs of the GTLD student. Because of the "consistently inconsistent" nature of most of these students, they may present a very different picture at home and school. Specifically, some students may function effectively at school, only to fall apart at home. Parents may complain to teachers that these students are frustrated, anxious, and/or depressed. Teachers may find this surprising and completely different from the students they see at school. For other students, the situation may be reversed: Some twice-exceptional learners may be fine in the quiet, familiar environment of home, but may appear apathetic, disengaged, or even defiant in the classroom. The conclusion when it comes to good communication is the same: Effective communication between home and school is an essential element to understanding the full picture of these complex learners. In sharing information about the student, it is important for the teacher and the parent to be as objective and specific as possible in describing behaviors that are impeding the student's progress, and both the teacher and the parent need to be open to accepting the portrayal described.

In communicating with parents, teachers and school staff should remember how difficult it can be for some parents to hear negative information about their child. This is especially true when a student has been identified as gifted, as there is even greater expectation that the child will be successful in school. Teachers can establish positive lines of communication when they utilize a strengths-based perspective when describing the student, especially when explaining a student's difficulties. Weishaar (2010) described the usefulness of practicing reframing when talking to parents about their children's negative behaviors or academic difficulties. The author noted that most negative behaviors can be viewed through a more positive lens. Take, for example, a twice-exceptional student who is talkative and enthusiastic in the classroom but experiences severe behavioral outbursts in unstructured settings in the school, such as the cafeteria and the bus line at the end of the day. It would be easy—and perhaps not inaccurate—to describe the child as being "out of control and oppositional." However, rather than present the issue as reflective of a child's lack of desire to follow rules, one would describe how active this child's mind is. A conversation with parents will likely be more productive if it is framed by the child's craving for constant intellectual stimulation. Then, the parent and the teacher could brainstorm some ideas for how to effectively structure downtimes at school, which are especially tough for the student. In short, the purpose of reframing is not to sugarcoat problematic behavior, but to communicate about the child from a strengths-based perspective. Doing so sets the stage for a collaborative and more effective working relationship with parents.

Staff Collaboration and Professional Development Is Important for Success

Effective communication among teachers and between teachers and other school staff is also an important foundation for the collaborative culture that is important for a successful GTLD program. Because these students can be so perplexing, teachers need to feel they can seek the support of fellow teachers and school administrators without concern that they are being judged for any difficulties they are experiencing in working with a student. Having an open dialogue with colleagues enables teachers to learn from one another and brainstorm ways to be more effective with students. Ultimately, this creates a more effective environment for both teaching and learning.

Along these lines, another element important to the culture of a good GTLD program is developing and maintaining a community of learning and support for teachers and school staff. Twice-exceptional learners are often demanding and require a level of skill, creativity, and patience that must be fostered and developed in teachers. Individuals who are most successful in working with this population need to be flexible, but organized, and have clear and realistic expectations for students, but also empathy for the students' learning struggles. These teachers need to be serious about their work, but not take themselves too seriously. Good perspective-taking skills are important, as is a sense of humor and an ability to not take things personally. Although there are some teachers who seem to have an inherent knack for working with this population of students, the skills to be an effective GTLD teacher can also be developed with appropriate training and support.

Weinfeld, Barnes-Robinson, Jeweler, and Shevitz (2002) emphasized the importance of ongoing learning opportunities for those who work closely with twice-exceptional students: The success of a GTLD program is "dependent upon professional development of those who work with this special student population" (p. 232). Training and learning can happen at many levels: attendance at state or national conferences, in-school training sessions, specialized in-service workshops, staff meetings where specific "from the field" challenges are discussed, and peer supervision/collaboration among teachers and other school staff about particular student issues. Developing a collaborative school culture where staff members feel comfortable sharing their difficulties and frustrations in working with these students helps improve their confidence and efficacy with this population.

Case Study: Herbert Hoover Middle School, Potomac, MD

Herbert Hoover Middle School in Potomac, MD, is a large public middle school in an affluent suburb of Washington, DC. Within one of the highest performing counties in the state of Maryland, Hoover is one of the most highly performing middle schools: Virtually all students have met the No Child Left Behind standards for both reading and math, and almost all students who took the state algebra assessment passed. Hoover has modest ethnic and socioeconomic diversity. Special education students make up about 10% of the population, and Hoover has one of the highest numbers of twice-exceptional students in the county. As a result of the relatively high performance of students overall, Hoover works to encourage students to move toward more accelerated and enriched coursework with the expectation that all students should have experience with advanced curriculum. Gifted programming at Hoover is provided in the general education classroom with coteaching provided by the special education teacher to address the needs of GTLD students.

Maribeth Tamilevich, special education teacher, and Gloria Bryant, general education/gifted teacher, were interviewed regarding their experiences with twice-exceptional learners in an inclusion setting at Hoover. Tamilevich's and Bryant's responses underscored the importance of a communicative and collaborative culture; they indicated that one of the most important variables in working with twice-exceptional students was good teamwork.

Hoover has had successful inclusion instruction for learning disabled students for many years, which helped set up the structures and expectations that made GTLD programming successful. In addition to the classroom team, the IEP team was anchored by solid assessment by a school psychologist knowledgeable about GTLD issues and a gifted education expert also participated on the team. A team that includes the gifted coordinator meets on a monthly basis to review student progress.

In the classroom, teamwork required that both teachers share responsibility equally in terms of planning and implementing instruction. Tamilevich and Bryant indicated that it was important that both teachers took responsibility for teaching the entire class, rather than the special educator only working with LD students, and that both focused on increasing the rigor in student thinking and products. This collaborative approach to instruction required that the teachers set aside time as a team to plan assignments and grade student work. Tamilevich and Bryant also indicated that it was important to develop a shared understanding of the students, both in terms of gifts and learning challenges. Teachers needed to get past the expectation that bright students are always organized, write well, and are well behaved. Both teachers noted it was important to focus on student strengths, but also to consciously differentiate for student learning challenges. They felt it was important to use a problem-solving approach where they were willing to evaluate everything and to try something else if their approach did not seem to be working.

Tamilevich and Bryant discussed a number of strategies they found to be successful with twice-exceptional learners. They have found that it is important to anticipate emotional tipping points for GTLD students—where they go from being intellectually stimulated and working well with other bright peers to quickly disintegrating into frustration and shutting down. Coping breakdowns can be avoided by building choice into assignments (e.g., letting students select a topic of personal interest, giving a choice of reading materials). Writing assignments can be modified to allow a variety of written output (e.g., PowerPoint presentations, 360-degree questions). Students who have difficulty reading primary source documents can still be expected to work with these materials, but they might be asked to work with a smaller number of them. Tamilevich and Bryant also found that GTLD students cope better when role assignments in group work are varied and when students are grouped with a variety of students rather than one group that always works together.

One challenge of the inclusion classroom they noted was getting twice-exceptional students to buy into remedial instruction. Tamilevich and Bryant's response to this challenge again emphasizes the importance of open communication—they discuss their own learning challenges to help normalize the issue of learning difficulties. Bryant also finds it very useful to include examples of famous people with disabilities when discussing different challenges with students. Teachers emphasize that no one is good at everything and feel that this attitude frees children to explore their own strengths and weaknesses.

Bryant and Tamilevich point to the advantages of a collaborative approach in that each teacher gains from the enthusiasm and dedication of the other. Because Hoover is essentially a very high-achieving school with excellent test scores, teachers have the opportunity to look deeply at their student population to find students who are not reaching their potential. The collaborative efforts of the team make it possible for accommodations to be made in an atmosphere of understanding and individualization.

Conclusion

A key element in developing a successful program for twice-exceptional learners is creating an open school culture that encourages communication at all levels. Good communication between teachers and students creates an environment where students feel both challenged and supported and where they can begin to develop good self-advocacy skills. Effective and frequent communication between parents and teachers can help both parties better understand twice-exceptional students and support their learning needs. Finally, good communication at the school level—between teachers, administrators, and school staff—helps set up an environment of collaboration, learning, and support that can help teachers become more effective at meeting the needs of these challenging students.

chapter 14

Best Practice for GTLD Programming 3:
Address Twice-Exceptional Learners' Social and Emotional Needs

GTLD students can face a number of social and emotional challenges, often the result of biological predisposition, poor information processing, and environmental stressors due to school and home difficulties. Many GTLD students face a complex array of biologically based challenges including ADHD and autism spectrum disorders, sometimes in combination. Other students with specific learning disabilities also struggle with regulating emotions, poor frustration tolerance, low self-esteem, poor coping and social skills, and obsessive or perfectionist tendencies. It is important to address these concerns on multiple fronts. Longitudinal research outlined earlier in this book indicated that students with significant social and emotional difficulties often have more limited educational attainment and life success.

GTLD Students Should Be Taught Strategies to Manage Emotional Intensity

Currently, there is a lively debate about the importance of addressing intensity in gifted students. For example, the organization Supporting Emotional Needs of the Gifted, or SENG (http://www.sengifted.org), has hosted recent webinars on the topic of living with the intensity of gifted students. It is likely true that gifted students, particularly students with learning challenges, struggle with managing their emotions and experiences more than is typical for average-performing students. They are likely to have passions that drive their creativity and talent, but that may also make them hard to live with on a daily basis. However, it is important to avoid the trap of categorical thinking; the fact that giftedness often is accompanied by a range of social and emotional challenges does not suggest that these intensity features are immutable. Many children and adults struggle with emotional dysregulation, and there are effective interventions that can help students manage their emotions and behavior in a more productive manner.

In *The Art of Learning*, Josh Waitzkin (2007), a chess prodigy whose experiences were documented in the book and film *Searching for Bobby Fischer*, uses his own experiences in advanced pursuits in chess and martial arts to identify important factors needed for the production of talent. His writing puts a personal face on well-known principles used in psychotherapy and performance psychology, namely resilience and mindfulness. Waitzkin has developed The Art of Learning Project (http://www.artoflearningproject.org) to provide teachers, parents, and students with materials to help students develop skills to further the development of their talent. The use of these techniques in the pursuit of a student's own personal goals is resonant with therapeutic approaches particularly effective with teens in terms of motivational or solutions-focused therapy. Waitzkin placed these concepts in a normalized context. Many of these concepts can be used by parents and teachers to create an environment to help students improve their ability to manage their complex emotional experiences.

The concept of resilience developed out of research on depression that found that when some individuals faced incredible—and even devastating—adversity, they were able to maintain a positive stance toward life. Research on resilience has led to a better understanding of the thoughts and behaviors that contribute to productive lives in the face of challenge (Chansky, 2008). In the area of resilience, Waitzkin (2007) advocated valuing process over results and rewarding sustained effort. Mistakes should not be viewed as failures but rather as opportunities for learning and growth. Adults should model evaluating their own setbacks with a focus on trying to improve. Performance should be reviewed calmly and discussed in terms of what led to a less than optimal performance. Waitzkin also identified the importance of developing emotional equilibrium in order to manage the inevitable setbacks that accompany advanced talent development, as well as to deal with unexpected events that lead to interruptions in challenging endeavors. Many of these issues are particularly important for twice-exceptional students whose learning challenges introduce more inconsistency in their performance, sometimes even in areas of talent. In addition, the need to remediate basic academics for some GTLD students can feel particularly disruptive to the flow of the pursuits they value.

Waitzkin (2007) also spoke to the value of developing a fluid sense of emotional control. He advocated developing an awareness of emotional states and an acceptance of internal states rather than an effort to change or fight these experiences. He indicated that it is important to be aware when past failures or experiences of loss are controlling the present and advocates finding a personal trigger, or a relaxation activity that relieves stress. To develop advanced skills, Waitzkin advocated alternating periods of intense effort with periods of recovery or relaxation. Taking an accepting observer's stance toward one's emotional experience and thought processes is also an important part of the mindfulness approach to psychotherapy, which often is incorporated into cognitive-behavioral treatments of anxiety and depression in adults and children (Thompson & Gauntlett-Gilbert, 2008). Mindfulness techniques encourage focus on the full range of experience in the present without allowing thoughts to get in the way. These techniques can be particularly helpful for twice-exceptional learners with repetitive thought patterns due to anxiety, depression, or obsessiveness.

Case Study: Marmaduke School District, Marmaduke, AR

Our search for a school using *The Art of Learning* led to a small farm town in northeastern Arkansas. Char Green, the gifted and talented coordinator for the school district of 700 students, heard Josh Waitzkin speak at the National Association for Gifted Children convention and was immediately taken with the relevance of Waitzkin's ideas to the affective challenges of her gifted students. Green indicated that even though her students live in a remote and economically deprived area, they connected readily with the life experiences of Josh Waitzkin as a privileged child growing up in Manhattan. These connections suggest the universality of the challenges of managing giftedness.

Green often uses passages from *The Art of Learning* both as a way to warm students up to a challenge and also as a focal activity. She is particularly attuned to the learning styles of her students and makes an assessment at the beginning of the year to identify the students' preferred modalities. Green tries to provide a range of activities in each 3-hour weekly pull-out session to engage the different types of students in the class. She indicated that extreme differentiation was very important for each class session. Green said that in her experience, gifted students had much greater diversity in their learning styles and social-emotional needs than the mainstream population. Lessons from *The Art of Learning* help students find the language to address their conflicted feelings about performance.

Green identified two passages that she felt particularly connected with her students. In the first, the "anorexic hermit crab," Waitzkin (2007) described a phenomenon he encountered as a chess competitor. He often played students who were the best in their schools and who had received extensive praise for their performance. These students had been taught flashy and aggressive opening moves in chess that allowed them to beat many competitors. However, if a competitor like Waitzkin managed to survive the opening attack, these students often crumbled and lost the game. Waitzkin was able to win because he had pursued a different course of focusing on the long-term learning process. In his view, when students focus on results rather than the learning process, they begin to limit themselves to avoid failure. He likens this phenomenon to a hermit crab's situation in finding a larger shell and a transition period where the crab might be without a shell and vulnerable. In his image of the anorexic hermit crab, Waitzkin described students who limit their challenges to guarantee success as being like a hermit crab who would stop eating to avoid having to find a larger shell. Green brought a hermit crab to her class to help students understand this analogy. She indicated that her students struggled to step out of their comfort zone because they feared looking like a failure.

In a second story that Green's students particularly connected to, Waitzkin (2007) talked about the importance of regaining composure when an error is made rather than allowing the emotional reaction to the error to lead to further errors in a downward spiral. He describes an experience where he watched a young woman who was listening to her iPod step out into a busy street. Because she was distracted, she looked the wrong direction on a one-way street. She was narrowly missed by a bicycle and began to yell at the bicyclist. She was so intent on her anger about the past situation that rather than step back on the curb, the woman made the further error of walking into the street and was struck by a taxicab. Waitzkin pointed out that the difference between winning and losing is often small, and it is often possible to turn an error into a success. However, allowing feelings about past mistakes to linger creates the potential for further errors. Green indicated that this lesson was particularly important for her gifted students who struggle with perfectionism.

Families and Teachers Play an Important Role in Building Resilience

Although Waitzkin's experiences as a gifted individual resonate with students, other writers share Waitzkin's emphasis on the importance of family and teachers in helping students develop greater resilience and emotional self-awareness. In *Building Resilience in Children and Teens*, Kenneth Ginsberg

(2011) talked about the 7 C's model of resilience. These factors include competence, confidence, connection, character, contribution, coping, and control. He emphasized the importance for families to provide children with acceptance and support, set high expectations for personal qualities of character rather than achievement, and model effective coping.

Sylvia Rimm (2008b) emphasized the role of an appropriate balance of praise, power, and freedom. In her view, many difficulties with motivation arise when children are given extravagant praise not based on actual performance, are allowed too many choices, and are given too much freedom. In the concept of the "V of love," she indicated that young children should begin at the bottom of the V, with moderate praise, limited power, and limited freedom. As children mature and develop greater competence, they should gradually move up to a broader range of freedom and power. Rimm (2000b) pointed out that when children receive extravagant praise that is not specific to particular efforts, they experience the praise as a form of pressure. When children receive too much freedom too early, they often become accustomed to having their own way, but tend to make bad choices in adolescence. Rimm (2000b) indicated that bright children often receive too much power and freedom because their advanced intellectual ability can make them appear more competent than they actually are in terms of social judgment and emotional maturity.

Explicit Social Skills Instruction Is Important for Twice-Exceptional Students

In addition to factors related to developing resilience and emotional control, social skills are important to develop in the classroom. Many aspects of Positive Behavior Support (e.g., Sprick, 2009) help students understand expectations and learn self-control. However, teachers and parents can also help students by modeling strategies such as active listening and helping students to use these skills in their daily peer interactions. Engaging students in social problem solving when a conflict emerges also provides important learning experiences. Rather than adults providing the solution, a peer mediation session where students are coached to come up with a solution that all members of the conflict can live with is an important opportunity to develop listening skills and perspective-taking.

The principles described above could be viewed as Tier 1 interventions in an RtI model. These interventions can be implemented classroom-wide and are beneficial to all students. Students encounter challenges in facing adversity and dealing with social problems on a daily basis and have ample opportunity to work on these skills at school. Parents can often be an important adjunct in providing a sounding board for their children to share difficult experiences at school and can help their children consider their own contribution to the problem. Parents can help students evaluate their own performance in a non-judgmental and problem-solving manner. It is important to listen to one's child with empathy and to demonstrate that his or her feelings and point of view are understood. It is another thing to accept his or her analysis of the situation blindly without considering what the parent knows about the child's challenges.

Beyond classroom-wide interventions, some students may need more targeted intervention to address coping and social skill deficits. As we have seen, students with learning disabilities often need explicit skill instruction and do not always draw the lessons from their experiences that might be desired. Social skills groups often provide an avenue for developing important skills within a context of guided practice. For example, Alvord, Zucker, and Grados (2011) in their "Resilience Builder" groups provided a model for teaching students important skills for increasing resilience, as well as social competence. This cognitive-behavioral approach is user-friendly and presents important concepts and skills in a structured format. The model has five structural components: interactive-didactic, free play and behavioral rehearsal, relaxation and self-regulation techniques, generalization, and parent involvement. Self-regulation techniques taught include progressive muscle relaxation, guided imagery, and positive self-talk.

Students on the autism spectrum also can profit from a social skills format. For example, Baker (2003) has developed an extensive program of social skills lessons for students with social communication disorders like Asperger's syndrome. These lessons are taught via structured learning, which includes didactic instruction, modeling, role-playing with feedback, and practice assignments for outside of the group. Skills taught range from communication skills such as "giving background information about what you are saying" to starting and ending conversations. Cooperative play skills, such as initiating play with others and compromising, are included, as is friendship management (e.g., getting attention, respecting personal boundaries). Emotion management skills such as self-regulation (e.g., coping with making a mistake), empathy skills, and conflict management are also topics of lessons.

Baker (2003) indicated that it is important to provide intervention both to the special needs student and to typical peers to increase social success in the classroom. Baker pointed out that it is often easier for typical peers to grasp concepts and change behaviors than for students on the autism spectrum. Although special needs students need direct skill instruction, typical peers need sensitivity training to be more accepting of students with special needs. In addition, specific activities need to be set up to practice sensitivity skills, with an incentive program as needed to gain the cooperation of typical peers.

Sensitivity training involves teaching the class about why a particular student has difficulty in the classroom. Although potential stigma might be a concern, Baker pointed out that typical peers are already aware of the behaviors that distinguish students with autism spectrum disorders. He recommended getting parental permission and preparing the student with AS for what will be said. Baker pointed to additional classroom activities that can be helpful in promoting peer acceptance of students with AS, such as lunch buddy programs or a classroom marble jar for exhibiting kind behavior.

For students with more oppositional behavior or who struggle to contain anger and impulsivity, a structured behavior program is often helpful. Ross Greene's (2008) Collaborative Problem Solving approach moves beyond the traditional behavior modification approach in viewing challenging behavior not as an act of will or an effort to get attention, but rather as an indication of a skills deficit. Greene's belief is that "kids will do well, if they can" (p. 11). In Greene's view, many challenging behaviors result from delays in the development of executive skills in shifting cognitive sets and organization; language skills centered around emotions and problem solving; emotion regulation skills; cognitive flexibility skills; and social skills. The Collaborative Problem Solving approach to challenging behavior requires an empathic approach where adults seek to identify and address the student's concern and to recognize skills deficits that contribute to the challenging behavior. The focus of intervention becomes developing a strategy to develop the needed skills.

Case Study: The Lang School, New York City, NY

The Lang School in the Tribeca neighborhood of Manhattan is a small private school for gifted students with learning disabilities. Founded in 2010 by Micaela Bracamonte, herself a twice-exceptional person, the Lang School has grown from 10 students to about 30 for the current year. Bracamonte indicated that the success of their program has arisen from the opportunities to modify and refine the curriculum and service delivery model available with a small population. Students at Lang typically come from public gifted schools, public or private special education programs, or academically rigorous general education settings. In addition to giftedness, students come to Lang with ADHD, anxiety disorder, Asperger's syndrome, and mild dyslexia. Many of these students have had negative experiences in their prior school settings. Bracamonte described the school's overall perspective to be serving as an advocate for the student and tailoring the educational program to meet each student's needs.

Bracamonte described the school's attempts to use a more structured or traditional gifted curriculum as unsuccessful. She said that Lang teachers required greater flexibility to adapt to the learning styles of the students, but indicated that teachers use portions of these programs such as aspects of the Schoolwide Enrichment Model for Reading (SEM-R; Reis et al., 2005). The operational principle for the school is Ross Greene's (2008) Collaborative Problem Solving approach, which emphasizes empathic engagement with students to identify and address the underlying causes of challenging behaviors. Bracamonte uses this approach for both staff interactions and working with students in the classroom. In addition to Collaborative Problem Solving, Lang invests heavily in intensive psychotherapy for its students; each student receives biweekly individual therapy sessions with staff psychologists, as well as participates in group sessions. For students who are too literal to do the perspective taking needed in Collaborative Problem Solving, it is particularly important to have psychotherapy to develop the skills needed for successful problem solving.

Each Lang classroom has both a gifted educator and a special educator who equally share classroom responsibilities. In addition, speech/language therapists, occupational therapists, and psychologists all "push in" services during the school day. Particularly impulsive students profit from a one-to-one aide. For students who need a behavior plan, an outside consultant is employed to develop an appropriate plan to ensure that students are not being inadvertently rewarded for negative behavior. Bracamonte believes it is essential for behavior plans to include parents in the reward system. Bracamonte firmly believes in only using positives in reinforcement systems (no response-cost programs) but does provide consequences for bullying, as well as verbal and physical aggression.

Because many students are overly active, Lang accommodates to their need to move. Students receive between 2–4 hours per week of physical education. In the classroom, students use AlphaBetter desks, which allow students to stand while working if they choose and have a swing bar that functions as a fidget object. Students are allowed to move in the classroom and choose their own work position as long as they are attending and on task. Each student has a personal fidget box with a selection of fidget objects and snacks preferred by the student.

Bracamonte described a rigorous selection process for hiring new teachers. She looks for teachers who have pursued their own passion or talent, as well as for teachers who are flexible in their approach and who are respectful of the students' inquisitiveness. In addition, successful Lang teachers should be able to function as facilitators and not have a high need to be seen as authority figures. Lang teachers need to be able to maintain a neutral face even when annoyed, because many students are quite anxious when teachers show strong reactions to behavior. Lang teachers need to be able to keep students engaged. Bracamonte indicated that she finds twice-exceptional adults who are open about their learning challenges make good teachers and provide role models for students. To develop teacher competence in working with complex twice-exceptional students, Lang provides intensive staff development on a regular basis. Bracamonte indicated that teaching complex students is quite demanding on teachers and Lang provides yoga and Pilates classes to help teachers unwind.

GTLD Students May Need Individual Counseling

Although classroom and group interventions can be very effective, some students require an even greater intensity of intervention. Often, for these students, negative coping patterns have consolidated into symptoms that warrant a diagnosis of depression, anxiety, and oppositional disorders. In her excellent books on internalizing disorders in children, Chansky (2000, 2004, 2008) explained that maladaptive patterns of coping develop in children in response to stress and biological predisposition. Over time, the repetition of maladaptive patterns, such as negative thinking, develop increased efficiency in neural pathways leading to these maladaptive approaches becoming the predominant manner of dealing with experiences. For example, children don't become clinically depressed overnight, but gradually develop depression as a result of habitual negative thinking. The good news of cognitive-behavior therapy is that children can learn new patterns of thinking that will lead to more adaptive functioning. For twice-exceptional students who need more intensive intervention, it is important to seek out a mental health provider who is knowledgeable about learning disabilities and giftedness.

Medication Increases Availability for Learning for Some Twice-Exceptional Students

The issue of medication is a sensitive topic. When school staff members suggest that parents seek a medication consultation, parents often experience this suggestion as a rejection of their child. We have worked with many families who felt that the school was giving up on their children, even though teachers and staff may have acted with the best intentions. In our view, medication is an important tool; for some students struggling with significant social and emotional issues, medication provides needed assistance to increase their availability for learning. For children with ADHD, medication can decrease impulsivity and give the students the ability to more carefully consider their actions. For other students who struggle with anxiety, depression, and obsessive thoughts, the right medication can calm them down, give them additional energy, and/ or allow their minds to open to more productive avenues of thinking. Children on the autism spectrum often struggle to manage extreme sensory reactions, internal distraction, and cognitive rigidity; all of which can be ameliorated with appropriate treatment.

Although medication can increase availability for learning, it does not teach new skills and as such should only be viewed as one component in an effective treatment plan. Students who have been distracted by internal thoughts and feelings or who spend time acting out are not engaged in the here and now in a manner that facilitates learning. These students often develop coping and social skill deficits as they fall behind in developing more mature social skills; they need psychotherapy that improves their emotional awareness and develops their insight and problem-solving capacity. Twice-exceptional children often profit from more structured skill-building therapies; just as in other types of instruction, they need modeling, practice, and feedback to develop new social and coping skills.

In our experience, parents are often more receptive to considering options like psychotherapy and medication when children have an independent diagnostic evaluation. When parents have the option to select their own psychologist, they feel that a neutral party has been able to view potential bias on the part of school staff and will have gathered additional data needed to determine the needs of the student. School staff members are more likely to be able to maintain an alliance with parents when a request for an evaluation is couched in terms of the need for more information to identify interventions rather than as a need to see if the child needs medication. When we recommend a medication evaluation in the context of the findings of a private comprehensive psychoeducational evaluation, we recommend that parents fully educate themselves before declaring that medication would never be a part of their child's treatment. A consultation with a child psychiatrist can provide a forum for parents to discuss options and their concerns about the dangers of medication. The National Institute of Mental Health website (http://www.nimh.nih.gov) provides extensive research-based information on mental health medications.

If a trial of medication is considered, it is important to collect baseline data on the prevalence of target behaviors prior to the initiation of treatment, and parents should ask their treating physician how progress will be monitored. Although some child psychiatrists maintain active contact with teachers to assess the impact of medication, many do not. It is also important to realize that identifying an effective dose often requires several months and several medications or combinations may be attempted before the right medication is identified. For students with highly complex behavioral difficulties—for example, students with both ADHD and autism spectrum disorders—a combination of medications may be needed. When a child is experiencing negative reactions to medications, it is important for parents to talk with the doctor about their concerns.

Conclusion

Twice-exceptional students face a number of social and emotional challenges. Like many mainstream gifted students, they often face the challenge of managing emotional intensity or sensitivity. Yet these students may also struggle with additional emotional burdens due to their biology, information processing challenges, and environmental stressors. Effective programming for twice-exceptional students requires specific attention to developing their coping and social skill resources. These students may profit from exploring the experiences of other gifted individuals, such as Josh Waitzkin in *The Art of Learning*, but they may also need a more highly structured and programmatic approach to building their resilience and social skills. As was found at The Lang School, some students need additional interventions including individual and group psychotherapy and may need medication to increase their availability for learning. It is important to keep in mind that social and emotional skills can be learned and that social-emotional difficulties can be an even greater roadblock to learning than a specific learning disability.

chapter 15

Best Practice for GTLD Programming 4: Work Around Weaknesses by Providing Accommodation and Adaptation of the Gifted Curriculum

The issue of accommodations for bright students is often fraught with misconceptions compounded with the resentment directed toward gifted people in general. Teachers may be reluctant to allow students to use specific accommodations because they view these interventions as crutches and feel that students should just work harder or better. Of course, there is variability in the motivation of twice-exceptional students, but many are actually quite motivated and hard working. The amount of effort they invest is often hidden from teachers because they spend hours on homework or have extra support from their parents.

Distinctions Between Accommodations and Adaptations

In the discussion of how GTLD programs can help to work around student weaknesses, it is important to distinguish between accommodations and adaptations. An accommodation is something that removes a barrier to performance, but does not change the substance of the course content or expectations. Use of a keyboard for writing is an example of an accommodation. A adaptation, or modification, is a change to expectations or course content. An example of an adaptation is reducing the number of math problems a student may need to do to demonstrate mastery.

Extended Time Accommodations Are Important for GTLD Students

Extended time is the most controversial accommodation for twice-exceptional students. Lovett (2012) described extended time as a double-edged sword. On the one hand, when used appropriately, it can remove barriers for students to demonstrate knowledge. At the same time, extended time also can be an adaptation that changes the validity of what tests measure. Lovett (2012) recommended that teachers consider when speed is important. If fluency in a task is an essential component, then extended time is not appropriate for any students; otherwise, students should be given ample time for tasks. Lovett (2012) also raised the concern that extended time is an "easy out" that substitutes an accommodation for effective interventions that would have more longstanding benefit. He indicated that test anxiety is often cited as a reason for extended time accommodations, yet there are effective interventions that students can learn to reduce anxiety. Similarly, extended time accommodations for slow reading rate may result in lack of services to increase reading fluency, a skill that can be improved even in high school.

Although it is true that extended time accommodations should not be viewed as a panacea, we find a broad range of students with learning disabilities do need additional time due to weak executive skills, poor working memory, and language processing weaknesses. A good assessment can identify the student who would best be served by this accommodation. However, it is important to provide students with instruction in strategies to make use of extra time; more time to do ineffectual things is not useful.

Adaptations Should Be Part of a Skill-Building Program

Students who are twice-exceptional are likely to need both accommodations and adaptations to be successful in traditional gifted programs. It may be helpful to view accommodations as supports for ongoing needs and adaptations as short-term interventions to facilitate the development of skills. Adaptations should be made carefully and should not be viewed as an ultimate solution, as they do mean that the GTLD student is not meeting the same standards as other gifted students. Adaptations should be made as part of a skill-building plan and should be viewed as meeting students where they are, but the ultimate goal should be to move the student into the standard program. Accommodations, such as extended time, will likely continue to be needed, even when students have developed more advanced strategies for learning.

GTLD Students Need Accommodations and Adaptations for Academic Acceleration

The research on gifted programming has identified two primary avenues for teaching to the strengths of gifted students: academic acceleration and academic enrichment (VanTassel-Baska & Stambaugh, 2008). In academic acceleration, students who have mastered grade-level content are placed in more advanced courses. For some students, this may mean grade advancement. Although skipping grades may be desirable for some gifted students, these students also may have social maturity that will make them fit in well with older peers. As we pointed out, many twice-exceptional students are more socially immature than their age peers and could struggle with the social demands of an older grade placement. Especially in high school courses featuring group projects and discussions, it would be important to provide support for GTLD students who may not have the prerequisite social skills. Twice-exceptional students may do well with acceleration in particular areas of strength. Often, acceleration in math courses is fairly easy to accomplish. Again, thought should be given to whether the GTLD student needs support on work habits and managing social challenges in the classroom.

Programs such as Advanced Placement and International Baccalaureate can be both wonderful and disastrous for twice-exceptional learners. They can be wonderful when they provide like-minded peers, intellectual stimulation, and creative outlets for demonstration of mastery. GTLD students benefit greatly from being in a learning environment that offers community, affinity, and opportunities to connect with other bright students who may share their passionate interests. However, packaged curriculum programs that adhere to very strict standards, systematized requirements, and heavy emphasis on production for students may not be the best choice for bright students with learning challenges. Sometimes these programs emphasize production and handing in numerous assignments. This may be quite intellectual in nature, but the demands may be too much for students who have executive functioning challenges.

Twice-exceptional students often struggle with writing, organization, reading, and memory (Weinfeld, Barnes-Robinson, Jeweler, & Shevitz, 2006). One of the obstacles to successful participation in AP and IB courses is the emphasis on writing with a large number of written assignments and a heavy workload. Accommodations such as recorded books or computerized text readers (e.g., Kurzweil 3000, see http://www.kurzweiledu.com) can be helpful for students (Lewis, 1998). Twice-exceptional students may also need more structure with writing assignments. It will be necessary for teachers to provide advanced organizers, varied avenues for accessing information from text, and supports for students who struggle with retaining information. This can all be done without sacrificing rigor, significance, richness, and quality of content.

Online courses provide an exciting avenue to provide acceleration to gifted students with a format that accommodates for many learning challenges. There are a number of organizations across the country, many housed within talent search programs, that provide acceleration to gifted students of all ages through online courses. Because online programs are frequently individually paced and make use of technological resources, they can usually accommodate the needs of students with disabilities without any sort of formal accommodation plan. For older students, many free college courses are taught online and provide a setting that can accommodate many learning challenges. For example, Coursera (http://www.coursera.org) has contracted with major universities to provide free online courses on a broad range of subjects. The online lectures are interactive and stop to ask students questions to help keep them focused on the lectures. Students are graded on the basis of mastery—the courses have multiple versions of assignments that students can keep taking until they pass them (untimed, of course). For open-ended assignments, students are graded by multiple peer reviewers as a way for both the writer and the reviewer to learn from examples. *The New York Times* (Lewin, 2012) recently reported that some universities are exploring ways to give college credit for these courses by having exams provided at academic testing centers. These courses provide the flexibility for students who need repetition of information, extra time, and immediate feedback to be successful.

GTLD Need Accommodations and Adaptations for Gifted Academic Enrichment

An alternative approach to gifted programming is the use of enrichment programs. Generally, these can be grouped by the integrated curriculum models, which apply advanced learning principles to standard academic content, and project-oriented programs that are driven by student interests. Each of these types of programs can be successful for GTLD students but many students will likely require accommodations and adaptations to the curriculum.

Integrated Curriculum

The College of William and Mary's Integrated Curriculum Model, one example of an integrated curriculum approach, which was created by Joyce VanTassel-Baska, provides gifted activities designed around specific curriculum standards (i.e., a gifted approach is applied to core content). In this method, which does include projects and hands-on learning, the assignments and questions are preselected for students. In addition, the reading material and assignments come as packaged units, which increase consistency in teachers' delivery of gifted instruction. Research conducted by VanTassel-Baska (VanTassel-Baska, 2003; VanTassel-Baska & Brown, 2007) and others has found that a more structured packaged curriculum is superior to teacher-created gifted programming. Many of the materials provide graphic organizers, again predesigned for teachers and students, to facilitate the development of higher order thinking skills.

Although consistency is an advantage for this approach, there are some features that present challenges for twice-exceptional students, particularly the linkage of specific texts to the gifted activities. When students have reading difficulties that limit their ability to independently access the texts in the William and Mary units, teachers may find it difficult to substitute other texts. The use of accommodations, such as text-to-voice software, can assist GTLD students in accessing this type of programming. The highly organized structure of the program can also cause difficulties when twice-exceptional students work more slowly than their peers and require longer periods of time to complete complex gifted assignments. Some GTLD students may dislike the highly structured nature of the William and Mary units, as it may not present information of particular interest to them. For some students with features of autism, the worksheet nature of tasks can be a way of avoiding social interaction and social problem solving.

Project-Based Enrichment

Project-based programs, such as the Renzulli Schoolwide Enrichment Model, approach gifted education from a more student-centered approach. In a pull-out model, students are allowed to pursue their own areas of interests and develop independent projects that evidence higher order thinking. One challenge for twice-exceptional students with this approach is the open-ended nature of the tasks. For students who have difficulty with executive functioning, it is easy to become overwhelmed by infinite possibilities and to have difficulty selecting a topic or project.

The Renzulli Learning System (http://www.renzullilearning.com), a web-based search engine designed by Joseph Renzulli and Sally Reis at the University of Connecticut, attempts to rein in the abundance of options by tailoring student searches on the Internet based on a student's interest profile, preferred learning styles, and preferred product style. Each student's web searches are filtered through this profile from a large inventory of prescreened websites. The system has a Project Wizard that attempts to provide structure to guide students through their projects. The web-based approach can be readily adapted for dyslexic students via text-to-voice software. Students with significant executive functioning challenges may need additional support to select a particular project and stay with it through all of the steps to completion. Students with a more limited range of interests may be tempted to stay within their comfort zone and may be resistant to learning about new topics. The challenge of moving students to the most advanced levels of higher order thinking and creativity is not limited to students with learning disabilities. Newman (2005) found that a large group of students in gifted programs that used the Renzulli Schoolwide Enrichment Model had difficulty advancing to the most sophisticated level of independent projects. She found that additional instruction in higher order thinking via the Talents Unlimited model, a structured program for teaching thinking skills, improved the quality of student independent projects.

GTLD Students Need Proactive and Effective Accommodations and Adaptations

For accommodations to be effective, they need to be carefully planned. The paradox of simultaneously accepting limitations and being aware of strengths is a framework that helps to guide decisions about the use of adaptations and accommodations for twice-exceptional students. One of the best approaches is to utilize a strengths inventory to assess needs and then to use corresponding approaches to compensate for areas of weakness. Students who have formal IEPs should have accommodations that address needs while also building on their strengths.

Many IEP forms list a standard set of accommodations that can be quickly and easily selected for a given student. However, the identification of *useful* accommodations requires a greater understanding of the individual student and consideration of the information processing demands of each setting. Students may need certain accommodations in one setting and not others, so it is important to collect information from a variety of sources. In planning accommodations and supports, it is also critical to consider students' strengths; building on students' strengths can help prevent the cycle of failure that creeps in when bright students have disabilities.

As students get older, it is important to include the student in the discussion of appropriate accommodations. Gifted students are usually painfully aware of their deficits. They may have the gift of advanced intellect, yet their lack of executive functioning skills and self-regulation can bring about patterns of overreliance on adults and resentment of the help they depend upon to meet standards that are often below their actual potential. When implementing accommodations, the goal of self-advocacy needs to be an integral part of the plans put in place to support GTLD students.

Case Study: The Kingsbury Day School, Washington, DC

The Kingsbury Day School is a private, full-time special education program for prekindergarten through high school students. A large proportion of students are publicly funded by their local school jurisdiction because their needs cannot be met with the services provided within the system. Kingsbury students typically have complex language-based learning disabilities and/or ADHD requiring integrated services, including speech/language therapy, occupational therapy, and individual and group psychotherapy. Some students have an autism spectrum disorder. Students are taught using multisensory techniques, and accommodations are built into the school routine.

Using a combination of cognitive test scores and teacher rating scales for qualities of giftedness, a group of students were identified who showed gifted potential. These students also had complex learning profiles, including basic academic fluency issues, attentional difficulties, and social-emotional challenges. The GTLD program allowed Kingsbury to focus on student strengths, which sometimes got left behind in remediating academic deficits. However, Kingsbury found that a gifted program required adaptation to meet the challenges for these complex students. Because of their learning needs, Kingsbury students require a high degree of structure and scaffolding to work around their learning challenges. The students were somewhat intimidated by large amounts of text and threatened by open-ended tasks that required them to take initiative.

Kingsbury selected the Renzulli Schoolwide Enrichment Model as the best curriculum fit, given its focus on student interest-based independent learning. In this program, students work on self-selected independent projects in a pull-out model. It was felt that allowing students to focus on preferred topics would increase their engagement in challenging work. Student projects have included studying the history of British Imperialism in Africa, designing a museum to illustrate differences between African and North American animals, building a trebuchet, and building a model of a California mission.

Kingsbury's gifted coordinator, Jillian Sorrenti, is a veteran special education teacher with extensive classroom experience. Sorrenti received training in gifted education through a graduate course taught by an expert in GTLD programming and an author of this book, Karin Tulchinsky Cohen. Sorrenti also attended gifted training in summer programs at The College of William and Mary and at Confratute, the Renzulli training program at the University of Connecticut. Sorrenti consults regularly with a school psychologist who is a specialist in twice-exceptional learners, and together they conduct action research to constantly refine the program. Although the Renzulli SEM program provided the framework and goals to work toward, Sorrenti's extensive experience in classroom management in the special education classroom allowed her to provide additional scaffolding and social-emotional support to maintain student engagement. In an interview, Sorrenti said that being in the field of GTLD has

> added a new dimension for me as a teacher. I am focused on helping students to solve real problems. The ultimate goal of having the Schoolwide Enrichment Model is to work backward, meaning that we start with students' motivations and interests, and we move towards the goal of having all students engaged in meaningful problem solving of real-world problems. (Personal communication, September 2011)

Individualizing expression styles is an important feature of the Kingsbury GTLD program. Some students prefer oral reports; some prefer to write papers, others choose to make three-dimensional models or create electronic presentations to demonstrate mastery. Sorrenti uses a combination of individualized technological adaptations. These adaptations remove obstacles that thwart students' access to the curriculum and to demonstrating mastery. A wide variety of interventions, such as text-to-speech software, speech-to-text programs, and visual supports, provide access to the curriculum and scaffold complex concepts. When students are able to demonstrate their understanding in modalities that highlight their strengths, their disabilities are much less pronounced. Sorrenti observed that as students continue in the program, they expand their expression styles. This enables them to shift from remediation to actualization of their giftedness; students can focus on expressing mastery without being hindered by their disabilities.

To support student development of independent projects, Kingsbury uses the Renzulli Learning System, a personalized web-based search engine that selects web resources for students based on each student's personalized interests and preferred learning styles. Even though the Renzulli Learning System provided each student with a tailored set of resources, students still had difficulty prioritizing research material. Ms. Sorrenti indicated that backward planning from the end product helped these students focus on a relevant set of websites and materials. For example, a student decided to make a museum about African animals and was helped to walk back through the planning process to identify the relevant information he would need to know to guide his research, rather than extensively research animals and then decide what type of project to do. A more traditional research approach tended to get students off-track and confused.

The Kingsbury GTLD students gradually came to grasp the process of developing projects over a series of months, although some had difficulty staying with a project once they encountered challenges. Some students were frustrated by the need to elaborate on their ideas. To help students with this concept, they were all expected to prepare an oral presentation with a visual display to present to peers and families. Students were coached through their presentations to help them identify what information was needed to inform the listener. Sorrenti works with students to articulate their higher order thinking processes in their presentation. Although students initially indicated that they did not wish to present their projects, they all became animated and enthusiastic when they had their turn to perform. Figure 15.1 provides a photograph of a Renzulli project from the Kingsbury Day School, a model of a California mission constructed out of "found" materials.

Each student also completed a self-evaluation to reflect on her learning process during the project. Sorrenti noted that self-reflection was the hardest part of the process for students, as their feelings about their learning challenges emerged in thinking about the obstacles they had encountered in the project. Some students had difficulty taking an overview of the whole process because of poor memory skills. One of the most challenging aspects of the written self-reflections was the students' overall resistance to edit their writing. An aspect of their disability is that students often do not see the need to make changes. In

Figure 15.1. Kingsbury Day School third-grade Renzulli project: Model of a California mission.

the future, teachers will provide students with varying supports, such as ongoing short journal writing to keep track of their experiences as they work, to address the complications that arise from memory deficits. Sorrenti has devised a system to keep logs and has a daily check-in and check-out system. She will be doing semester reports that include reflective narratives with individual progress to strike a balance between empathy and individual accountability.

An important goal of the Kingsbury program was to advance the understanding of twice-exceptional issues in the school community and particularly to emphasize the focus on strengths-based instruction. Kingsbury provided professional development for teachers and programs for parents to understand the contradictions in the performance of GTLD students. The gifted coordinator worked in collaboration with classroom teachers to provide direct instruction in higher order thinking, executive functioning, and social skills. Classroom teachers also work with GTLD students on improving their writing, particularly in terms of organization and elaboration through structured instruction, such as using graphic organizers.

The Renzulli Schoolwide Enrichment Model provides mechanisms for infusing strength-based instruction into the school culture through enrichment clusters. During its first full year of implementation of the Renzulli SEM program, Kingsbury developed enrichment clusters for students as a whole. All students and staff in the school participated in a series of cluster activities for four sessions. Students were allowed to select their cluster based on interest and within their general age group. Sessions included cooking, line dancing, superheroes, gardening, and book clubs. Students who struggled in group settings received facilitation by having an adult mentor, often a psychologist or speech therapist, accompany them in the activity. Facilitators of the group were careful to plan tasks to ensure a strong organizational structure for each session and to engage students in problem solving and higher order thinking. For example, in a cooking class on types of noodles from around the world, students engaged in compare and contrast activities to describe their cooking experiences in the class. Facilitators of the groups found that even students who struggled both cognitively and academically showed growth in executive functioning in these preferred activities, and students made greater effort to explain their ideas in these enrichment activities.

Conclusion

Accommodations and adaptations provide important program modifications for GTLD students. Accommodations level the playing field for students who struggle with written text or who need additional time to access strategies, recall information from memory, and organize their ideas. Adaptations change the work to meet the student where he or she is. GTLD students can be successful with academic acceleration and enrichment, but will likely need modifications to the content in terms of the quantity of advanced work required of them. They may also need support to access text and deal with the large quantity of information available to them on any specific topic. As the experience of the Kingsbury Day School illustrates, these students can be sidetracked by the sheer volume of information available and need individualized support to develop a focused product even in an area of personal interest. As students mature, it is important to involve them in the process of developing a plan of accommodations in order to select the most effective interventions and for students to develop the skills to advocate for themselves as they progress to higher education.

chapter 16

Best Practice for GTLD Programming 5: Provide Explicit Instruction in Higher Order Thinking Skills and Metacognition

Training in Higher Order Thinking

One goal of gifted education is the development of higher order thinking skills. This concept can be somewhat elusive and can be confused with extensive factual knowledge. For example, comprehensive knowledge of battles and personnel in the Civil War may indicate a strong memory but does not necessarily indicate the capacity for analysis and synthesis of ideas. Bloom's (1956) taxonomy provides a useful starting point to understand the goals of gifted instruction in terms of developing higher order thinking and creativity. This model (see Figure 16.1), which was revised in 2001 by Anderson and Krathwohl, was developed to show the relationship between cognitive processes to encourage teachers to focus instruction on higher level skills.

King, Goodson, and Rohani (1998) have pointed out that the lower skills on the pyramid—Remember and Understand—constitute cognitive skills, but are not higher order skills in the sense of going beyond the information presented. As one progresses up the pyramid, the level of effort involved increases and there is an implication that the lower stages form a prerequisite for higher skills.

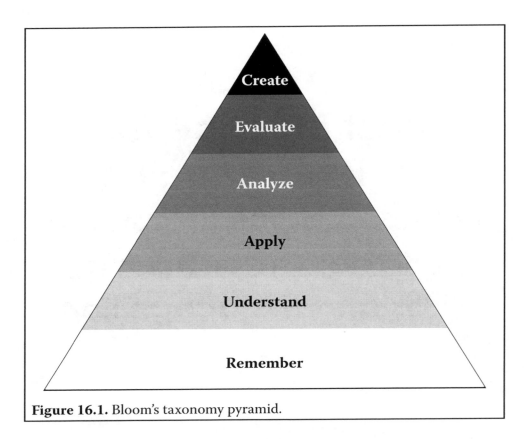

Figure 16.1. Bloom's taxonomy pyramid.

Many students with learning challenges find that the lower cognitive processes create a barrier to engaging in the higher order thinking skills that their intellectual and creative gifts might manifest. For example, poor working memory, a common feature of the cognitive profile of gifted students with learning and attentional challenges, can be a barrier to the acquisition of knowledge. These students have difficulty even getting "off the mark" when placed in a situation where they must listen, absorb information, and react instantly. Similarly, poor organizational strategies can contribute to inefficiently encoded memory, which prevents the effective recall of information on demand. Many gifted students are able to cover up this difficulty, at least temporarily, by using their excellent reasoning skills to fill in the gaps in their knowledge. One difficulty with this compensatory strategy is that these students are limited by their own prior knowledge. As we will note below, there are many ways to work around a working memory deficit that would allow gifted students to move on to more advanced thinking tasks.

Effective curriculum models for twice-exceptional students should incorporate higher order thinking skills into subject areas and investigate authentic problems, but should also provide a strong and obvious framework that teaches

Figure 16.2. TASC wheel. Reprinted with permission from Belle Wallace, TASC International.

students a process for investigating advanced problems. GTLD students are often confused by changes in format, so a consistent approach to organizing higher order tasks, preferably with a clear visual graphic, will have the greatest success. These students need specific instruction in how to engage in higher order thinking strategies. Moseley et al. (2005) reviewed a number of thinking skill models and programs. In this chapter, we will highlight a few promising programs that have been used schoolwide to good effect.

Thinking Actively in a Social Context (TASC)

The TASC model (http://www.tascwheel.com) provides a structured approach to problem solving based on the TASC wheel. Figure 16.2 illustrates the wheel as it is displayed in classrooms. The program was developed over many years of action research in a variety of settings in the United Kingdom, as well as internationally. It was originally developed to increase rigor in the instruction of students in third world countries. One advantage to the TASC model is its ability to function at multiple levels of complexity, allowing the program to be effective both with challenged and highly able learners.

TASC focuses on a process for student project development that can be adapted to any academic subject area. The TASC wheel is prominently displayed in the classroom and students are explicitly taught how to go through the steps of the problem-solving process embedded in the wheel concept. Students initially identify what they already know about the topic and then focus on a specific problem or topic. Research skills are developed as students seek to identify possible solutions to the problem. Students use evaluation skills to select a preferred solution and identify steps to implement it. The outcome is evaluated and critiqued, and students present their findings to peers to explain their reasoning in the way they chose to solve the problems. Key features of the program are the use of group problem solving and a process of self-evaluation and revision. Verbal expression and metacognition are facilitated through the expectation that projects must be presented to an audience. The TASC model teaches student to focus on continual review and improvement of their products, rather than getting an A.

Case study: St. Gwladys Primary School. Tucked into a Welsh valley, the town of Bargoed in Caerphilly, South Wales, was once a thriving center of commerce due to the development of coal mines in the area. Many individuals came from other areas of the United Kingdom and Eastern Europe during the 19th and early 20th century to work in the mines, bringing with them a strong value of education for their children as a way to improve their prospects. The miners of that period were intellectually curious and politically active through their labor unions. During the Thatcher government in the 1980s, the mines were closed, leading to the severe economic decline of the mining communities.

Like other towns in the area, Bargoed has suffered from the loss of more prosperous community members who left to seek employment elsewhere. Although a strong sense of community remains, the economic woes of the area have been accompanied by the disruption of family life for a number of families by the problems of marital and child abuse and parental substance use that often accompany economic hardship. Similar to problems in the inner city, there are multiple generations of family unemployment where families subsist on government benefits. Many parents have limited availability to provide for the academic needs of their children and do not place a strong family value on education. Schools provide additional support for students such as free meals.

Given the somewhat grim context, St. Gwladys Primary School, winner of the National Association for Able Children in Education (NACE) Challenge Award, is a surprising center of advanced curriculum and the provision of sophisticated services for gifted and talented students. With a population of 340 students ages 3–11, the school hums with calm enthusiasm as students engage in TASC projects throughout the school, even at the prekindergarten level. The school began using the TASC model 4–5 years ago as part of a Caerphilly district initiative. Although the school has about 8%–10% "highly able" students, TASC is used throughout the school and is embedded in academics throughout the school day and in all subject areas. All teachers went through a daylong training, and additional training was provided to master teachers who led training at the school level. Teachers engaged in ongoing professional development using the TASC model through professional learning communities where they shared the efforts to incorporate TASC project-based learning into all areas of the curriculum.

Kate Halpin, St. Gwladys school head, indicated that the initiation of the TASC program was a revelation to their teaching staff. Although there was a period of adjustment in the students to the structure of the program, she indicated that teachers quickly saw the emergence of strengths in students of all ability levels. Students were quickly able to grasp the TASC format and dramatic improvements were noted in students' ability to work in cooperative groups and to talk about their ideas and thinking processes. The school has been so pleased with the success of the program that it continues to invest in TASC teacher training even though district support is no longer provided.

Halpin indicated that she values TASC for its ability to give each student an individual voice. Particularly for more visually talented students, the TASC approach allowed them to use preferred learning and production styles, but also developed their capacity to use verbal expression through the expectation that students will explain their ideas to their classmates. She noted that even the 4-year-olds were able to use metacognitive strategies and had begun using more open-ended questioning (e.g., the five Ws) in discussing their peers' work. Because the TASC model is used throughout the school, the vocabulary and concepts form a common language to talk about the learning and thinking process.

Halpin also described TASC as developing resilience in students through the emphasis on evaluating outcomes and "rethinking" to try something to improve the results. In a 6-year-old classroom, students were well aware of the term *resilience* and were able to explain that it meant trying something else when something doesn't work. In TASC, there are no wrong answers. Instead, quality of each answer is assessed *by the students* and then modifications are proposed. One value of the program, according to Halpin, is the benefits for more academically talented students to learn that other students who may have learning challenges may have the best ideas. Students interviewed at the school indicated that they were not upset when their ideas did not prevail on a particular project because their ideas had been successful in other projects.

As examples of TASC projects, the 6-year-old class was engaged in the task of designing a presentation about invertebrates for a younger group of students. The teacher guided the students in identifying the important features such a program would need to have. Students spontaneously identified the need for clear language, visual images, and good organization. The students were divided into working groups who then organized themselves into different roles for the task. One student identified that he was the artist for his group. Halpin indicated that students learn the strengths and weaknesses of their peers and tend to naturally assign roles appropriate to student strengths. In an older class, a group of students were working on the design for a bridge out of paper that had to meet specific performance criteria. All students in the group, even some who appeared to have some verbal fluency challenges, were eager to share their ideas and experiences in experimentation. They all were able to clearly describe the process they had pursued and identify their future plan of action. Students were universally enthusiastic about TASC projects.

The TASC wheel was also in use in the prekindergarten class. The teacher used a modified wheel with visual icons to help students recall the steps in the TASC process. The students were assigned to work with a partner to design "mini beasts" (e.g., ladybugs, butterflies). In a class of 30 preschoolers, the level of attention and cooperation was striking. Students were attentive in the presentation phase and asked open-ended questions to assist the presenters in explaining their ideas. When asked how his group decided on their beast, a student explained that he had gone with his partner's idea "because he knew he would get a chance to use one of his ideas later." Students in this class were able to identify and explain the concept of symmetry, and one student was able to explain the purpose of antennae.

About one third of the students at St. Gwladys have special learning needs, including specific learning disabilities and autism spectrum disorders. In addition, because of the depressed area, many students enter the school with below average verbal expression skills. Special education is delivered by a resource specialist who works in an immersion model within the classroom. The school uses flexible age groupings to group students according to skill level. The resource teacher indicated that she also used TASC projects with her students, but felt that they needed additional scaffolding and explicit instruction in skills. She noted that student behavior challenges were often not evident during TASC work and that some students with traumatic histories were much more engaged and active in TASC group work than they were in other forms of social interaction. Students on the autism spectrum were somewhat challenged by the group approach and often struggled with rigidity and perspective taking, but the staff felt that these behaviors decreased through exposure to the TASC process. ASD students often liked the predictability inherent in the wheel.

TASC is also used at the secondary level. The Ysgol Gyfun Cwm Rhymni school is a Welsh-immersion program that was recently singled out by the national press as an example for the development of gifted and talented students at the secondary level. Matthew Webb, a science teacher at the school, indicated that TASC was used in the early secondary years (the equivalent of American junior high or middle school). Students at his school attended primary schools that used the TASC model. Webb indicated that TASC was very useful, particularly in science, because it complements the model of scientific inquiry. He developed a modified TASC wheel for students with learning challenges with simplified language. Students identified as gifted are placed in separate classes at Cwm Rhymni and receive academic acceleration. He uses the TASC wheel to help students organize research plans for projects. Students with writing challenges are not expected to make elaborate notes on the wheel.

In discussions with school staff and classroom observations, it is apparent that the strengths of the program at St. Gwladys lie in the universality of the program in forming a common language for discussing thinking and learning and the emphasis on constant reevaluation and improvement of products rather than seeking the "correct" answer. Students appeared to take ownership of their learning and were eager to share their ideas in a safe environment. Through the TASC process, students learn to give and receive constructive feedback and to develop leadership skills in working with others in group projects.

Teaching for Intellectual and Emotional Learning (TIEL)

Teaching for Intellectual and Emotional Learning (http://www.tielinstitute.com) is a curriculum model developed by Christy Folsom (2009) as a means to educate students in skills that will be required for success in the 21st century. In Folsom's view, these skills involve the incorporation of both higher order cognitive skills and aspects of affective or character education. The TIEL model uses project-based learning to teach students skills in decision making, planning, and self-evaluation that lead toward greater self-management.

The TIEL wheel (see Figure 16.3) combines the cognitive theories of J. P. Guilford and the humanistic approach of John Dewey. Guilford's Structure of Intellect theory identifies five specific thinking operations: cognition, memory, evaluation, convergent thinking, and divergent thinking. Dewey's educational philosophy focused on child-centered, hands-on learning with an emphasis on developing collaborative relationships. Affective components of the TIEL wheel derived from Dewey's philosophy include appreciation, mastery, ethical reasoning, empathy, and reflection.

Similar to teacher modifications to the TASC wheel, Folsom (2009) identified specific cognitive subskills that require explicit teacher modeling and instruction. The color coding of the wheel seeks to make connections between affective and cognitive processes. For example, she drew connections between the cognitive skill of evaluation and the character skill of ethical reasoning, pulling in the relationship between values and ethics in real-world decision-making. Although the TASC wheel identifies a specific, sequential process, the

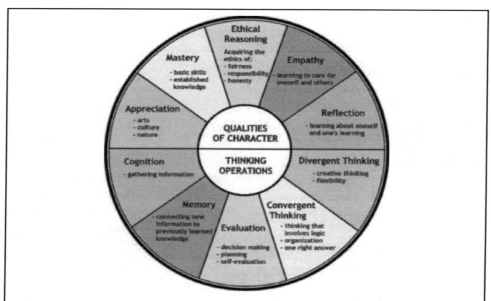

Figure 16.3. TIEL wheel. From *Teaching for Intellectual and Emotional Learning* (p. 33), by C. Folsom, 2009, Lanham, MD: Rowman and Littlefield Education. Copyright 2009 by Rowman and Littlefield Education. Reprinted with permission.

TIEL wheel is more conceptual and allows for students to make connections across the components of the wheel.

Folsom's (2009) book, an outgrowth of her qualitative research dissertation, provided extensive case studies of the implementation of the TIEL model in elementary education. An important feature of the program is the use of three visual aids: the TIEL wheel, a color-coded bulletin board, and color-coded puppets associated with different thinking skills, the latter to be used with primary students. Students implement the TIEL model through project-based learning with the TIEL concepts providing overall structure and guidance. Teachers use the TIEL wheel to identify skills to develop in creating lessons. They often use the TIEL concepts to develop graphic organizers for student projects.

Folsom's (2009) case studies provided a fascinating overview of the personal growth of the teachers as they became more conscious of their own thinking process. Her book illustrated that teachers need the time to develop their materials and need a forum—for example, with a master teacher—to reflect on their teaching process and how well they are using the TIEL model. Teachers who utilized the model indicated that they found value in the common language provided for students and teachers to talk about thinking, the visual concreteness of the wheel, the flexibility of the framework in addressing a broad range of student competence in thinking skills, and the way that the wheel concept facilitated generalization and the linkage of experiences.

The TIEL model helps educators understand these thinking skills and others necessary to complex learning. Using TIEL as a framework for curriculum design helps teachers balance content and process. TIEL helps teachers create learning experiences that span several basic thinking operations. When teachers plan curriculum using the TIEL framework, they create a classroom environment that encourages intellectual, emotional, and character development.

Thinking Maps®

Thinking Maps (http://www.thinkingmaps.com), developed by David Hyerle in the 1980s, have been utilized in more than 5,000 schools in the United States and throughout the world. The Thinking Maps concept is based upon earlier insights of concept mapping. Hyerle and Williams (2009) drew a distinction between graphic organizers and conceptual mapping. Graphic organizers tend to be charts or graphs designed by the teacher that students simply fill in. Conceptual mapping is a more active process where the students make their own decisions about which format works best with the material and form a visual representation of their thought processes.

Hyerle has identified eight Thinking Maps that represent major cognitive processes: Defining in Context, Describing Qualities, Comparing and Contrasting, Categorizing, Part-Whole, Sequencing, Cause-Effect, and Seeing Analogies (see Figure 16.4.). As students progress in their expertise in using the models, they begin to combine maps for more complex representations of connections between ideas.

In a 1999 journal article from the *New Hampshire Journal of Education*, Jeffrey Spiegel, principal of Hanover Street School, described his school's implementation of the Thinking Maps model. He cited the importance of both teachers and students becoming aware of their own thought process. Spiegel discussed the process of integrating a new method into a school. At Level 1, a stage that could last 1–2 years, teachers focus on learning the tool and tend to provide instruction designed to teach the use of the tool. As they progress to Level 2, teachers come to see the tool as a vehicle for helping students understand curriculum content. At this stage, teachers identify the goal of study and decide which maps would apply to the content. Gradually, teachers begin to give students more options, and by Level 3, teachers focus on more global learning goals (essential and guiding questions) and engage students in discussions about what they wish to learn. At this stage, the students who have been familiarized with the range of Thinking Maps are allowed to choose the map they think best fits the task. Progressively, students are encouraged to reflect on their

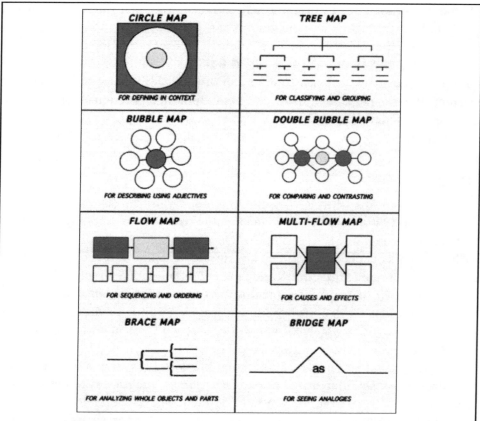

Figure 16.4. Thinking Maps.© Thinking Maps, Inc. Reprinted with permission.

choices and evaluate the outcomes. The process of reflection is very similar to the TASC model of "rethinking."

It is important to note that the introduction of a curriculum model is an evolving process that takes several years to implement. Spiegel (1999) pointed to the importance of community discussion among teachers as a way of becoming more conscious of the process of implementation and developing community standards of implementation. Professional learning communities where teachers have the opportunity to present their experiences and reflect on their teaching process are an important component to such a program.

The Thinking Foundation website highlights the effective use of Thinking Maps in the Pass Christian Public Schools in Mississippi. All students in this district used Thinking Maps, which were incorporated into all academic disciplines. Students overall scored relatively poorly on high-stakes state testing, but after the introduction of Thinking Maps, the district's performance rose to the highest in the state. Even after Hurricane Katrina totally demolished the school buildings in the district and instruction was disrupted, student performance on state tests remained strong.

Case study: Pass Christian Middle School, MS. A small village along the Mississippi Gulf Coast, Pass Christian was built on a peninsula deeded to a freed slave in the late 18th century. Prior to the Civil War, Pass Christian was a vacation destination for the wealthy residents of New Orleans. In the 20th century, the shrimping industry gradually declined, leading to economic deprivation in the area. About 11 years ago, when Thinking Maps were introduced, the schools were 70% free and reduced lunch and student academic performance was considerably below the state average. Suzanne Ishee, Pass Christian Middle School teacher and Thinking Maps trainer for her district, indicated that teachers were quickly won over by the major improvements in student thinking and writing that emerged with the use of Thinking Maps. Student performance dramatically improved, raising the Pass Christian district to the highest levels of performance in the state.

In 2005, Hurricane Katrina devastated Pass Christian, leaving most of the teachers and students with nothing. Of the four schools in the district, only one could be used after a 7-week hiatus, and teachers shared portable trailers with virtually no materials. Ishee recalled that "it was like going back to a slate and chalk with just a white board and two markers" (personal communication, August 21, 2012). Many students were emotionally devastated by the loss of family members and personal experiences of survival. Ishee described drawing a Circle Map with the word "Katrina" written in the middle to assist students in processing their experiences in the wake of the hurricane. Teachers found that the common language of Thinking Maps provided the continuity needed to keep students focused on learning despite chaotic conditions. Students continued to perform at advanced levels on state tests despite the disruption in their education. Ishee said that it is important not to view the Pass Christian Thinking Maps story as a "Katrina story," but rather indicated that Katrina was a bump in the road of a longstanding success story about improvements in student achievement brought about by the use of Thinking Maps.

Currently, Thinking Maps are used in all Pass Christian schools from prekindergarten to high school. Despite the ongoing community disruption in the aftermath of Katrina, the Pass Christian district has been rated as number one in the state for the past 3 years. Ishee indicated that the success of Thinking Maps lies in the fact that the maps are a visual representation of thinking that can be applied to any subject area. These tools are readily adaptable to working with the common core objectives. Teachers receive a daylong training and then work with mentors in a training the trainer model.

At Pass Christian Middle, Ishee teaches two enrichment courses using traditional gifted techniques, such as hands-on projects with authentic documents. One course focuses on fine arts and one on science and math. These courses are offered as electives open to any student interested in participating. Ishee indicated that students of all ability levels choose to take the class and that Thinking Maps assist students in demonstrating strengths. Student performance among a group performing in the lowest quartile rose to the 90th percentile. Ishee indicated that it is important not to underestimate students who may struggle in traditional academics. In the upcoming school year, Pass Christian students will conduct an oral history study of local experiences during the Civil Rights movement using Thinking Maps to illustrate varying perspectives in the community.

The National Research Center on the Gifted and Talented Thinking Skills Curriculum

This thinking skills curriculum was developed in the 1990s as part of a Jacob K. Javits grant at the University of Connecticut. It was influenced by the work of Barry Beyer, Edward DeBono, and Venezuela's Project Intelligence. Burns et al. (2006) provided a manual for explicit instruction of thinking skills. Their program teaches seven skills: cause and effect reasoning, decision making, comparing and contrasting, classifying, making observations, planning, and predicting. The program provides an instruction module for each skill, which progresses from direct instruction of the concept to guided practice of the skill with familiar content, to guided practice in a real-world application, and finally, prompted transfer to the current academic curriculum. The teaching techniques utilized include use of graphic organizers, debriefing, coaching, and feedback.

As an example of this approach, the teaching of cause and effect begins with an explanation of the purpose of the skill and examples of how it is used. Several prerequisite skills are identified as: (a) being able to identify the event, (b) understanding why it is important to find cause and effect, (c) identifying actions or events related to the event, (d) using appropriate information-gathering techniques, and (e) using data as evidence. Burns et al. (2006) indicated that some students may need explicit instruction in these prerequisite skills in order to advance to cause and effect reasoning. The teacher then goes on to a series of activities to help students understand what cause and effect means. In an exercise called "The Dog Ate It," students consider reasons for why a student might not turn in homework and what the effects of not turning in homework might be.

In subsequent activities, students go on to brainstorm and learn how to evaluate possible causes as good explanations. For example, students consider reasons for trees being cut down in a park and weed out the ideas that don't seem probable. They then go on to collect further information to try to discover why the parks department might choose to cut down trees. Gradually, students are led to activities that relate cause and effect thinking to more particular parts of the curriculum, such as why an author might have chosen to write a particular book they also are reading in class.

Instruction in Metacognitive Strategies

Metacognition refers to the ability to be consciously aware of mental processes. Previously, we talked about programs that made problem-solving procedures explicit. Here, we will discuss the benefits of explicit strategy instruction in other aspects of metacognition, specifically in addressing weaknesses in executive functioning.

Executive functioning refers to important skills for managing tasks and regulating emotions. For some teachers, this concept is baffling, and they wonder if it is a way to pathologize or make excuses for typical child or teen behavior. It can be hard to tell the difference between the student who is "late, lost, and unprepared" (Cooper-Kahn & Dietzel, 2008) because of typical teen issues like boyfriend problems or a sports failure and students who have a learning disability that includes executive functioning weaknesses. One issue to consider is the pervasiveness of the problem. Students who may be occasionally disorganized generally show higher functioning at other times. Students with brain-based executive function weaknesses often can't get it together, even for things they really care about.

Working with twice-exceptional students to understand and address their executive functioning challenges is a key component of helping them to understand their own unique learning profiles. Most bright students with learning difficulties struggle in some area of executive functioning. Students with ADHD often lack the inhibition of impulses and have difficulty sustaining attention to tasks that are not inherently interesting to them. They may have difficulty grasping task demands and getting started. For students with specific learning disabilities, executive functioning issues may manifest in challenges of planning and prioritizing, as they are not able to produce the work at the same rate as their peers. Many students have a poor sense of time and struggle to estimate the time needed for tasks and to manage their time effectively.

Students with weak executive skills often have difficulty with self-monitoring and do not always identify when their organization and planning difficulties are interfering with their performance. These students may feel overwhelmed, but may have difficulty identifying the source of their distress; they feel lost in a sea of disconnected information. As a result, these students profit from explicit instruction in managing tasks. Important areas to address are developing a sense of time, breaking down tasks into manageable components, developing self-monitoring skills, and improving emotional regulation.

Dawson and Guare's (2010) excellent book, *Executive Skills in Children and Adolescents*, provides guidance for parents and teachers in interventions to improve executive functions in children of all ages. Using an RtI model, they discuss a general approach applicable to a broad range of executive skill issues, including task management and emotional self-regulation. In their model, Tier 1 interventions involve classroom-based interventions. These strategies involve modifying the environment or changing the teacher's behavior. Environmental modifications include changing the nature of the task to limit executive function demands and using verbal and visual cues to prompt students to follow procedures. Teachers use a process of rehearsal, guided practice, and debriefing to help make specific strategies more obvious to students. With Tier 2 interventions targeted toward students struggling to manage executive skills, teachers work with small groups of students in a coaching modality. Teachers help students formulate their own plans and procedures to address their executive function difficulties. With teacher guidance, students learn to make plans and timelines, develop strategies for remembering tasks, and make their own checklists to keep track of materials.

For Tier 3 interventions, needed for students with deficits in executive skills, a more formalized plan is introduced. Students at this level require instruction in specific behavioral routines. Teachers will need to formulate scripted routines, such as a "Desk Cleaning Routine" or "Managing Open-Ended Tasks." To instruct students, teachers will model these routines and develop scripts for students to learn. As students practice these routines, the teacher provides corrective feedback and gradually fades supervision. Students with severe executive function deficits should work on a small number of specific skills and may require an incentive or reinforcement system to stick with new behaviors.

As a specific example from Dawson and Guare's (2010) book, they provided guidance in how to teach students to pay attention (see pp. 82–83 of that volume). The student is initially instructed in the importance of paying attention and asked for specific behavioral indicators that would demonstrate sustained attention (e.g., eyes on teacher). The student develops a description of what paying attention looks like with the support of the teacher. The student and teacher then select a particular time to practice the skill and identify criteria to evaluate his performance. They agree on how to measure attention, and the child is expected to use a checklist to self-monitor his performance. At the practice session, the teacher reminds the student of the goal. Following the practice session, the teacher and student compare notes to evaluate the student's performance.

Case Study: A Student With Deficits in Executive Skills

Carson is a third-grade student currently attending a full-time special education program due to Asperger's syndrome and ADHD, Combined Type. His parents sought a private placement for Carson after 2 unsuccessful years in a mainstream school setting. In his typical first-grade classroom, Carson stood out. While others were engaged in tasks, he would often fall off his chair in dramatic fashion or wander around the room seeking interaction and sensory stimulation at inappropriate times. His teacher indicated that although Carson had strong basic academic skills, he had great difficulty completing his work, often becoming distracted and off-task while pursuing his own personal interests. For example, he would often get out a preferred book rather than complete his work. At home, Carson struggled to complete homework, often spending hours avoiding getting down to work. Frequently, he engaged in tantrums or quickly dashed off his work with little effort to do it well.

Carson also struggled with reading social cues, and a frequent complaint from classmates was his constant touching and violation of their personal space. When Carson encountered a negative reaction to his behavior, he often escalated the behaviors. Carson loved rules and was quite "bossy" to others. In the lunchroom, he would attempt to initiate conversation with dramatic monologues and extreme facial gestures, but he was oblivious to his reception, even when students literally turned away from him. He had difficulty with turn taking; in games, when passed the ball, he tended to keep it. Carson frequently engaged adults, asking for explanations for why he was expected to do specific tasks; these conversations were often interpreted by his teacher as disrespectful, and power struggles were common.

Carson's parents brought him for testing to determine a better way to help Carson with his challenges and to learn strategies to assist him in applying his intellect to academic tasks. On the WISC-IV, Carson obtained a General Ability Index of 126, which fell at the 96th percentile, with very superior nonverbal reasoning ability (Perceptual Reasoning Index of 131—98th percentile) and high average verbal comprehension (Verbal Comprehension Index of 112—79th percentile). His working memory and processing speed scores were average. These results illustrate some of the challenges in interpreting test scores noted earlier in this book. Although Carson only scored in the high average range on formal verbal testing, even a cursory casual conversation revealed that Carson had advanced vocabulary, sophisticated reasoning, and a vast depth of knowledge for his preferred topics. On structured verbal tests where he had to comply with external expectations, he hemmed and hawed, often providing a very concrete answer or one that was tangential to the topic. He often missed easy items, but was able to answer a number of items that children his age would not be expected to know. Similarly, Carson demonstrated exceptional nonverbal reasoning ability, but would sometimes lose credit on tasks because he pursued his own interests or thoughts (e.g., rotating a block design because he wanted it to look like a house). Academically, Carson had strong basic reading skills, but struggled with drawing inferences in reading. His conceptual understanding of math was quite strong, but he often made minor calculation errors. Carson had relatively strong skills in written composition, but struggled with handwriting.

Measures of executive functioning indicated that Carson had difficulty multitasking and had an "in and out" quality to sustaining attention. Parent and teacher ratings on the Behavior Rating Inventory of Executive Function (BRIEF; Gioia, Isquith, Guy, & Kenworthy, 2000), a series of behavior scales assessing executive skills in daily life, indicated major concerns in the two primary domains of behavioral regulation and metacognition. In the area of behavioral regulation, Carson had difficulty inhibiting behaviors, shifting the focus of his attention, and controlling his emotions. In the metacognitive domain, he had difficulty initiating and planning tasks, using working memory, and monitoring his performance.

The transition to a smaller, specialized school program was not a panacea; Carson continued to struggle with off-task behavior, impulsivity, and peer difficulties. Medication for ADHD helped somewhat, but teachers also worked with Carson throughout the school day to develop better behavioral regulation and metacognition. Carson was often provocative and annoying to other students and had great difficulty coping with the sensory stimulation of more unstructured classes like art and music. Transitions were particularly challenging for Carson, and he often expressed worries about changes in classroom plans. When doing independent work in the classroom, he would frequently become distracted by his preferred topics and had difficulty with task completion. Molly Girona, Carson's classroom teacher at the Kingsbury Day School, implemented a number of strategies to assist him in adapting to the classroom.

To help Carson with emotional regulation challenges, Girona worked with him to be able to identify his feelings and to choose an appropriate response. He often sought out creating a conflict with a peer as a means of avoiding challenging work or when he was anxious. She used a joint behavior plan involving the two students to increase their motivation to choose other solutions to feeling "silly." Carson also struggled with transitions, participating in group activities, and choosing appropriate behavior in classroom activities. Girona created social stories for each situation (e.g., walking in the hall, completing a writing assignment). In each story, she felt that it was important to give Carson her expectations for his behavior, as well as a rationale regarding why it was important for him to engage in the preferred behaviors. She also identified strengths that he could use to meet teacher expectations.

One important component of the intervention was Girona's efforts to develop a relationship with Carson in order to motivate him to meet her expectations. She began the year with private lunches and with rewards that allowed Carson to use things that belonged to her. For example, Carson was an eager Rubik's cube practitioner and enjoyed earning the opportunity to use Girona's stopwatch to time himself. She also had private conversations with Carson about his strengths and weaknesses and helped him develop personal goals in the classroom. For example, he wanted to be able to play a game at recess without someone getting upset and he wanted to work as a partner with a friend with whom he had a challenging relationship. Girona used these conversations to help Carson monitor his progress toward his goals. Girona indicated that Carson responded well when she gave him responsibility in the classroom and showed him that she trusted and believed in him.

Although Carson had highly developed basic academic skills, he did have some challenges in the more conceptual aspects of his academics. He had difficulty with problem solving in math and with reading comprehension. In math, Carson was quite impatient to get to the finish line and often missed important information in word problems. Girona taught Carson to use a problem-solving method (figure out the question, circle the important information, eliminate extraneous information, and choose a problem-solving strategy). Carson was expected to pick a problem-solving strategy from a menu listed on the board (e.g., act it out, draw it, work backward, make a list). These strategies were explicitly taught to the whole class at the beginning of the school year. Carson could be brought to focus on the problem-solving process when he was expected to explain to the class how he solved the problem using the problem-solving model. Girona indicated that she had to teach Carson how and why to use scratch paper, as he would attempt to hold complex information in his mind. In reading comprehension, Carson struggled to understand what comprehension questions were asking. Girona taught him how to "unpack" the question to be sure he understood everything that the question involved. Carson tended to give one-word answers and needed guidance on how to identify details to support a point. He had a hard time identifying the main idea and needed explicit instruction on how to know if something was important.

Conclusion

Many students struggle to develop higher order thinking skills, not only students with learning challenges. However, because of their weak executive skills, twice-exceptional students often fail to develop effective strategies for approaching complex tasks through their own initiative and typically require training in metacognitive strategies. Research on learning disabled college students has found that learning these explicit strategies was viewed as essential for their college success. Often these strategies can be taught through fairly simple programmatic approaches that incorporate a step-by-step method that can be applied in multiple academic contexts, use a visual graphic, and are used consistently throughout the school for several years at a time. As our case studies in Wales and Mississippi illustrate, these programs are cost effective and often provide benefits for all students in the school.

chapter 17

Best Practice for GTLD Programming 6:
Embed Supports and Accommodations Into the School Program Rather Than Only on an Individual Basis

Individualized adaptations and accommodations to existing curriculum are important supports for students with learning disabilities. However, classroom teachers often find it difficult to implement multiple individually tailored menus of accommodations. Further, many twice-exceptional learners do not have official diagnoses or plans and may be traveling under the radar in terms of teacher awareness of their need for accommodations. These students may prosper when accommodations are embedded in the structure of how information is presented and how they are asked to demonstrate knowledge.

Case Study: Eleanor Roosevelt High School, Greenbelt, MD

Eleanor Roosevelt High School is a large comprehensive high school in Prince George's County, MD, a large and highly diverse suburban county of metropolitan Washington, DC. Roosevelt is consistently listed among *Newsweek's* America's Best High Schools and was recently recognized by the College Board for its strong success with African American students passing the AP Chemistry examination. With more than 2,500 students, 80% of whom are minorities, Roosevelt provides a solid role model for meeting the learning needs of a broad range of students.

The Roosevelt Science and Technology program (about 1,000 students) is a magnet program with competitive admission based on middle school grades and performance on timed tests of reading comprehension and mathematics. In the program, students are required to take 4 years of mathematics and science, including three advanced science courses. In addition to the standard menu of AP courses, Roosevelt offers other advanced science courses, including Bioorganic Chemistry, Genetics, Geology, Microbiology, and Forensics. Students who have completed the AP Calculus sequence can go on to college courses in multivariable calculus and differential equations taught at Roosevelt by a professor from a local university. During the senior year, each Science and Tech student is expected to complete a yearlong research project under the mentorship of a scientist. Students have completed their research at labs at the National Institutes of Health; the University of Maryland, College Park; the USDA; and NASA.

The school environment strongly values academic success, and students indicate that it is "cool to be a geek" at Roosevelt. It is typical for students in the Science and Tech program to take (and pass the examination for) 10 or more AP courses during their high school years. In addition to a strong academic program, students are encouraged to develop their talents through the arts, sports, and service organizations. Many students attend courses in "zero period," an additional course period prior to the beginning of the school day, or skip lunch in order to continue both their academics and extracurricular activities.

Twice-exceptional students can successfully test into the Roosevelt Science and Tech program, often with the testing accommodations specified in their IEPs. Jane Hemelt, the Science and Technology Coordinator at Roosevelt, indicated that GTLD students successfully complete the rigorous high school program meeting the same requirements as other students. One striking impression in speaking with Hemelt was the sense that she did not see the twice-exceptional learners as a separate group within the Science and Tech program. She indicated that GTLD students who were motivated and who took advantage of the opportunities provided were as successful at taking AP courses and in being accepted to good colleges as other students. Some twice-exceptional students could not handle the stress of the rigorous demands and left the program, but she indicated that this issue was not specific to students with learning challenges; other students also left because they struggled to handle the workload.

Hemelt indicated that twice-exceptional learners in the Science and Tech program can receive a number of supports and accommodations. Students often receive extended time accommodations for tests, the logistics of which they are expected to work out with their teachers on their own. Hemelt expressed concern about students receiving extended time for long-term projects because she said students often were unrealistic in expecting to complete large amounts of work as the semester drew to a close. Students are also allowed to use assistive technology, such as books on tape. She indicated that teachers typically work with students to address their learning challenges when they are made aware of them. She noted that it is important for parents to take an active role in establishing regular contact with teachers and in monitoring their students' performance via the school system's database, which provides parents with access to the teachers' gradebooks on a daily basis. Students with IEPs are eligible to take a resource class taught by a special education teacher that focuses on time management, study skills, and self-advocacy.

One reason for GTLD student success in the Science and Tech program is that students are likely pursuing areas of personal interest because students selectively apply to the program for its science and math focus. In addition, Roosevelt embeds considerable support into the program that is available to all students. Teachers offer opportunities for students to correct their work and improve their grades on some assignments and provide specific rubrics regarding expectations for assignments. In writing assignments, students are expected to write multiple drafts and engage in peer editing as a part of the process. Students are allowed product choice in some assignments (e.g., making a movie or creating a work of art). In addition, students can receive extra credit for participating in enrichment activities, such as the Physics Is Phun program at the University of Maryland, which provides hands-on activities to teach elementary physics concepts. For advanced courses, teachers provide afterschool review sessions for AP tests. Every Saturday throughout the school year, a math teacher (on a volunteer basis) provides review sessions for AP Physics and Calculus courses. The National Honor Society also provides free tutoring to all students.

Twice-exceptional students also have success in completing the yearlong research project that culminates in a paper written in the style of a professional journal article, a professional poster, and a PowerPoint presentation shared with peers. Students work with scientist-mentors who help them design their research, but Roosevelt also provides a daily class for seniors to help them produce their paper and presentations. The teachers provide structure in giving students examples of quality work and exercises to assist them in developing the prerequisite skills to complete these complex tasks. Students go through a process of revising and editing each chapter in their research paper over the course of the year and practice their presentations to receive feedback. Many students go on to continue their research after graduation.

Universal Design for Learning

A newer approach to providing accommodations, Universal Design for Learning (UDL; http://www.udlcenter.org), is based upon insights from neuroscience that suggest that there is considerable variability in how people learn best and that a barrier is created for many types of students by unvarying presentation and assessment of information. To illustrate this point, take a simple example from daily life. Think about the variability in how people access driving directions: One person needs the names of streets and distances, another person does best with a map drawn with landmarks identified, another with a GPS system that speaks the directions aloud. UDL provides a framework for building accommodations into tasks so that they are available to all students. This approach may not totally replace individualized accommodations, but will make it easier for teachers and students to use accommodations.

To some extent, UDL formalizes strategies that many teachers have used for years. Good teachers have always known that the best way to reach the largest audience is to mix it up and approach concepts from different angles. Universal Design for Learning formalizes this insight and encourages teachers to plan for a variety in learning styles in three ways: how information is presented, how students demonstrate knowledge, and how students are emotionally engaged in the learning process. When flexibility is built in, teachers don't have to worry about tracking the accommodation needs of each student individually. With UDL, students don't have to wait or be singled out to have the best learning environment to meet their learning style. In the next section, we will review the three basic principles of UDL and discuss how these principles can be valuable for the GTLD student.

UDL Principle I: Multiple Means of Representation

UDL recognizes that information can be conveyed through a variety of media and formats. One particular barrier for many students is text. With modern technology, there are many ways to electronically modify and adapt text to meet the diverse needs of learners. For example, enlarging font, text-to-voice capability, and embedding dictionaries in reading material are all ways to proactively facilitate students' access to text. For students to make the greatest connection to the material, UDL encourages teachers to illustrate points through multiple types of examples, to highlight critical features of concepts, to use multiple media and formats in the presentation of material, and to support connections to students' prior knowledge by providing context (Hall, Strangman, & Meyer, 2003).

Many bright students who struggle with reading and writing are stuck at the gate when their only means for learning are textbooks and workbooks. This greatly limits their access and can create disillusionment with learning overall. Fortunately, there are numerous technological supports that address weaknesses in reading, writing, revising, and even generating ideas. When the world of technology is opened for twice-exceptional students, they can achieve a level of independence that in another time period would not have been possible.

The emphasis on multisensory presentation of information is very helpful with twice-exceptional learners who may have difficulty accessing auditory and/or visual information. These students may need information presented visually in one subject area and auditorily in another. Clarity of purpose when using technology can support teachers in addressing the often sharply varying needs of GTLD students. One challenge for teachers is to keep abreast of the rapidly changing technology resources that can be adapted for learning. For example, there has been a recent explosion of information in using iPhone and iPad applications to meet educational needs.

Twice-exceptional students, particularly students with weak executive functions and attentional difficulties, struggle with the skills needed to sort through the vast store of information now available on any topic through the Internet and to effectively select relevant information for a particular purpose. Teachers need to help students organize the process of acquiring information into manageable steps that can be achieved in small increments. Providing scaffolds can ensure access for GTLD learners to construct meaning from the glut of information presented to students in an information-rich world.

When twice-exceptional students struggle with accessing the curriculum, compacting the amount of information required can greatly improve the chances of the students accessing the critical parts that are building blocks for further learning. UDL addresses this concept when it stresses the importance of varying demands and resources to optimize challenge. This is where an educator's expertise in differentiation and flexibility comes into play. Although it is best to address these needs proactively, often the obstacles a student encounters can only be detected when she hits bumps in the road. Strategies such as compacting, tiering lessons, and using an array of assistive technologies can be resources that optimize challenge. Rather than hitting roadblocks, these challenges can be seen as opportunities for better understanding a student's learning style and preferences.

UDL Principle II: Multiple Means of Action and Expression

UDL also prescribes the use of variety in how students demonstrate their knowledge (Hall et al., 2003). Teachers should provide options for the presentation of knowledge (e.g., allowing oral reports or videography instead of a paper). In addition, teachers are encouraged to provide models of successful projects or assignments in a variety of formats and to provide opportunities for students to practice skills needed to produce quality work. Teachers should make sure that students possess the skills needed to successfully complete their project(s). In addition, teachers should provide ongoing and relevant feedback to help students keep on track and to help them better understand the expectations for the task.

UDL stresses the importance of providing options for expression and communication. Weinfeld et al. (2006) pointed to the difficulty many twice-exceptional students have with written expression. In many ways, writing is the most complex academic task, as it involves the coordination of multiple brain systems (i.e., language, motor, executive functions, higher order thinking). Often, GTLD students have weaknesses in areas that compromise their ability to work quickly and to access their higher order skills. When students are struggling with handwriting or basic writing mechanics, less mental energy is available to convey their ideas. Typically, twice-exceptional learners cope with these challenges by writing the shortest amount possible. Although they may be able to verbally communicate elaborate narratives, their written product is often succinct and lacking in detail.

UDL highlights the need to allow students to choose their means of expression. For example, they could develop projects using video representations, or they could use graphic art to express new knowledge and insights. By using multiple tools for the expression of their ideas, GTLD students are freed from the barriers of writing that may constrict their expression of newly integrated knowledge. However, it is not enough to simply provide access to technology. Students will need direct instruction and scaffolding to become comfortable using these tools. Breaking down technology skills into individual steps can facilitate student acquisition of skills. Many twice-exceptional learners will need a slow and thoughtful process with purposeful practice to independently perform at desired levels.

Focusing on mastery can also lead to sustained effort and persistence. Many GTLD students struggle when the work demands focus on completing numerous and lengthy assignments. Mastery-oriented feedback helps both students and teachers to be clear about what really matters when setting standards for achievement. When twice-exceptional students are given assignments that test their endurance and not their mastery of a concept, they are much more likely to underachieve. Focusing on quantity can be demoralizing for these students. For example, students can become frustrated and oppositional when given a worksheet with 50 items to demonstrate understanding of a basic spelling concept when it would be obvious to an observer after a few problems that students clearly grasped the relevant concept. When given "busy work," students may have difficulty persisting and errors may be introduced as their attention wanes.

UDL Principle III: Multiple Means of Engagement

UDL also focuses on strategies to engage and motivate learners. As mentioned earlier in this section, twice-exceptional learners need avenues that tap into their interests and strengths—not only to optimize achievement levels, but also to minimize emotional barriers they may have to learning. Students require tasks that engage their interest and provide an appropriate level of challenge. They may need support to sustain motivation over time. When GTLD learners are stimulated and invested in their own learning, they are much less likely to get bogged down in the areas that negatively impact their achievement.

Twice-exceptional students vary in personality and temperament. Some students are inspired to learn when put in situations that are novel and tap into their love for spontaneity. Other GTLD students need highly structured environments and learn best when they feel the comfort of predictable routines. Some twice-exceptional students are introverts and need time to work alone to make academic progress. Others are extroverts and need opportunities for social interaction to achieve their highest potential. Taking these differences into account when planning assessments, units, and structuring the learning atmosphere will help teachers to optimize the classroom environment.

UDL also emphasizes the importance of relevance, value, and authenticity. Traditionally, curricula for gifted students have focused on the need for authentic products, the use of primary source materials, and the connection to real-world problems. Twice-exceptional students can thrive when asked to engage in problem solving about important real problems and often are very successful with hands-on learning. Students are more likely to be motivated when they see how learning connects to their own lives.

Implementation of UDL

The basic principles of UDL are to provide variety in how information is presented, how students demonstrate knowledge, and how students are engaged in the learning process. The CAST UDL training modules (http://www.udlonline.cast.org) provide an example of how a teacher might implement UDL. In the example, a ninth-grade English teacher wishes to provide instruction on a grammatical concept that her students are struggling with: appropriate subject-verb agreement. She initially planned to go over the concept and have students do sample items in their grammar books. However, by using the UDL checklist from CAST, she was able to evaluate her lesson in a way that guided her to recognize that the assignment was too easy for some students and too hard for others, due to its reliance on written text, and that the lesson was likely to have limited student engagement.

Following the principles of UDL, the teacher increased the engagement of her students by finding a relevant context for subject-verb agreement—writing an accident report for insurance. Her students were learning to drive and she knew there was a high probability that the students would be involved in an accident at some point. She was able to help them see the relevance of good writing in this context where accuracy would be important. The teacher then showed a YouTube video of a car crash and asked students to complete a crash diagram and write a crash narrative. Then she had students read an online article (with text-to-voice software if needed) and identify subjects and verbs in the article. Students were allowed to work in groups if they chose. The teacher then provided strategies and models by having students visualize the scene or draw a picture and then write a sentence that matched their mental picture. She provided model and nonmodel sentences ("The car is wrecked" vs. "The cars is wrecked") and then asked students to make up their own examples. To provide relevant practice, the culminating activity was to show the class a crash video and divide the class into small groups with each group assigned to a different role: describing the road, describing the scene, and describing the actions of each of the vehicles.

This lesson illustrates a number of features likely to be important to twice-exceptional students. The teacher used multisensory presentation of the material and incorporated multiple output modes (i.e., writing a description, oral presentation, drawing a model). Students were allowed accommodations for reading difficulties. Students could seek the support of a group where other more competent students could help them, or they could work alone if they were uncomfortable with the group process. However, one thing to consider is that students should also be encouraged to develop skills in their areas of weakness. So a student who is uncomfortable in group interactions should be provided with scaffolding and practice to be able to participate effectively in a group.

In addition to receiving benefits of accommodations and supports at the level of individual lessons, GTLD students can profit from interventions embedded at the program level. Programmatic components can include additional instruction opportunities, online supports, and peer tutoring. Many of these interventions can be helpful for other underserved populations in advanced programs.

Case Study: Bartholomew Consolidated School Corporation, Columbus, IN

Columbus is a small Midwestern city in southeastern Indiana. With a primary manufacturing base, Columbus has seen a recent increase in immigration from Latin America resulting in an increase of ELL students (Center for Teaching and Learning & SuCasa Columbus, 2007). The town boasts a combination of Victorian architecture combined with modernist architectural landmarks commissioned by the founder of the Cummins fire engine manufacturing company. Columbus has buildings by many major modernist architects including works by I. M. Pei and Eero Saarinen. Conde Nast Traveler (Hussain, 2012) rated Columbus as one of the world's best cities for architecture lovers. In 2012, The Bartholomew Consolidated School Corporation, in the Columbus public school system, received a Bill and Melinda Gates Foundation grant in partnership with CAST (formerly Center for Applied Special Technology; http://www.cast.org) to improve student literacy through professional development using UDL.

Rhonda Laswell, UDL Coordinator for the Bartholomew Consolidated School Corporation, initially used UDL in her seventh- and eighth-grade science classes. She described UDL as resonating with many of her own instructional principles, such as inquiry-based and hands-on learning, as well as the use of Maslow's (1943) hierarchy of needs. However, she found that UDL added a missing piece—the affective component of engagement. She realized that she had been focused on conveying the content and standards, but did not always help students see the content as authentic and relevant to their lives. Through UDL, she began instruction by engaging students through personal reflections in journals, eliciting personal experiences of students relevant to the topic, or providing examples from everyday life that helped students see the value in what they were learning. For example, in a lesson on genetics, she focused on students' personal experiences with genetic disorders, rather than simply starting with vocabulary.

Laswell emphasized that UDL is about removing barriers and that an important component to UDL implementation, and indeed all teaching, is the establishment of an appropriate classroom culture. Laswell advised that it is important to establish an atmosphere where students feel safe to take risks and to work through failure experiences. It is important for teachers to be transparent about their expectations; Laswell described telling her students her own pet peeves in the classroom so that there were no surprises. Stress that interferes with learning often occurs when there is a gap between what the student expects and what actually happens in the classroom. At the beginning of the school year, she asks students to write things that make them feel unsafe or uncomfortable in the classroom on an index card. Laswell then uses these barriers as individual goals for her students, and she provides scaffolding to help them overcome the barriers. For example, for a student who indicated that she felt uncomfortable presenting to the class, Laswell scaffolded the experience by initially having her present only to the teacher, then to a small group, then to the class with a buddy, then presenting to the class alone with a buddy sitting nearby, and finally presenting to the class as a whole.

Laswell became interested in accommodations because she found that many of the modifications she made for special education students might also apply to others in the classroom. She indicated that UDL means that the broad range of variations in learning are addressed in the design of the lessons and teachers don't need to be constantly consulting the students' IEPs because concerns will be addressed automatically. As a coordinator, Laswell provides mentoring to teachers in all disciplines and grades, indicating that using the UDL Guidelines (see http://www.udlcenter.org/aboutudl/udlguidelines/downloads) provided a means of evaluating the quality of teaching. When teachers look at lessons through the UDL framework, they see the deficiencies in the lesson, not in the student, and the framework provides guidance to improve instruction to meet the needs of the most students. As Laswell put it, "if you use Universal Design, students will learn."

Laswell is active in professional development regarding UDL and said that teachers also have barriers to learning that need to be addressed. Not every teacher connects with the UDL framework in the same manner. For example, because Laswell was a science teacher, she was attracted to the neuroscience underlying the UDL principles, but other teachers might be drawn to other aspects of the program. She recommended the UDL Exchange website (http://udlexchange.cast.org/home) as a clearinghouse and forum for teachers to find and share lesson plans and to access resources to implement UDL. Laswell described her experience with UDL as a revelation and said she could never return to teaching the old way. She indicated that UDL is not just about technology (although she finds technology allows students the privacy and flexibility to meet their own learning needs), but about helping students connect with learning in the way that they function at their best.

Conclusion

Although each of our case studies across Chapters 12–17 illustrates a particular strand of best practice, we were impressed by common themes that emerged in our interviews. Teachers addressing the needs of complex learners in all settings spoke to the need to use student interests as a way to increase motivation and recognized that learners of all types had strengths that might not be evident with traditional methods of instruction. Teachers also recognized the importance of social and emotional issues and prioritized their efforts to address these concerns in order to increase student motivation. The teachers we interviewed were also aware of the need to follow a consistent and organized curriculum and to provide repeated exposure to underlying basic concepts. Our case studies illustrate that creative efforts are being made to address complex learners in a variety of settings despite budget limitations and that many of these strategies could be successfully implemented schoolwide.

chapter 18

Preparing Twice-Exceptional Students for College

Many GTLD students rightfully aspire to attend college, and educational programs serving these learners should help them prepare for this transition. An important fact to keep in mind when advising and helping twice-exceptional students prepare for college is that receiving services in high school under IDEA does not a guarantee that they will qualify for supports in college. The Americans with Disabilities Act (ADA), which governs the provision of support for adults, uses a different standard for determining eligibility for protection— a "functional impairment in a major life skill" rather than a specific learning disability in a subject area as required by IDEA. Although a specific learning disability often entails a functional impairment, this is not always the case. Students with learning disabilities who compensate well enough to perform in the average range may not qualify for accommodations under ADA. On the other hand, students who did not meet criteria for a specific learning disability under IDEA may be able to qualify as having a functional impairment under ADA. In fact, a large portion of college students with learning disabilities are initially identified at the college level.

Documentation of Eligibility for Accommodations

College-bound students with disabilities are caught in a difficult situation as a result of differing expectations for documentation for secondary schools under revisions of IDEA and demands of postsecondary institutions to meet the requirements for eligibility for accommodations under ADA. Requirements for formal testing, once a required part of eligibility for special education services, have been relaxed under IDEA with a greater focus on progress monitoring consistent with the RtI model of service delivery. Because of this shift in focus, students do not necessarily go through a diagnostic process, but rather their academic performance challenges are addressed in a more functional way. Graduating students receive a Summary of Performance (SOP) that gives an overview of their academic skills and recommendations for their postsecondary needs.

Following the requirements of the 2004 revision of the Americans with Disabilities Act and subsequent litigation that led to court-imposed strict standards, most universities developed requirements for accommodations that included (a) a formal diagnosis provided by a qualified professional, (b) evidence of current functional impact, and (c) the use of adult norms for evaluating the student's cognitive and academic skills. In addition, the need for extended time accommodations had to be demonstrated through the use of timed and untimed academic measures. The dilemma for current students with disabilities is that this level of information is not provided as part of their free and appropriate education under IDEA. IDEA (2004) specifically indicated that it is not the secondary school's responsibility to provide testing for postsecondary concerns. Documentation of a disability for postsecondary purposes falls on the disabled student and his or her family, who must arrange for a private diagnostic evaluation.

ADA was amended by Congress in 2008 (ADAA) to address some of the concerns about the use of rigid definitions of eligibility for accommodations and indicated that postsecondary institutions could not impose a uniform requirement for extensive testing. Congress indicated that documentation requirements could not be unduly "burdensome" for the disabled person and that the eligibility criteria should be broadly applied. Disabilities were to be viewed as lifelong conditions that might be in remission under certain circumstances. The focus for documentation moved from eligibility to demonstrating the current impact and identifying appropriate accommodations. The Association on Higher Education and Disability (AHEAD; 2012), the group that develops best practice standards for postsecondary institutions, recently released new standards based on the new understanding of ADAA. These standards address problems with the type of documentation now emerging from secondary schools. Under these new guidelines, the college disability counselor determines whether a student requires accommodations based primarily on the student's self-report of his history of learning problems and accommodations received in the past. The second line of evidence is the counselor's own observations and impressions of the student with a third line of evidence arising out of documents from third parties (e.g., IEPs, psychoeducational evaluations). The standard to be applied is whether there is sufficient evidence that a reasonable person would conclude that a problem exists and that the proposed accommodations would likely improve the situation.

Although these changes may be forthcoming, a review of disabilities documentation requirements in a sample of selective colleges in 2012 we did indicated that postsecondary institutions and the Educational Testing Service still require a formal diagnosis of a learning disability or ADHD with a recent comprehensive psychoeducational evaluation. However, for school systems using the RtI model, students may not have formal testing but will leave high school with a document called the Summary of Performance (SOP), which discusses the student's academic progress, ongoing needs, and accommodations. According to Shaw, Keenan, Madaus, and Banerjee (2010), college administrators question the adequacy of the SOP as a document for determining eligibility for accommodations in college, due to its subjective nature and lack of detail. A national summit was organized to develop an SOP template, which can be found on the Council for Exceptional Children's website (http://www. cec.sped.org), but implementation of the document likely varies with the level of record keeping of the secondary school system. In addition, it is the student's responsibility to amass the necessary documentation, and many students may have difficulty compiling the relevant information. A further concern for twice-exceptional students is that they may not be identified under the RtI model and may not have written documentation to provide to colleges.

The gap between secondary and postsecondary documentation creates a barrier for many students of limited means who do not have the resources to pay for a diagnostic evaluation. To address this inequity, a stakeholder group facilitated by a Denver Office of Economic Development Youth Transitions Grant met in 2008 to identify ways to bridge the documentation gap for students with learning disabilities (Colorado State Board of Education, 2010). This group included staff from the Colorado Department of Education and college/ university disability services officers. The goal was to identify ways that learning disabled students could document their eligibility for accommodations without costly private testing. The group concluded that with additional materials from student records, enough information could be compiled to meet the documentation standards for postsecondary education.

The Colorado work group developed a documentation checklist to assist families and secondary school administrators in compiling enough information to meet postsecondary requirements. The checklist (which can be downloaded from http://www.cde.state.co.us/cdesped/download/pdf/Guidelines_DocumentationGuidelinesForPostsecondary.pdf) includes:

❖ various norm-referenced testing that might have been used to determine eligibility in the past (e.g., Test of Written Language, Gray Oral Reading Tests);

❖ curriculum-based measurement (CBM) assessment, which includes a list of attempted interventions and achievement test scores with percentiles;

❖ specific learning disability determination forms, disability documentation from outside professionals, and accommodation information from the present level of performance section of the IEP;

❖ ACT or SAT accommodation request forms and approval letters;

❖ recent IEP and triennial IEP;

❖ SOP; and

❖ secondary foreign language waiver, if applicable.

GTLD Programs Should Compile Documents for College Accommodations

Although student files may contain adequate information for postsecondary purposes, it is likely to be beyond the practical capacity of many families of disabled students to compile these documents on their own. An important case management function for GTLD programs would be the compilation of a packet of documents. Secondary documentation of accommodations is particularly important, especially because twice-exceptional students may not be formally identified to have RtI forms or IEPs. If schools move toward a Universal Design in Learning model where accommodations are built in to academic tasks, the formal documentation of accommodations will be even more limited. In the new AHEAD (2012) standards, students are responsible for discussing their own experiences with accommodations, so it would be important for schools to highlight what accommodations students currently receive and why. Missouri AHEAD (http://www.moahead.org) has developed a downloadable student packet with very useful checklists and timelines to assist students and their families in compiling documentation for college eligibility. One important component is a form for documenting accommodations.

Parents Should Be Apprised of Their Responsibility to Obtain Documentation

Many parents of students with identified learning disabilities have become accustomed to the school system managing the provision of services and can be taken by surprise with the idea that they will need to make arrangements for testing required for college admissions exams and accommodations for their children. Private psychoeducational testing is expensive and often takes a few months between scheduling an appointment for testing and receiving the final report. It is important to make parents aware of the costs and advanced planning required in a timely manner, ideally during the sophomore or junior year of high school. Students can begin taking adult measures of intelligence at age 16 (these tests compare their performance to other 16-year-olds).

For families of limited means, there are some resources available for paying for private diagnostic testing. Typically, psychologists are not able to offer reduced fees for psychological evaluations due to the very small profit margin in testing. Young adults are often more time-consuming to test and require more extensive testing to document their learning challenges. Diagnostic testing is very labor-intensive, and it is difficult to take shortcuts without compromising the quality of the evaluation. Although a few health insurance companies cover psychological testing, most managed care groups do not. However, psychological services are allowable expenses under flexible spending accounts. Some students may also qualify for vocational rehabilitation services that will pay for diagnostic testing.

One less than ideal option for students who have inadequate documentation is to request psychological testing once they are admitted to college. Some university counseling centers provide diagnostic testing for learning disabilities and ADHD with reduced fees. Students with demonstrated financial need could potentially have their fee waived similar to their other college expenses. For example, Purdue University gives priority for students with financial need in the wait list for diagnostic testing. One thing to consider, however, is that the wait list for testing is likely to be increasing due to documentation gaps emerging from secondary schools.

Psychoeducational Testing Identifies Important Supports and Accommodations for College-Bound GTLD Students

In addition to the documentation function for ADA eligibility, psychoeducational testing for college purposes serves other important needs. Postsecondary institutions are only required to provide accommodations, but a good evaluation can identify other supports and strategies that will facilitate the student's success in college. Also, diagnostic testing, particularly neuropsychological testing, can point to accommodations that may not have been attempted in the secondary school program. The evaluation process often helps students identify their own strengths and learning challenges. As students move into the college setting, they are increasingly expected to advocate for their own needs and to manage the provision of their accommodations. High school students should receive a personal feedback session as part of their evaluations so that they begin to understand their own needs and to learn the language to speak about their challenges.

Diagnostic testing can also look at the social-emotional challenges that may become increasingly problematic as students make the transition to greater independence. Many twice-exceptional students manage to cope in the high school setting, but their families are very aware of the social-emotional costs of maintaining a high level of academic performance. Because they are able to make it through the school day and many high school classes are large, significant social and emotional issues can go undetected at school. As a result, these issues may not be addressed by school-based intervention. A comprehensive psychoeducational evaluation provides a forum for demonstrating that a student has both academic and social-emotional needs that require accommodation. Integrating the whole person in the analysis provides college disability counselors with information needed to help students manage the challenges of college demands.

Students with autism spectrum disorders form a group who is particularly likely to profit from a good psychoeducational evaluation before entering college. A number of these students who may have been identified in the past will not meet the new, more restrictive diagnostic criteria in the DSM-V, but will still face significant challenges in social interactions and coping with complex sensory experiences. A number of accommodations and supports for these students are unlikely to be a part of their secondary school experience, and a psychologist with expertise in working with autism spectrum disorders will be able to make helpful recommendations for issues around social interactions and independent living in the college environment. For example, students with ASD may need special living arrangements or may need greater structure in monitoring their academic progress on a weekly basis.

Types of College Accommodations

Many college students will be familiar with accommodations they received in high school. Extended time accommodations are usually very important for twice-exceptional college students, as extra time can help them compensate for various learning challenges, including slow reading or processing speed, poor attention, and weak executive skills. One important factor to consider is that in college extended time may be offered at the Office of Disability Services and may be proctored by a staff member rather than the professor. For students who profit from the chance to have questions clarified, the presence of an instructor may be needed. Many GTLD students also use audiobooks or assistive technology, such as text-to-voice and voice-to-text software. They may require note-taking support as well.

Other less familiar accommodations include priority registration. It is often important for twice-exceptional students to consult with the Office of Disability Services about instructors who teach in a format compatible with their learning style. Students with learning disabilities often are most successful with teachers who are highly organized and who provide multisensory instruction. Students with learning disabilities also often qualify for a waiver of a foreign language requirement. Barr (1993) indicated that research has found that LD students need modification of the foreign language requirement; they typically struggle beyond the first year of a college foreign language course.

Transition to College

The transition to college can be quite challenging for many twice-exceptional learners, particularly those students with significant executive function weaknesses—take the messy classroom desk and lost backpack and fast-forward to a chaotic college dorm room with lots of unstructured time and assignments. In addition, many students with learning challenges rely heavily on parental support to organize their study time and assist with large-scale projects and studying for tests. In college, students are expected to manage their own time and to take the first step in advocating for their own learning needs.

Secondary GTLD programs can provide needed training for students and their parents to make the transition. For example, the Achieving

College Transitions Now (ACT Now) curriculum designed by Northampton Community College through a grant from the U.S. Department of Education provides a structured program with modules for secondary educators, students, and parents focusing on skills needed to make a successful transition to college. The course helps students identify their strengths and weaknesses, as well as develop self-advocacy skills. Parents and teachers are provided with information regarding differences between IDEA and ADA and documentation requirements for college accommodations. For more information about this program, see http://www.northampton.edu/Student-Resources/Disability-Services/Special-Projects/ACT-Now.htm.

Students should also consider college programs that provide additional support beyond accommodations. For example, a number of colleges receive federal funding through the Department of Education TRIO grants (http://www2.ed.gov/about/offices/list/ope/trio/index.html). These programs are designed to provide additional support to low-income, first-generation college students and individuals with disabilities to increase college retention and graduation rates. These programs provide academic tutoring and study skills training, as well as structured academic counseling.

Conclusion

It is important to keep in mind that many GTLD students have the capacity to attend college and there are colleges with supports for learning disabilities across a broad spectrum of needs. Although some colleges and universities provide minimal supports, others provide a broad range of programs including weekly mentoring, tutoring, and assistance with technology. Twice-exceptional students and their parents often struggle to identify resources and may not understand the changing mandates for supports as the students transition from high school to college. It is important for GTLD programs to recognize that twice-exceptional students need additional guidance to identify colleges that provide the level of services the students require and to help families organize the necessary documentation for accommodation eligibility. It should also be recognized that college is not for everyone, and GTLD students can also be eligible for accommodations in the workplace under the Americans with Disabilities Act.

Conclusion

Although some may question the concept of GTLD and attribute fluctuations in performance to normal variation, we hope our analysis has provided convincing evidence that there is more to the story—that there are gifted students who face exceptional challenges that deserve attention. GTLD students are elusive. It can seem that they are trying as hard to remain hidden as teachers are trying to find them. They share features that stretch the definitions of both giftedness and learning disabilities. Without intervention and support, these students often fail to reach their potential and a valuable resource for our society is lost. The social and emotional consequences of their struggles can turn these students' challenges into a burden for society. We believe that it is worthwhile to pay attention to these students because sensitive handling and fairly simple resource allocation can lead to major gains.

Twice-exceptional students can serve as a focal point for teaching a variety of important concepts that are useful to the school population as a whole. Attention to GTLD issues requires teachers and administers to use child-centered observation and to go beyond easy answers to explore alternate explanations. Further, greater understanding of the information processing issues underlying learning provides guidance to teachers in selecting more effective interventions. This approach is particularly helpful for teachers using the RtI model, which deemphasizes diagnostic testing. In addition, attention to GTLD issues also requires the recognition of the importance of contextual and personality factors that affect the ability of all students to demonstrate their strengths.

The topic of twice-exceptionality highlights the need for further integration of insights from RtI and hypothesis testing/cognitive testing models. RtI brings a number of benefits to the table; intervention moves forward based on functional performance rather than getting bogged down in categories. In addition, RtI recognizes the importance of organizing the environment as an intervention for these students. Teachers are encouraged to use classroom- and school-based structural changes as much as possible. A major contribution is the focus on the measurement of progress on a consistent basis; frequent assessment sets expectations for student improvement that can get lost with a more categorical approach.

Although RtI is typically used only to address underachievement, The Association for the Gifted, a division of the Council for Exceptional Children (CEC-TAG; 2009), developed a joint position paper indicating that RtI should be expanded to meet the needs of gifted students (http://cectag.com/wp-content/uploads/2012/04/RTI.pdf). This broadening of the RtI model could actually benefit gifted students in the sense that all students should be working toward improvement and students at the upper end of achievement should not be viewed as performing adequately unless they are also making improvement at their level. Requiring all students to have RtI goals would force increased rigor and differentiation in the classroom. Currently, the emphasis on specific goals for low-performing students directs teacher energy toward meeting those specific goals. Having specific goals for high achievers would create incentives for teachers to also focus on more advanced students. To some extent the issues of equity emerge—shouldn't all students have goals to advance their skills?

Although RtI has a number of features to recommend it, the concept of GTLD points out the limitations of the RtI model as currently envisioned. If RtI only applies to students who are underperforming in a general sense, only the most disabled gifted students will be identified. The majority—those who are able to compensate to some extent—also do not perform at their ability level, but will not be recognized. It is unfortunate that some proponents of RtI seem to feel that these gifted students and their families should be satisfied with mediocrity.

Diagnostic testing can provide important guidance for RtI. When students don't respond to Tier 1 and 2 interventions, a neuropsychological approach to testing provides fundamental information to differentiate why a particular learner is struggling in a particular subject. We have already seen how the understanding of neuropsychological processes in reading, namely phonological processing and rapid retrieval, led to major advances in reading remediation. Some of the important information processing components are nonspecific and will have an impact on students across the board. Nevertheless, understanding a student's facility with verbal versus nonverbal information can guide teachers to pick the best fit for a particular student, thereby increasing their efficiency in selecting interventions.

The neuropsychological approach is based on a focus on process. This orientation does not require formal neuropsychological training, but does require professional development for teachers and staff on information processing. Noticing how a student approaches a learning task is something teachers may do automatically, but they will have greater insight to guide student instruction when they consider student performance from an information processing perspective. The red flags we identified for recognizing twice-exceptional students in the classroom are based on underlying information processing issues. A neuropsychological orientation can also improve teacher performance in effectively addressing student behaviors. For example, at the Kingsbury Day School, teachers who have been trained to understand the role of executive functions in student behavior are much better able to move beyond seeing challenging behavior as a discipline problem to considering it as an instance of a processing problem for a learning disabled student. This change in perspective provides teachers with a wealth of options to intervene rather than simply engaging in a power struggle or a disciplinary procedure. Simply changing the task format or recognizing the student's need for increased scaffolding can often lead to a happy and productive resolution to many behavior problems.

A neuropsychological approach to testing moves away from a focus on scores as an endpoint. The effective assessment of GTLD students requires attention to points that are really principles of good test interpretation; it is important to take a sophisticated approach to score interpretation and to recognize factors that introduce complexity in test performance. Test scores are always approximations and clinical judgment should never be left out of the equation in making decisions about what test scores say about a student's potential. For example, it is important to recognize that composite tests scores, while psychometrically the most stable test scores, lose their stability when there is wide-ranging variability in component scores. In addition, standardized tests have difficulty measuring real-world performance, particularly for older bright students, and it is important to collect information from parents and teachers about a student's typical performance. In addition, it is important to keep in mind that a student's information processing challenges also impact her performance on standardized tests, limiting the validity of the test scores. Qualitative information about test performance is important to consider in evaluating the validity of particular scores.

A comprehensive neuropsychological battery is a valuable resource to guide instruction and identify supports and accommodations for students. A good evaluation provides a road map for many years in the future and is often a good investment for families. In addition to providing valuable information for teachers and schools, the increased understanding family members gain as a result of a diagnostic evaluation often leads to greater empathy and support for students. Helping families develop appropriate expectations can be both a relief and empowering for students. A student's understanding of his own learning profile, derived from neuropsychological testing, provides the groundwork for self-advocacy throughout his academic and working life.

Although neuropsychological testing is a great resource, we recognize that it is expensive and not always easy to access for many of the students who might profit from it. However, increased understanding of neuropsychological processing for teachers developed through professional development can lead to a neuropsychological awareness even if there are no test scores. In addition, we have pointed to measures commonly available to school psychologists that are relatively brief and readily available that could supplement the basic IQ and achievement testing and provide a relatively inexpensive way to gain a great deal of information.

We fundamentally disagree with critics of testing who feel that overall intelligence does not need to be accessed to remediate learning problems. We agree that it makes sense to use the tried and true interventions as soon as students appear to be falling behind. But this approach only addresses learning at the grossest level and is most effective in the primary grades. Learning issues of older students are considerably more complex, particularly for those students for whom best practices remediation have not worked. Having an understanding of a student's overall potential provides very important information that can orient teachers to appropriate expectations for students and to set goals for intervention.

The paradoxical nature of twice-exceptional students can be confusing to teachers. These students need both flexibility and structure in the learning environment. They need high expectations, but also an empathic approach that recognizes their frustration. GTLD students often desire connection to a community, but struggle with social skills and assertiveness in groups.

Twice-exceptional students often struggle with the complex nature of their learning profile; they need help both to recognize their strengths and to be willing to demonstrate them. These students also need to come to terms with their learning challenges. Although some teachers are born to be flexible and observant of student diversity, other teachers require professional development to become more sensitive to the needs of their students. The GTLD model provides an efficient means of addressing a range of issues that are also more broadly applicable at a general level.

In developing our best practices, we used interviews and observations across a range of settings to identify effective strategies to meet the needs of twice-exceptional students. We looked at general education settings, specialized programs for gifted or high-ability students, as well as a special education setting. We felt it was important to profile programs across a broad spectrum, from a well-funded high-achieving program with limited diversity challenges to programs with a broad range of diversity. Some of the schools we profiled provide inventive programming in areas of complex challenge, whether economic decline or natural disaster has distressed the community. We presented the case studies with an eye to the perspective of the classroom teacher and the challenges of program implementation. As a result of our research, we identified six best practices to meet the needs of twice-exceptional students. Many of these principles likely strike a common note—they are also likely to benefit students with a variety of needs.

First, students should be taught in ways that engage their strengths and their interests. Although this perhaps seems obvious, the strengths of learning disabled students are often lost in the push to remediate academic weaknesses. The focus on NCLB has perhaps encouraged this focus on deficits. However, programs that use student interests as a way to engage them seem to be more successful in getting students to take risks and demonstrate their strengths. The success of twice-exceptional students in the Johns Hopkins University Center for Talented Youth's summer programs provides a wonderful example of how students with learning disabilities can excel when immersed in a learning experience that captures their interests and plays to their strengths. Students are often willing to put forth the extra effort to overcome learning challenges when they are excited about a topic.

A second best practice is the importance of developing a supportive context. Twice-exceptional students do best when there is good communication between teaching staff who are able to share responsibility for remediating learning challenges and demanding rigor from students. Parents need to be in the loop and the GTLD concept can help parents recognize the potential and the needs of their students. Hoover Middle School in Maryland provides a wonderful example of the teamwork possible in an inclusion setting and the importance of creating an environment that conveys appreciation of student strengths, as well as a normalization of learning challenges. At Hoover, students are taught that everyone has strengths and weaknesses.

Gifted students with learning disabilities need to have a range of accommodations and adaptations. This topic is somewhat controversial, as individuals who do not appreciate the hidden learning challenges of twice-exceptional students may raise issues of equity. We drew a distinction between accommodations, interventions that remove barriers, and adaptations, interventions that

modify task demands. We recommended that accommodations be viewed as more long-standing needs with adaptations being viewed as an aspect of scaffolding to facilitate student progress. As we noted at the Kingsbury Day School, students who have not had a history of exposure to the demands of gifted programming need a longer trajectory to develop the basic skills to produce products at a gifted level of performance. For these students, the criteria for gifted work become goals to work toward.

Students with learning disabilities profit from multisensory instruction and explicit instruction in strategies. These students often have difficulty informally picking up on procedures and patterns on their own. One challenge for gifted programs across the board is the encouragement of students' higher order thinking. Bloom's taxonomy delineates the hierarchy of thinking processes. Many students struggle to make the leap beyond current information to inferences and creative thinking. This issue is particularly problematic for twice-exceptional students who may be reluctant to go beyond the obvious. We feel that the programs most likely to engage GTLD students share the characteristics of a high level of consistency, a clearly delineated problem-solving process, a common language that can be used across academic subjects, and project-based learning following the students' interests. Traditional gifted programs can be adapted for students with learning challenges, and this has been a trend in recent research on the use of traditional gifted curriculum with a broader spectrum of students. Students with significant learning challenges need additional scaffolding and need more modeling and experience with the concept of a long-term project, as indicated at the Kingsbury Day School.

An exciting finding for us was discovering other programs that develop higher order thinking in school-based programs, such as the TASC program in the United Kingdom, and the TIEL program and Thinking Maps in the United States. Each of these approaches introduces problem-solving processes that can be used by all students in the school. TASC and Thinking Maps are introduced at the preschool level. Students are encouraged to engage in authentic problem solving about topics of personal interest and often work together in groups. The schoolwide use of these programs is likely to be highly effective with learning disabled students because students use the same method in all courses and over a period of years. The model becomes a common language and the visual representation provides a lodestone for students to orient to the stages in the process. The group process facilitates the development of social and expressive language skills. Students in the TASC program were quite impressive in their ability to verbalize metacognitive processes, a factor shown to contribute to the success of college students. Equally impressive in the TASC and Thinking Map schools was the increased academic performance of students on high-stakes testing. It is important to note that it seems to take about 3 years to fully introduce a new

curriculum model and teachers require ongoing professional development to effectively implement these programs. Train-the-trainer models seem to be the best method to introduce new models where teachers have the opportunity for modeling and a supportive environment to address problems they encounter with implementation.

As seen in the TASC and Thinking Map approaches, embedding interventions throughout the school program is very important. Similarly, embedding accommodations and support for twice-exceptional students into the program is both more efficient and avoids some of the stigma that students experience in dealing with their learning challenges. The Universal Design for Learning approach takes the inclusion of accommodations to a new level with the concept of proactively embedding multisensory access and output into the curriculum. One barrier for students with disabilities is rigid curriculum that forces teachers to reactively work around students' needs. UDL attempts to build in flexibility to address a variety of learning challenges; however, it poses problems with the documentation of accommodations for college—when accommodations are built in to the school program, students do not have a paper trail to provide to colleges. The Science and Technology program at Eleanor Roosevelt High School provides an example of how supports can be embedded in a program without sacrificing standards; GTLD students at Roosevelt complete the same rigorous requirements as their mainstream peers.

Many of the practices described could be introduced in school programs without formal identification of a student being gifted or learning disabled. What is the value of the concept of GTLD? Is it important to develop one more interest group? In an ideal world, instruction would be differentiated for all students and there would be no need for special interest identification. However, teacher surveys indicate that teachers struggle to differentiate instruction and tend to focus on low-performing students due to the emphasis on NCLB standards in their evaluations. Gifted students in general are given short shrift due to limited teacher preparation in techniques for providing gifted instruction. Twice-exceptional students who are not even identified in many current settings are likely to suffer doubly due to their complex needs. The GTLD concept highlights the needs of these students who often go on to underachieve. Their lost potential for society is important as we attempt to reclaim advanced standing in academic performance internationally. With a sensitive educational environment and fairly practical accommodations, many of which can be built in to instruction with advances in technology, these students can go on to successful college and career experiences.

References

Association on Higher Education and Disability. (2012). *Supporting accommodation requests: Guidance on documentation practices.* Retrieved from http://www.ahead.org/uploads/docs/resources/Final_AHEAD_Supporting%20Accommodation%20Requests%20with%20Q&A%2009_12.pdf

Alvord, M. K., Zucker, B., & Grados, J. J. (2011). *Resilience builder program for children and adolescents: Enhancing social competence and self-regulation.* Champaign, IL: Research Press.

American Psychiatric Association. (2000). *Diagnostic and statistical manual of mental disorders* (4th ed., Text rev.). Washington, DC: Author.

Americans with Disabilities Act, 42 U.S.C. §§ 12102 et seq. (1990).

Americans with Disabilities Amendments Act, Pub. Law 110-325 (September 25, 2008).

Anderson, L., & Krathwohl, D. (Eds.). (2001). *A taxonomy for learning, teaching, and assessing: A revision of Bloom's taxonomy of educational objectives* (Complete ed.). New York, NY: Longman.

Antshel, K. M., Faraone, S. V., Stallone, K., Nave, A., Kaufmann, F. A., Doyle, A., . . . Biederman, J. (2007). Is attention deficit hyperactivity disorder a valid diagnosis in the presence of high IQ? Results from the MGH Longitudinal Family Studies of ADHD. *Journal of Child and Adolescent Psychiatry, 48,* 687–694.

Assouline, S. G., Foley Nicpon, M., Colangelo, N., & O'Brien, M. (2008). *The paradox of giftedness and autism: Packet of information for professionals.* Iowa City: The University of Iowa, The Connie Belin & Jacqueline N. Blank International Center for Gifted Education and Talent Development. Retrieved from http://www.education.uiowa.edu/html/belinblank/Clinic/Resources.aspx

Assouline, S. G., Foley Nicpon, M., & Whiteman, C. (2010). Cognitive and psychosocial characteristics of gifted students with written language disability. *Gifted Child Quarterly, 54,* 102–115.

Assouline, S. G., Foley Nicpon, M., & Whiteman, C. (2011). Cognitive and psychosocial characteristics of gifted students with written language disability: A reply to Lovett's response. *Gifted Child Quarterly, 55,* 152–157.

Autism Central. (2012). *Asperger's syndrome documentary—David Jordan.* Retrieved from http://www.autism-central.com/aspergers-syndrome-documentary-david-jordan/997

Baker, J. (2003). *Social skills training for children and adolescents with Asperger syndrome and social-communications problems.* Shawnee Mission, KS: Autism Asperger Publishing.

Barr, V. (1993). *Foreign language requirements and students with learning disabilities.* Washington, DC: Center for Applied Linguistics. Retrieved from http://www.cal.org/resources/digest/barr0001.html

Baum, S. M., Cooper, C. R., & Neu, T. W. (2001). Dual differentiation: An approach for meeting the curricular needs of gifted students with learning disabilities. *Psychology in the Schools, 38,* 477–490.

Baum, S. M., Olenchak, F. R., & Owen, S. V. (1998). Gifted students with attention deficits: Fact and/or fiction? Or, can we see the forest for the trees? *Gifted Child Quarterly, 42,* 96–104.

Baum, S. M., Renzulli, J. S., & Hébert, T. P. (1995a). *The prism metaphor: A new paradigm for reversing underachievement* (CRS95310). Storrs: University of Connecticut, The National Research Center on the Gifted and Talented.

Baum, S. M., Renzulli, J. S., & Hébert, T. P. (1995b). Reversing underachievement: Creative productivity as a systematic intervention. *Gifted Child Quarterly, 39,* 224–235.

Beauchamp, M. H., & Anderson, V. (2010). SOCIAL: An integrative framework for the development of social skills. *Psychological Bulletin, 136,* 39–64.

Bianco, M., Carothers, D. E., & Smiley, L. R. (2009). Gifted students with Asperger's syndrome: Strategies for strength-based programming. *Intervention in School and Clinic, 44,* 206–215.

Bloom, B. (Ed.). (1956). *Taxonomy of educational objectives: The classification of educational goals. Handbook I: Cognitive domain.* New York, NY: Longmans Green.

Brody, L. E., & Mills, C. J. (1997). Gifted children with learning disabilities: A review of the issues. *Journal of Learning Disabilities, 30,* 282–296.

Brophy, D. R. (2001). Comparing the attributes, activities, and performance of divergent, convergent, and combination thinkers. *Creativity Research Journal, 13,* 439–455.

Brown, M., & Rice, G. (2004). *Developmental dyslexia in adults: A research review.* London, England: National Research and Development Centre for Adult Literacy and Numeracy. Retrieved from http://www.nrdc.org.uk/uploads/documents/doc_166.pdf

Burns, D. E., Leppien, J., Omdal, S., Gubbins, E. J., Muller, L., & Vahidi, S. (2006). *Teacher's guide for the explicit teaching of thinking skills.* Storrs: University of Connecticut, The National Research Center for Gifted Education. Retrieved from http://www.gifted.uconn.edu/nrcgt/reports/rm06218/rm06218.pdf

Center for Talented Youth. (n.d.a). *Student life.* Retrieved from http://cty.jhu.edu/summer/grades7-12/intensive/catalog/studentlife.html

Center for Talented Youth. (n.d.b). *Summer programs.* Retrieved from http://cty.jhu.edu/summer/index.html

Center for Teaching and Learning, & SuCasa Columbus. (2007). *Logrando Secundaria—Achieving high school: Key findings and recommendations from a study of Indiana schools and Latino high school students.* Retrieved from http://www.iupuc.edu/ctl/files/LograndoSecundariaFinalReport.pdf

Chansky, T. E. (2000). *Freeing your child from obsessive-compulsive disorder.* New York, NY: Three Rivers Press.

Chansky, T. E. (2004). *Freeing your child from anxiety.* New York, NY: Broadway Books.

Chansky, T. E. (2008). *Freeing your child from negative thinking.* Cambridge, MA: Da Capo Press.

Charwarska, K., Klin, A., & Volkmar, F. (2003). Automatic attention cueing through eye movement in 2-year-old children with autism. *Child Development, 74,* 1108–1122.

Colangelo, N., Kerr, B., Christensen, P., & Maxey, J. (1993). A comparison of gifted underachievers and gifted high achievers. *Gifted Child Quarterly, 37,* 155–160.

Coleman, C., Lindstrom, J., Nelson, J., Lindstrom, W., & Gregg, K. N. (2010). Passageless comprehension on the Nelson-Denny Reading Test: Well above chance for university students. *Journal of Learning Disabilities, 43,* 244–249.

Colorado State Board of Education. (2010). *High school to college transition for students with specific learning disabilities: Best practice documentation guidelines for Colorado postsecondary institutions.* Retrieved from http://www.cde.state.co.us/cdesped/download/pdf/Guidelines_DocumentationGuidelinesForPostsecondary.pdf

Cooper-Kahn, J., & Dietzel, L. (2008). *Late, lost, and unprepared: A parents' guide to helping children with executive functioning*. Bethesda, MD: Woodbine House.

Council for Exceptional Children, The Association for the Gifted. (2009). *Response to Intervention for gifted children*. Retrieved from http://cectag.com/wp-content/uploads/2012/04/RTI.pdf

Cox, A. (2008). *No mind left behind: Understanding and fostering executive control—The eight essential brain skills every child needs to thrive*. New York, NY: Penguin Press.

Cramond, B. (1995). *The coincidence of Attention Deficit Hyperactivity Disorder and creativity* (RBDM9508). Storrs: University of Connecticut, The National Research Center for the Gifted and Talented.

Crepeau-Hobson, F., & Bianco, M. (2011). Identification of gifted students with learning disabilities in a Response-to-Intervention era. *Psychology in the Schools, 48*, 102–109.

Cross, T. L., & Coleman, L. J. (2005). School-based conception of giftedness. In R. J. Sternberg & J. E. Davidson (Eds.), *Conceptions of giftedness* (2nd ed., pp. 52–63). Cambridge, UK: Cambridge University Press.

Dabrowski, K., & Piechowski, M. M. (1977). *Theory of levels of emotional development: From primary integration to self-actualization: Vol. 2*. Oceanside, NY: Dabor Science.

Dawson, M., Soulières, I., Gernsbacher, M. A., & Mottron, L. (2007). The level and nature of autistic intelligence. *Psychological Science, 18*, 657–662.

Dawson, P., & Guare, R. (2010). *Executive skills in children and adolescents* (2nd ed.). New York, NY: Guilford Press.

Duffett, A., Farkas, S., & Loveless, T. (2008). *High-achieving students in the era of No Child Left Behind*. Washington, DC: Thomas Fordham Institute.

Dyson, L. L. (1996). The experiences of families of children with learning disabilities: Parental stress, family functioning, and sibling self-concept. *Journal of Learning Disabilities, 29*, 280–286.

Education for All Handicapped Children Act of 1975, Pub. Law 94-142 (November 29, 1975).

Eide, F., & Eide, B. (2011). *The dyslexic advantage: Unlocking the hidden potential of the dyslexic brain*. New York, NY: Penguin Group.

Emerick, L. J. (1992). Academic underachievement among the gifted: Students' perceptions of factors that reverse the pattern. *Gifted Child Quarterly, 36*, 140–146.

Fletcher, J. M., Francis, D. J., Morris, R. D., & Lyon, G. R. (2005). Evidence-based assessment of learning disabilities in children and adolescents. *Journal of Clinical Child and Adolescent Psychology, 34*, 506–522.

Foley Nicpon, M., Allmon, A., Sieck, B., & Stinson, R. D. (2010). Empirical investigation of twice-exceptionality: Where have we been and where are we going? *Gifted Child Quarterly, 55,* 3–17.

Foley Nicpon, M., Doobay, A., & Assouline, S. G. (2010). Teacher, parent, and self perceptions of psychosocial functioning in intellectually gifted children and adolescents with autism spectrum disorder. *Journal of Autism and Developmental Disabilities, 40,* 1028–1038.

Folsom, C. (2009). *Teaching for intellectual and emotional learning: A model for creating powerful curriculum.* Lanham, MD: Rowman and Littlefield Education.

Freed, J., & Parsons, L. (1997). *Right brained children in a left brained world: Unlocking the potential of your ADD child.* New York, NY: Simon and Schuster.

Freitag, C. M. (2007). The genetics of autistic disorders and its clinical relevance: A review of the literature. *Molecular Psychiatry, 12,* 2–22.

Ganesalingam, K., Yeates, K., Taylor, H., Walz, N., Stancin, T., & Wade, S. (2011). Executive functions and social competence in young children 6 months following traumatic brain injury. *Neuropsychology, 25,* 466–476.

Gentry, M., & Neu, T. W. (1998). Project High Hopes summer institute: Curriculum for developing talent in students with special needs. *Roeper Review, 20,* 291–295.

Ginsburg, K. R. (2011). *Building resilience in children and teens: Giving kids roots and wings.* Elk Grove, IL: American Academy of Pediatrics.

Gioia, G. A., Isquith, P. K., Guy, S. C., & Kenworthy, L. (2000). *Behavior Rating Inventory of Executive Function.* Lutz, FL: Psychological Assessment Resources.

Goldstein, G., Allen, D. N., Minshew, N. J., Williams, D. L., Volkmar, F., Klin, A., & Schultz, R. T. (2008). The structure of intelligence in children and adults with high functioning autism. *Neuropsychology, 22,* 301–312.

Gordon, M., Lewandowski, L., & Keiser, S. (1999). The LD label for relatively well-functioning students: A critical analysis. *Journal of Learning Disabilities, 32,* 485–490.

Grandin, T. (1996). *Thinking in pictures: And other reports from my life with autism.* New York, NY: Doubleday.

Grandin, T. (2006). *Thinking in pictures: My life with autism* (Expanded ed.). New York, NY: Random House.

Greene, R. (2008). *Lost at school: Why our kids with behavioral challenges are falling through the cracks and how we can help them.* New York, NY: Scribner.

Hall, T., Strangman, N., & Meyer, A. (2003). *Differentiated instruction and implications for UDL implementation.* Wakefield, MA: National Center

on Accessing the General Curriculum. Retrieved from http://aim.cast.org/learn/historyarchive/backgroundpapers/differentiated_instruction_udl

Heller, K. A. (2004). Identification of gifted and talented students. *Psychology Science, 46,* 302–323.

Heller, K. A., Perleth, C., & Lim, T. K. (2005). The Munich Model of Giftedness designed to identify and promote gifted students. In R. Sternberg & J. Davidson (Eds.), *Conceptions of giftedness* (2nd ed., pp. 147–170). Cambridge, UK: Cambridge University Press.

Howlin, P., Goode, S., Hutton, J., & Rutter, M. (2009). Savant skills in autism: Psychometric approaches and parental reports. *Philosophical Transactions of the Royal Society of Biological Sciences, 364,* 1359–1367.

Hussain, B. (2012, June 4). World's best cities for architecture lovers. *Conde Nast Traveler.* Retrieved from http://www.cntraveler.com/daily-traveler/2012/06/cities-architecture-design-lovers-photos?mbid=nl_daily_traveler#slide=9

Hyerle, D., & Williams, K. (2009). *Bifocal assessment in the cognitive age: Thinking maps for assessing content learning and cognitive processes.* Retrieved from http://www.thinkingfoundation.org/david/books/TMapsAssessJournal.pdf

Individuals with Disabilities Education Act, 20 U.S.C. §1401 et seq. (1990).

Individuals with Disabilities Education Improvement Act, Pub. Law 108-446 (December 3, 2004).

Jeltova, I., & Grigorenko, E. L. (2005). Systemic approaches to giftedness: Contributions of Russian psychology. In R. J. Sternberg & J. E. Davidson (Eds.), *Conceptions of giftedness* (2nd ed., pp. 171–186). Cambridge, UK: Cambridge University Press.

Johnson, E. S., Humphrey, M., Mellard, D. F., Woods, K., & Swanson, H. L. (2010). Cognitive processing deficits and students with specific learning disabilities: A selective meta-analysis of the literature. *Learning Disability Quarterly, 33,* 3–18.

Kalbfleisch, M. L. (2000). *Electroencephalographic differences between males with and without ADHD with average and high aptitude during task transitions* (Unpublished doctoral dissertation). University of Virginia, Charlottesville.

Kaufmann, F., & Castellanos, F. X. (2000). Attention Deficit/Hyperactivity Disorder and gifted students. In K. A. Heller, F. J. Mönks, R. J. Sternberg, & R. F. Subotnik (Eds.), *International handbook of giftedness and talent* (2nd ed., pp. 621–632). Amsterdam, The Netherlands: Elsevier.

Kaufmann, F., Kalbfleisch, M. L., & Castellanos, F. X. (2000). *Attention Deficit Disorders and gifted students: What do we really know?* Storrs: University of Connecticut, The National Research Center on the Gifted and Talented.

Kavale, K. A., & Forness, S. R. (1998). The politics of learning disabilities. *Learning Disability Quarterly, 21,* 245–273.

Keenan, J. M., & Betjemann, R. S. (2006). Comprehending the Gray Oral Reading Test without reading it: Why comprehension tests should not include passage-independent items. *Scientific Studies of Reading, 10,* 363–380.

King, E. W. (2005). Addressing the social and emotional needs of twice-exceptional students. *TEACHING Exceptional Children, 38*(1), 16–20.

King, F. J., Goodson, L., & Rohani, F. (1998). *Higher order thinking skills.* Retrieved from http://www.cala.fsu.edu/files/higher_order_thinking_skills.pdf

Kinsbourne, M. (1973). School problems. *Pediatrics, 52,* 697–710.

Kulik, J. A. (1992). *An analysis of the research on ability grouping: Historical and contemporary perspectives* (RBDM 9204). Storrs: University of Connecticut, The National Research Center on the Gifted and Talented.

Learning Disabilities Association of America. (2010). *The Learning Disabilities Association of America's white paper on evaluation, identification, and eligibility criteria for students with specific learning disabilities.* Retrieved from http://www.ldanatl.org/pdf/LDA%20White%20Paper%20on%20IDEA%20Evaluation%20Criteria%20for%20SLD.pdf

Levine, M. (2002a). *Educational care: A system for understanding and helping children with learning differences at home and in school* (2nd ed.). Cambridge, England: Educators Publishing Service.

Levine, M. (2002b). *A mind at a time: America's top learning expert shows how every child can succeed.* New York, NY: Simon and Schuster.

Levine, M., & Reed, M. (2001). *Developmental variation and learning disorders* (2nd ed.). Toronto, Ontario: Educators Publishing Service.

Lewin, T. (2012, July 17). Universities reshaping education on the web. *The New York Times.* Retrieved from http://www.nytimes.com/2012/07/17/education/consortium-of-colleges-takes-online-education-to-new-level.html?_r=1&pagewanted=all

Lewis, R. B. (1998). Assistive technology and learning disabilities: Today's realities and tomorrow's promises. *Journal of Learning Disabilities, 31,* 16–26.

Little, C. A., Kearney, K. L., & Britner, P. A. (2010). Student self-concept and perceptions of mentoring relationships in a summer mentorship program for talented adolescents. *Roeper Review, 32,* 189–199.

Lovett, B. J. (2011). On the diagnosis of learning disabilities in gifted students: Reply to Assouline et al. (2010). *Gifted Child Quarterly, 55,* 149–151.

Lovett, B. J. (2012). Extended time testing accommodations: What does the research say? *NASP Communique Online, 39.*

Lovett, B. J., & Lewandowski, L. J. (2006). Gifted students with learning disabilities: Who are they? *Journal of Learning Disabilities, 39,* 515–527.

Lyon, G. R., & Moats, L. C. (1997). Critical conceptual and methodological considerations in reading intervention research. *Journal of Learning Disabilities, 30,* 578–588.

Mannuzza, S., Klein, R. G., Bessler, A., Malloy, P., & LaPadula, M. (1998). Adult psychiatric status of hyperactive boys grown up. *American Journal of Psychiatry, 155,* 493–498.

Maslow, A. (1943). A theory of human motivation. *Psychological Review, 50,* 370–396.

McCoach, D. B., Kehle, T. J., Bray, M. A., & Siegle, D. (2001). Best practices in the identification of gifted students with learning disabilities. *Psychology in the Schools, 38,* 403–411.

McKenzie, R. G. (2009). Obscuring vital distinctions: The oversimplification of learning disabilities within RTI. *Learning Disabilities Quarterly, 32,* 203–215.

McKenzie, R. G. (2010). Insufficiency of Response to Intervention in identifying gifted students with learning disabilities. *Learning Disabilities Research & Practice, 25,* 161–168.

Mirsky, A. F., Anthony, B. J., Duncan, C. C., Ahearn, M. B., & Kellam, S. G. (1991). Analysis of the elements of attention: A neuropsychological approach. *Neuropsychology Review, 2,* 109–145.

Moon, S. M., & Dillon, D. R. (1995). Multiple exceptionalities: A case study. *Journal for the Education of the Gifted, 18,* 111–130.

Moon, S. M., Zentall, S., Grskovic, J., Hall, A., & Stormont-Spurgin, M. (2001). Emotional, social, and family characteristics of boys with AD/HD and giftedness: A comparative case study. *Journal for Education of the Gifted, 24,* 207–247.

Moseley, D., Baumfield, V., Elliott, J., Gregson, M., Higgins, S., Miller, J., & Newton, D. P. (2005). *Frameworks for thinking.* Cambridge, UK: Cambridge University Press.

Mottron, L., Dawson, M., Soulières, I., Hubert, B., & Burack, J. (2006). Enhanced perceptual functioning in autism: An update, and eight principles of autistic perception. *Journal of Autism and Developmental Disorders, 36,* 27–43.

National Association for Gifted Children. (2008). *The role of assessments in the identification of gifted students.* Washington, DC: Author. Retrieved from http://www.nagc.org/index.aspx?id=4022

National Center for Educational Statistics. (1999). *Students with disabilities in postsecondary education: A profile of preparation, participation, and outcomes.* Washington, DC: Author. Retrieved from http://nces.ed.gov/pubs99/1999187.pdf

National Council on Disability. (2003). *People with disabilities and postsecondary education.* Retrieved from http://www.ncd.gov/publications/2003/Sept152003

National Education Association. (2006). *The twice-exceptional dilemma.* Retrieved from http://www.nea.org/assets/docs/twiceexceptional.pdf

Neihart, M. (2000). Gifted children with Asperger's syndrome. *Gifted Child Quarterly, 44,* 222–230.

Neihart, M. (2008). Identifying and providing services to twice exceptional children. In S. Pfeiffer (Ed.), *Handbook of giftedness in children* (pp. 115–138). New York, NY: Springer Science and Business Media.

Newman, J. L. (2005). Talents and Type III's: The effects of the Talents Unlimited model on creative productivity in gifted youngsters. *Roeper Review, 27,* 84–90.

Nicolson, R., & Fawcett, A. (2008). *Dyslexia, learning, and the brain.* Boston, MA: MIT Press.

Nielsen, M. E. (2002). Gifted students with learning disabilities: Recommendations for identification and programming. *Exceptionality, 10,* 93–111.

No Child Left Behind Act, 20 U.S.C. §6301 (2001).

Olenchak, F. R., & Reis, S. M. (2002). Gifted students with learning disabilities. In M. Neihart, S. M. Reis, N. M. Robinson, & S. M. Moon (Eds.), *The social and emotional development of gifted children: What do we know?* (pp. 177–191). Waco, TX: Prufrock Press.

Pirozzo, R. (1982). Gifted underachievers. *Roeper Review, 4*(4), 18–21.

Raiford, S. E., Weiss, L. G., Rolfhus, E., & Coalson, D. (2005). *WISC-IV technical report #4: General Ability Index.* Lebanon, IN: Pearson Education.

Ramsden, S., Richardson, F. M., Josse, G., Thomas, M. S. C., Ellis, C., Shakeshaft, C., . . . Price, C. J. (2011). Verbal and non-verbal intelligence changes in the teenage brain. *Nature, 479*(7371), 113–116.

Reis, S. M. (1998). Underachievement for some—dropping out with dignity for others. *Communicator, 29,* 19–24.

Reis, S. M., Eckert, R. D., Schreiber, F. J., Jacobs, J., Briggs, C., Gubbins, E. J., . . . Muller, L. (2005). *The Schoolwide Enrichment Model reading study* (RM05214). Storrs: University of Connecticut, The National Research Center on the Gifted and Talented.

Reis, S. M., Hébert, T. P., Diaz, E. P., Maxfield, L. R., & Ratley, M. E. (1995). *Case studies of talented students who achieve and underachieve in an urban high school* (Research Monograph 95120). Storrs: University of Connecticut, The National Research Center for the Gifted and Talented.

Reis, S., McCoach, D. B., Coyne, M., Schreiber, F. J., Eckert, R. D., & Gubbins, E. J. (2007). Using planned enrichment strategies with direct instruction to

improve reading fluency, comprehension, and attitude toward reading: An evidence-based study. *The Elementary School Journal, 108,* 3–23.

Reis, S. M., McGuire, J. M., & Neu, T. W. (2000). Compensation strategies used by high-ability students with learning disabilities who succeed in college. *Gifted Child Quarterly, 44,* 123–134.

Renzulli, J. S. (1977). *The Enrichment Triad Model: A guide for developing defensible programs for the gifted and talented.* Mansfield Center, CT: Creative Learning Press.

Renzulli, J. S. (2005). The Three-Ring Conception of Giftedness: A developmental model for promoting creative productivity. In R. J. Sternberg & J. E. Davidson (Eds.), *Conceptions of giftedness* (2nd ed., pp. 246–279). Cambridge, UK: Cambridge University Press.

Renzulli, J. S., & Reis, S. M. (1997). *The Schoolwide Enrichment Model* (2nd ed.). Mansfield Center, CT: Creative Learning Press.

Rhodes, V., Stevens, D., & Hemmings, A. (2011). Creating positive culture in a new urban high school. *The High School Journal, 94*(3), 82–94.

Rimm, S. (1995). *Why bright kids fail and what you can do about it.* New York, NY: Crown.

Rimm, S. (2008a). Underachievement syndrome: A psychological defensive pattern. In S. Pfeiffer (Ed.), *Handbook of giftedness in children: Psychoeducational theory, research, and best practices* (pp. 139–160). New York, NY: Springer Science and Business Media.

Rimm, S. (2008b). *How to parent so children will learn* (3rd ed.). Scottsdale, AZ: Great Potential Press.

Roan, S. (2011, November 3). Dyslexia not related to intelligence, study finds. *Los Angeles Times.* Retrieved from http://latimes.com/health/boostershots/la-heb-dyslexia-20111103,0,157.story

Rourke, B. (1989). *Nonverbal learning disabilities: The syndrome and the model.* New York, NY: Guilford Press.

Rowe, E. W., Kingsley, J. M., & Thompson, D. F. (2010). Predictive ability of the General Ability Index (GAI) versus full scale IQ among gifted referrals. *School Psychology Quarterly, 25,* 119–128.

Ruban, L. M., & Reis, S. M. (2005). Identification and assessment of gifted students with learning disabilities. *Theory Into Practice, 44,* 115–124.

Sahyoun, C. P., Belliveau, J. W., Soulières, I., Schwartz, S., & Mody, M. (2010). Neuroimaging of the functional and structural networks underlying visuospatial vs. linguistic reasoning in high-functioning autism. *Neuropsychologia, 48,* 86–95.

Seltzer, M. M., Almeida, D. M., Greenberg, J. S., Savla, J., Stawski, R. S., Hong, J., & Taylor, J. L. (2009). Psychosocial and biological markers of daily lives